Distance-Learning Programs

Edited by Lynn E. Henrichsen

Case Studies in TESOL Practice Series

Jill Burton, Series Editor

Teachers of English to Speakers of Other Languages, Inc.

Typeset in Berkeley and Belwe
by Capitol Communication Systems, Inc., Crofton, Maryland USA
Printed by Kirby Lithographic Company, Inc. USA
Indexed by Coughlin Indexing Services, Annapolis, Maryland USA

Teachers of English to Speakers of Other Languages, Inc.
700 South Washington Street, Suite 200
Alexandria, Virginia 22314 USA
Tel 703-836-0774 • Fax 703-836-6447 • E-mail tesol@tesol.org • http://www.tesol.org/

Director of Communications and Marketing: Helen Kornblum
Managing Editor: Marilyn Kupetz
Copy Editor: Marcella Fecteau
Additional Reader: Marcia Annis
Cover Design: Kathryn Ellsworth

ISBN 0-939791-93-5
Library of Congress Control No. 2001094380

Dedication

To all who teach and learn at a distance

Table of Contents

Acknowledgments   vii

Series Editor's Preface   ix

CHAPTER 1: Beyond Adding Telecommunications to a
Traditional Course: Insights Into Human and Instructional
Factors Affecting Distance Learning in TESOL   1
  Lynn E. Henrichsen

PART 1: TEACHING ESOL AT A DISTANCE

CHAPTER 2: Technology With a Human Touch: Reaching ESL Students
in Their Own Communities Through Interactive Television   13
  Janet L. Eyring

CHAPTER 3: Closing the Distance in Adult ESL: Two Approaches to
Video-Based Learning   25
  Sylvia Ramirez and K. Lynn Savage

CHAPTER 4: "Show the Baby," the Wave, and 1,000 Thanks:
Three Reasons to Teach via Satellite Television and the Internet   39
  Christine Uber Grosse

CHAPTER 5: Make It a Conference Call: An English Conversation
Course by Telephone in South Korea   51
  Robert J. Dickey

CHAPTER 6: Using the World Wide Web as a Resource for
Models and Interaction in a Writing Course   61
  Janet Raskin

CHAPTER 7: Teaching Tomorrow's Class Today:
English by Telephone and Computer From Hawaii to Tonga   71
  Brent A. Green, Kory J. Collier, and Norman Evans

CHAPTER 8: An Academic Writing Course in Cyberspace 83
    David Catterick

PART 2: PREPARING ESOL TEACHERS AT A DISTANCE

CHAPTER 9: Making Distance Learning Dynamic:
The Evolution of the TelESOL Web-Based Teacher Education Program 97
    Joyce W. Nutta

CHAPTER 10: Expanding Horizons: Delivering Professional Teacher
Development via Satellite Technology and E-Mail in Israel 113
    Yael Bejarano, Esther Klein-Wohl, and Lily Vered

CHAPTER 11: Teacher Education at a Distance in
Canada and Thailand: How Two Cases Measure Up to
Quality Distance Education Indicators 127
    Ruth Epstein

CHAPTER 12: The Pedagogy and Technology of
Distance Learning for Teacher Education: The Evolution of
Instructional Processes and Products 141
    C. Ray Graham, Annela Teemant, Melanie Harris,
    and Ramona M. Cutri

CHAPTER 13: Expanding the Horizon of the
TESOL Practicum via Distance Learning 151
    Michael Janopoulos

CHAPTER 14: Practicing What We Preach:
Optimal Learning Conditions for Web-Based Teacher Education 161
    Joy Egbert and Chin-chi Chao

CHAPTER 15: Avoiding the Pitfalls of Test Writing in a Distance-Learning
Situation: Our Experience at United Arab Emirates University 173
    Lisa Barlow and Christine Canning-Wilson

References 185

Index 191

Acknowledgments

A published book is rarely, if ever, the work of a single individual working alone. A volume of case studies such as this one, however, requires an extraordinary degree of collaboration among many people. As editor of this volume, I am deeply indebted to the host of fine professionals who have contributed to this work in various ways.

First, I need to express my thanks to the contributors of the 14 case studies that appear in this volume. Their real-world experiences with distance teaching and learning form the foundation for this book's content and authenticity. Further, the case study authors' willingness to write up their experiences and share them with the world made it possible for those experiences to benefit others struggling with similar distance education challenges. I also wish to acknowledge the many TESOL professionals who submitted excellent, interesting case studies that could not be included in this volume simply because there was not enough space.

I owe a large debt of gratitude to Alice Feathers, my editorial assistant at Brigham Young University (BYU). Her diligent thoroughness, intelligent questioning, and keen eye for detail greatly increased the quality of the final manuscripts for this book. Likewise, the support I received from the Linguistics Department at BYU was invaluable.

I would also like to recognize the work of Jill Burton, the editor of the Case Studies in TESOL Practice Series, and Marilyn Kupetz, TESOL's managing editor, for their patience and guidance throughout the long process of putting this volume together. Marcella Weiner and Marcia Annis, who put the finishing editorial touches on the work, deserve to be recognized, too.

Finally, I wish to confirm my great appreciation for my wonderful family, who sacrificed much time and attention to support me while I was working on this volume.

Series Editor's Preface

The Case Studies in TESOL Practice series offers innovative and effective examples of practice from the point of view of the practitioner. The series brings together from around the world communities of practitioners who have reflected and written on particular aspects of their teaching. Each volume in the series will cover one specialized teaching focus.

◈ CASE STUDIES

Why a TESOL series focusing on case studies of teaching practice?

Much has been written about case studies and where they fit in a mainstream research tradition (e.g., Nunan, 1992; Stake, 1995; Yin, 1994). Perhaps more important, case studies publicly recognize the value of teachers' reflection on their practice and also constitute a new form of teacher research—or teacher valuing. Case studies support teachers in valuing the uniqueness of their classes, learning from them, and showing how their experience and knowledge can be made accessible to other practitioners in simple but disciplined ways. They are particularly suited to practitioners who want to understand and solve teaching problems in their own contexts.

These case studies are written by practitioners who are able to portray real experience by providing detailed descriptions of teaching practice. These qualities invest the cases with teacher credibility and make them convincing and professionally interesting. The cases also represent multiple views and offer immediate solutions, thus providing perspective on the issues and examples of useful approaches. Informative by nature, they can provide an initial database for further, sustained research. Accessible to wider audiences than many traditional research reports, however, case studies have democratic appeal.

◈ HOW THIS SERIES CAN BE USED

The case studies lend themselves to pre- and in-service teacher education. Because the context of each case is described in detail, it is easy for readers to compare the cases with and evaluate them against their own circumstances. To respond to the wide range of settings in which TESOL functions, cases have been selected from diverse EFL and ESL settings around the world.

The 12 or so case studies in each volume are easy to follow. Teacher writers describe their teaching context and analyze its distinctive features: the particular demands of their context, the issues they have encountered, how they have effectively addressed the issues, and what they have learned. Each case study also offers readers practical suggestions—developed from teaching experience—to adapt and apply to their own teaching.

Already published or in preparation are volumes on

- action research
- academic writing programs
- assessment practices
- bilingual education
- community partnerships
- content-based language instruction
- English for specific purposes
- global English
- intensive English teaching
- interaction and language learning
- international teaching assistants
- journal writing
- mainstreaming
- teacher education
- technology-enhanced learning environments
- teaching English as a foreign language in primary schools
- teaching grammar
- teaching literature

◈ THIS VOLUME

From around the world, teachers and their learners in this volume bridge the tyrannies of distance—language, culture, location, and time—to develop linguistic and teaching skills via electronic and televisual communication, and other techno-logical means. The volume vividly portrays the importance of teamwork and is a tribute to the dedication of teachers in making learning individually relevant in the global contexts in which they teach—to the extent that in the chapters, international education appears as satisfying, real, and intimate as face-to-face classroom interaction.

Jill Burton
University of South Australia, Adelaide

CHAPTER 1

Beyond Adding Telecommunications to a Traditional Course: Insights Into Human and Instructional Factors Affecting Distance Learning in TESOL

Lynn E. Henrichsen

◈ THE DEVELOPMENT OF DISTANCE LEARNING

In its broadest, most classic sense, distance education[1] is any "formal instruction in which a majority of the teaching occurs while educator and learner are at a distance from one another" (Verduin & Clark, 1991, p. 19). This distance may involve both time and space and can be bridged in various ways to accomplish instructional purposes (Heinich, Molenda, Russell, & Smaldino, 1999; Newby, Stepich, Lehman, & Russell, 2000).

By no means a purely modern phenomenon, distance learning began centuries ago in the form of instructional correspondence between traveling members of royal families and their tutors back home. In the 1800s, paper-based postal tuition or correspondence study courses became very popular among the working masses in Europe and America. In the 20th century, telecommunications technology—first radio, then television, and finally computer networks—entered the distance-learning equation. As the 1990s began, the International Council for Distance Education estimated that 10 million people worldwide were studying at a distance every year. (For a thorough review of the history of distance education, see Verduin & Clark, 1991, pp. 15–17.)

Now, as the 21st century dawns, it seems impossible to determine with accuracy how many millions of learners around the world are involved in distance learning in all of its current manifestations. Traditional paper-based correspondence courses are still popular, as are radio broadcasts and audio teleconferences. One- and two-way video teleconferences are also widely used, as are videotapes. Computer-based distance learning has mushroomed with the proliferation of the Internet (Heinich

---

[1] Although some experts make a distinction between *distance education* and *distance learning* (Verduin & Clark, 1991, pp. 10–11), in popular current usage, these two terms (along with others, such as *distance teaching* and *open learning*) are used interchangeably (Heinich, Molenda, Russell, & Smaldino, 1999, p. 404).

et al., 1999). The World Wide Web has created a new range of options, from chat rooms to streaming video. Besides synchronous instruction, in which teacher and learners interact at the same time, asynchronous learning networks allow people to work with remote learning resources at any time, from any place, and at any pace.

◈ DISTANCE LEARNING IN TESOL

As this volume of case studies from around the world illustrates, distance learning is very much a part of TESOL practice today. In fact, in today's world, where the demand for English language skills and prepared teachers of those skills is growing tremendously, distance education is an attractive notion. It offers a powerful answer to the challenge of providing language instruction and teacher preparation for the large numbers of people around the world who need them.

The diverse cases in this volume also show that distance learning in TESOL takes a variety of forms. Practitioners employ the full range of available communications media and information systems. In addition, TESOL educators use distance learning for diverse purposes—ranging from the development of basic language skills to the preparation of ESOL teachers. Accordingly, the first seven cases in this book involve various aspects of teaching ESOL and the final seven concern ESOL teacher preparation programs.

◈ TEN INSIGHTS FROM THE CASE STUDIES

Out of the diversity in these 14 cases emerge 10 insights of value to all TESOL professionals involved in education at a distance. Underlying all these insights is a fundamental idea—that quality distance education involves considerably more than simply taking a program developed in a live, face-to-face context and then delivering it at a distance using telecommunications. Achieving success in distance education involves dealing with interrelated cultural, psychological, pedagogical, and pragmatic factors (Chen, Mashhadi, Ang, & Harkrider, 1999; Henderson, 1996). These will be explained as each insight is discussed.

1. Various information-communications technology options exist for delivering language instruction and teacher education at a distance, each with its own strengths.

In a well-designed program, the strengths of various technology options will be recognized and inform design decisions. The choice of instructional medium should be based on factors such as course content, student population, institutional facilities, and available staff. Bejarano, Klein-Wohl, and Vered (chapter 10) describe a course in Israel that employed two different distance-learning technologies— synchronous satellite television broadcasts and asynchronous e-mail communications. The satellite broadcasts allowed for visual input, for instance, whereas the e-mail discussions allowed students time to think and rethink.

In a well-designed distance-learning course, different media can work together in a complementary fashion as did Uber Grosse's program in Arizona and Mexico (chapter 4), employing satellite television, a Web-based discussion board, and e-mail.

Likewise, Ramirez and Savage (chapter 3) used print materials, videotapes, audio-tapes, telephone voice mail, and face-to-face instruction—each for different purposes.

2. Advanced, complicated information-communications systems are not necessarily better, especially in some international settings.

A corollary to these cases is the recognition that the use of more complicated technology does not necessarily translate into better teaching or learning (Ham, 2000). In fact, in many remote areas, simple communication systems may actually work better than the newest information technology.

For example, Epstein's distance-learning programs in Canada and Thailand (chapter 11) were primarily print based to ensure accessibility in remote areas. Print was also advantageous for ease of revision and cost.

Other authors had similar experiences. In Korea, Dickey (chapter 5) chose telephones over computers because neither he nor his students had access to high-speed Internet service. In Tonga, where technological options were limited and sometimes unreliable, Green, Collier, and Evans (chapter 7) achieved success using telephone connections for transmitting voice data and computer data. Even when sophisticated communications systems exist, simpler is sometimes better. As Graham, Teemant, Harris, and Cutri (chapter 12) describe, after teaching over a state network that allowed instantaneous two-way video and audio communications but was difficult to use, having videotapes that could be played locally by a site facilitator was a step forward in terms of usability and instructional effectiveness. Like other educators (Bender, McLaughlin, & Ehrhart, 1993; Collis, 1999; Soh & Soon, 1991), they have recognized that so-called low-end technology definitely has its place.

3. Regardless of the technology used, solid instructional design and effective teaching methods are crucial.

Perhaps the paramount lesson emerging from these diverse cases is that, in any setting, the instructional approaches employed are just as important as the content or communications systems themselves (Ham, 2000). Even technologically simple distance education can be advanced in terms of its instructional design, and when even the most advanced technology is used with poorly designed instruction, the outcome is often weak teaching and learning.

A number of chapters support this point. Nutta (chapter 9) emphasizes the importance of using established instructional design processes. Bejarano et al. (chapter 10) highly recommend conducting needs analyses, while Eyring (chapter 2) concurs that such a foundation goes a long way toward making distance education truly learner centered.

In their chapter, Graham et al. note that successful distance learning depends less on the delivery system than it does on the system's pedagogy. Other authors agree that using teaching methods appropriate to the distance-learning situation and the learners in it is crucial: In California, Ramirez and Savage noted that many of their learners were not prepared for distant study and often felt isolated, so these educators designed special forms to promote and reinforce independent learning. In Korea, Dickey found that his usual teaching approach, which relied on using visual presentations, was not viable when teaching by telephone, so he developed new procedures. In Israel, Bejarano et al. increased comprehension and retention by using a "review/preview" procedure, keeping television broadcasts short and lively and minimizing the classic, boring talking head. Several other authors make the point that effective distance instruction must be active and do much more than merely deliver information. Eyring enlivened her television ESL course by including interesting videos, music, and visual aids and by engaging her distant students in experiential learning. Nutta, in her teacher preparation course, engaged the teachers in site-based field experiences and reflection, role-plays, case studies, interviews, and actual lessons. Epstein's program gave participants opportunities to try out new teaching practices and to reflect on them. Similarly, Egbert and Chao (chapter 14) used scenarios and case journals in their teacher preparation course.

Many other distance educators have written about issues of instructional design and information presentation in distance learning (e.g., Davis, 1990; Wagner, 1993). Some have focused on cultural issues (Chen, Mashhadi, Ang, & Harkrider, 1999; Collis, 1999; Wild, 1999). For a good general set of instructional design guidelines for distance learning, see Thomas (1999).

4. Distance education involves teachers and learners in new or modified roles for which they must be prepared and that must be taken into account in program planning.

In distance-learning programs, teachers and learners often find themselves in roles that are not typical in traditional face-to-face instruction. Distance educators have many duties that go beyond what classroom teachers normally do. As many cases in this book attest, these duties include carefully organizing and structuring class activities far in advance as well as planning and scripting instruction to a high level of detail. Graham et al. note that, in comparison with regular teaching, designing their distance-learning courses required "as much as 10 times the planning effort." In addition, a distance educator's responsibilities may include massive record keeping. Simply keeping track of all the incoming assignments in a distance-learning course enrolling a large number of students can become a gargantuan task. Uber Grosse, Green et al., and Nutta had to come up with special protocols for dealing with the avalanche of e-mail messages. Other new roles include training facilitators at remote sites, designing materials, and supervising facilitators. These additional responsibilities are time consuming, and several authors note that distance educators need release time, extra resources and funding, and additional compensation. Many distance educators also find that they have to deal with complicated, intimidating communications media. Eyring notes that television teaching requires special training, and Graham et al. report that learning to teach to the camera is often difficult.

Another special challenge for teachers of distance courses, which may enroll hundreds of students who may be thousands of miles away, is getting to know class members. Teachers may never see students' faces or have any contact with them outside of class. In such circumstances, even learning students' names is unusually difficult.

Asking productive questions appropriately is yet another challenge for distance educators. Eyring found that the open-ended, broadcast-style questions that had served her so well in live, face-to-face classes were "met with silence" when she taught via television. Her solution was to always call on individual students at remote sites by name. Of course, when a distance-learning course includes several sites and many students, even calling on someone by name can be difficult and confusing for the teacher. One solution is to give a name to each remote site and create seating charts of students at each site.

Giving clear instructions when students are far away and communications channels are limited is yet another challenge, especially in asynchronous programs. When developing Web-based teacher education, Nutta worried about how to ensure comprehension and avoid confusion. Responding to this challenge requires different effort and care than that typically required in face-to-face, real-time settings.

Motivating students who are geographically or temporally distant is also difficult but often crucial. Nutta took on the role of "cheerleader." At the same time, distance-learning students must assume greater responsibility for their own motivation and discipline, particularly in asynchronous, independent study-type programs where students have little direct contact with the teacher or classmates. In such programs, designers need to build motivational features into course activities and materials. Ramirez and Savage did this by creating specially designed forms that encouraged independent learning.

Finally, working as a member of an instructional development and delivery team that includes technicians, facilitators, materials producers, and so forth is a role that is foreign to most traditional classroom teachers. This team member role is discussed in the next insight.

5. Working as a member of an instructional development and delivery team is an essential but challenging new role for many teachers involved in distance education.

In traditional classrooms, teachers work mainly on their own. In distance-learning programs, however, course development and delivery is usually such a large, complex task that a team of workers is required. These team members fulfill diverse roles, including content expert, instructional designer, editor, media specialist, course producer, computer technician, telephone specialist, camera operator, and graphic artist. When teamwork becomes a necessity, teachers no longer have autonomy or sole responsibility for instruction. Case authors frequently comment on the need for collaboration and the importance of cultivating friendly, cooperative relationships and healthy communication. Distance educators ignore this challenge at their peril.

Team teaching among teachers is also common in distance-learning programs. For example, Bejarano et al. taught their distance-learning course together. Uber Grosse relied heavily on a team of seven teaching assistants. Epstein's programs employed a staff of tutor/markers. Many authors report using site facilitators at their programs' remote locations. Working with other teachers, tutors, and site facilitators lightens a teacher's load in some ways but additional coordination and communications needs also make it heavier.

6. Active, interactive learning is important but requires extra effort in distance-learning settings.

Many researchers and educators have noted the value of active engagement and interaction—in learning generally and in distance learning (Egbert, Chao, & Ngeow, 2000; Hazari & Schnorr, 1999; Kroder, Suess, & Sachs, 1998; Parker, 1997; Pearlman, 1994; Rodes, Knapczyk, Chapman, & Chung, 2000; Soliman, & Warschauer, 2000). Learners recognize this value also. Fulford and Zhang (1993) found a significant correlation between learners' perceptions of interaction and their satisfaction with distance-learning courses.

Nevertheless, actively involving learners and creating teacher-student and student-student interaction when these parties are widely separated is a daunting challenge that has long plagued distance education. In distance-learning courses using print media and the mail system, communications go back and forth at a slow pace. The lag between when a student asks a question and when the teacher answers it can be weeks. Modern communications media have virtually overcome this challenge. Satellite transmissions, such as those used by Bejarano et al. in Israel, allow distant educators and learners to communicate back and forth nearly instantaneously. Fiber optics networks of the type employed by Janopoulos in Iowa (chapter 13) permit two-way, real-time interaction to occur when students and teachers are hundreds of miles apart. And, as Raskin's case (chapter 6) illustrates, the World Wide Web enables students on different continents to communicate with one another with virtually no delay.

However, even when communications technology allows instantaneous message transmission, involvement and interaction do not occur automatically in distance-learning settings. Creating the degree of activity and human interaction that is usually taken for granted in face-to-face teaching situations is a challenge that most of the authors had to address. These challenges are especially great when designing asynchronous, automated, independent-study instruction. With varying degrees of success, creators of Web sites and computer programs have attempted to simulate a human interface that interacts with learners. Nevertheless, many of the authors who used synchronous, real-time instruction also experienced problems fostering involvement and interaction among students. They addressed this question in various ways depending on their particular setting. The students in the case of Green et al., for instance, were thousands of miles away from the teacher and could only be heard, not seen. Consequently, special protocols for encouraging and tracking participation had to be instituted. Even though Eyring had visual contact with the students in her television course, she had to modify her normal questioning procedure and call on particular students in distant classrooms by name. Uber Grosse's experience was similar. Bejarano et al. and their students were pleased with the quantity of interaction that took place in their course but were dissatisfied with its quality. They concluded that it was important not only to encourage participation in discussions but also advise students on which types of comments were most productive.

Involvement and interaction entail more than simple class discussion, of course, and case authors report an impressive variety of engaging, interactive activities. Egbert and Chao designed student-instructor interaction, problem-solving, application, and self-reflection activities into their Web-based course. They also incorporated joint hands-on activities, including MOO field trips. WebCT (2000) gave Catterick (chapter 8) and his students bulletin board, private mail, whiteboard, and chat room options for communicating with one another. Nutta gave her teachers in Florida the possibility of interacting with ESL students at Tel-Aviv University in Israel by means of key pal projects. The model developed by Graham et al. employed an active learning approach that pushed students to engage with content, reflect on their experiences, and interact with one another. Subsequent evaluations suggested that this cooperative approach to learning was one of the program's more valuable aspects.

Another teacher-student interaction challenge involves how and when to correct ESL learners' mistakes in English. In Catterick's case, this challenge was complicated because, in virtual chat rooms, students communicated in writing, but other aspects of their discourse were more characteristic of casual speech. His solution was a course policy that tolerated errors in chat sessions. In Raskin's writing course, on the other hand, correction of errors was expected. Her solution was to use double-column Netscape tables with the students' writing pasted into the left column and her comments in the right column. She also marked students' work electronically, providing them with clear guidance for revising it. Facing the challenge of responding to a large volume of student writing, Green et al. used macros to expedite the process.

7. Building a sense of community among distant learners and overcoming their sense of isolation is challenging but of great value.

The human contact and sense of community that are natural in face-to-face classrooms are not so easy to duplicate when people study at widely separated locations or different times (Killion, 1997). Participants in many distance-learning programs report feeling isolated. Several authors in this volume dealt with the challenge of creating community among separated learners, and they came up with a variety of solutions.

A typical first step was to acquaint students at different sites with one another. In her television course, Eyring had students at remote sites write letters introducing themselves. She then read some of these letters on the air. For the same reason, Ramirez and Savage had learners exchange photos, e-mail addresses, and assignments. Nutta took digital pictures of each team and sent members copies to post by their computers.

To create greater feelings of community and opportunities for interaction, Uber Grosse organized her class of 116 students into six "neighborhoods." Graduate student assistants served as neighborhood managers and gave students extensive, personalized feedback on their writing. To personalize instruction in the satellite sessions, Uber Grosse studied the roll in advance so that she could call on students at distant sites by name. Further personalizing the class, she took time in each session to celebrate weddings, births, birthdays, and holidays. Students responded favorably to all these devices. In Raskin's Web-based course, weekly, hour-long chat sessions served a valuable socializing function. This socialization laid a crucial foundation for the peer-review and partner-feedback processes that occurred later. In her teacher preparation courses, Nutta responded to the challenge of building community with a constructivist approach that required collaborative teamwork. Likewise, Graham et al. organized participants into cooperative groups that worked together throughout the course and continued to exist long after the formal instruction ended.

Whenever it was practical, educators in the cases arranged for face-to-face meetings with their distant-learning students to help build feelings of community. In their e-mail course in Israel, Bejarano et al. included five face-to-face class meetings that allowed participants to identify each other. All of the students in Nutta's course lived in the same state, so she conducted a mandatory, face-to-face orientation session at the beginning and end of the course to promote camaraderie. Likewise, in Thailand, Epstein found a face-to-face orientation seminar very useful, and Uber Grosse traveled to Mexico City to meet students face to face. Other distance educators (e.g., Cooper, 2000) also strongly recommend face-to-face meetings.

8. Flexibility in the design and delivery of distance-learning programs is crucial to their success.

Adaptability is crucial to success in distance education. Wise program designers allow for flexibility in the instructional program and the delivery system so that they can adjust to varying circumstances. These adjustments can be made necessary by geographical distances, the passage of time, or other factors, such as participants' cultures.

Distance-learning programs often involve participants from widely scattered geographic areas. Consequently, instruction originally designed for just one cultural or linguistic group may be delivered to learners from very different backgrounds. Distance educators need to be sensitive to such differences and anticipate the need for linguistic and cultural adjustments in the course content or delivery system. Henderson (1996) recommends incorporating multiple cultural perspectives in an eclectic paradigm so that students from different cultures can be accommodated. Collis (1999) discusses cultural dimensions to consider in program planning and gives a set of 10 design guidelines for culture-related flexibility.

In this volume, Barlow and Canning-Wilson's experience (chapter 15) illustrates the cultural challenges that distance educators face. Their challenge was to produce interesting yet culturally sensitive test material for students at nine different distance-learning centers in the United Arab Emirates. The conservative Islamic culture of the country precluded topics related to religion, sex, and politics. In addition, the authors had to make allowances for other cultural aspects (e.g., tribal/family alliances and political and social tensions specific to the Gulf).

Flexibility in program administration is also valuable. Bejarano et al. had to make quick, communications-system adjustments when they taught their e-mail course. Some students registered without realizing that having access to e-mail was a prerequisite, so the instructors arranged for them to participate using fax communications instead. "Rolling with the punches" when the technology crashes is also crucial to success in distance programs (Reinhardt & Isbell, 1999, p. 17). For instance, Graham et al. report that their two-way video system would occasionally fail, and they would lose communication with another site. When this happened, the facilitator at that site had to quickly improvise another activity.

Adjustments in program design and delivery also gradually occur. Nutta, for example, describes the evolution of her distance-learning program through three stages. The ability to adjust over time produced a markedly superior course. Graham et al. also recount the progression of their program through several generations of technology and pedagogy.

9. When learners are spread over a large geographic area, evaluating their progress or assessing program success entails some special challenges.

What do students learn from this program? What results does it produce? Such fundamental questions loom large in administrators' minds when they consider distance-learning programs, especially when those programs are not only innovative but also expensive (Hawkes & Cambre, 2000). Although recognizing that distance learning has its own set of assessment problems, distance educators often ask these questions themselves (e.g., Hazari & Schnorr, 1999; Sujo de Montes & Gonzales, 2000; Wade, 1999).

In this volume, Nutta wondered how to evaluate students fairly, while holding them to on-campus course objectives and standards. Barlow and Canning-Wilson, charged with creating and administering examinations that could be administered at nine different distance-learning centers throughout the United Arab Emirates, faced challenges of test security and cultural sensitivity heightened by distance. Students at different centers not only took tests at different times (and had cultural attitudes that encouraged "collaborative test-taking") but also came from different tribes in the seven federated emirates.

Just as evaluating students in distance-learning programs is more complicated than in traditional classrooms, distance-learning program evaluation also involves additional challenges. For instance, as Epstein notes, traditional course evaluation systems may not ask questions appropriate to distance learning. Ryan (2000) makes a similar point: Additional elements and perspectives need to be considered. For example, as noted in Insight 5, distance-learning courses often involve a team of instructional designers, on-site facilitators, and technicians, but traditional course evaluation forms may focus only on the instructor.

Indeed, whether it is appropriate to compare distance and traditional courses at all is a fundamental question. Epstein notes that distance education differs in many ways from traditional education and must be evaluated on its own terms, not simply by comparing it to face-to-face instruction. Other professionals and professional organizations agree (California Teachers of English to Speakers of Other Languages, 1995; Collis, 1999; National Council of State Supervisors of Foreign Language, 1990; Shale & Gomes, 1998) and have proposed sets of characteristics and performance indicators particular to distance-learning programs.

Despite these assessment challenges, several authors report successes in program evaluation and improvement. Bejarano et al. used a specially designed distance-learning course evaluation system that included multiple-choice items and interviews. Graham et al. employed video recordings of class sessions along with student evaluations and suggestions. Epstein's CERTESL program conducted formative evaluations of each course during its pilot year and summative evaluations in subsequent years. Nutta involved her students in renewing and updating the content of the course Web site.

10. Reducing or eliminating student attrition in distance-education programs requires effort.

A notoriously high dropout rate has traditionally plagued distance-learning programs. External incentives can pressure students to finish a distance program, but this sort of extrinsic motivation seems artificial and antithetical to the spirit of learning. Fortunately, distance-learning program designers can combat student attrition in other ways. Many of these are related to the previous nine insights. For example, as Dickey's case shows, using the right delivery system for a particular situation (Insights 1 and 2) can reduce student frustrations and thus encourage students to continue in a course. Engaging participants in active, interactive learning (Insight 6) is a proven way to increase their motivation, as is making them feel that they belong to a supportive community of learners (Insight 7). In contrast, distance-learning programs in which students feel isolated seem to have the highest rate of noncompletion.

Several of the chapters convincingly suggest that successfully implementing the principles contained in these insights can reduce or eliminate student attrition in distance-learning programs. For example, 72% of the students in the satellite course by Bejarano et al. attended all the sessions. Students in their e-mail course gave it a rating of 4.8 (on a 5-point scale), indicating a high degree of satisfaction, and 82% of them completed it. Similarly, by making her distance-learning course accessible and interactive, Nutta eliminated attrition entirely.

◈ CONCLUSION

The insights gained from studying and comparing these 14 different cases make it obvious that quality distance education involves considerably more than simply using information-communications technology to deliver a traditional classroom course at a distance. The experiences of these authors demonstrate that successful distance education requires overcoming challenges that do not normally occur in traditional classroom settings and that go far beyond using the right telecommunications system. Regardless of where and how their programs are offered, providers of ESOL instruction and teacher education at a distance frequently encounter difficulties involving human and instructional factors. A deeper understanding of these factors can lead to fewer problems and greater success in distance education efforts.

◈ CONTRIBUTOR

Lynn E. Henrichsen is a professor in the Department of Linguistics at Brigham Young University in Provo, Utah, in the United States. A former chair of TESOL's Teacher Education Interest Section, his 25-year career in language teaching, research, and materials development has taken him to Brazil, Mexico, China, Hawaii, Japan, Samoa, and Spain. For nearly two decades, he has been investigating the role of human, cultural, institutional, and instructional factors in the successful implementation of educational innovations.

PART 1

Teaching ESOL at a Distance

CHAPTER 2

Technology With a Human Touch: Reaching ESL Students in Their Own Communities Through Interactive Television

Janet L. Eyring

◈ INTRODUCTION

Imagine, if you will, a student named Hoa coming home after work and, instead of having to travel for miles to get to his ESL class, he has to walk only two blocks. Watch as he sits down with his neighbors in a makeshift classroom that is an office by day and a classroom by night. This convenient and unusual setting is not the only thing that distinguishes this class from other ESL classes. First, he is greeted by an administrator who knows his needs and possibly his name. Second, 2 of 4 nights a week a teacher learner from a local university instructs Hoa and his fellow students. The other 2 nights he is again greeted by the teacher learner/facilitator, but he listens to and views instruction from an experienced teacher being broadcast live from the university over a television monitor. Besides just watching the teacher on television, he can speak to her about his issues and problems. He can also interact with hundreds of other students seated in similar classrooms talking into similar microphones in neighborhoods across the area.

This scenario describes one field-based, distance-learning model implemented over three school sessions in Orange County, California. Key participants in the program included university and off-site administrators, media center technicians, an ESL television teacher, teacher learner facilitators, and adult ESL students. Attention to student needs through a problem-posing curriculum brought the human touch to this telecommunications-based model, which relied on three delivery types:

1. live studio (teacher was face to face with students)

2. interactive televised instruction (ITI) (instruction was facilitated live at a distant site)

3. video (videos of broadcasts were played and facilitated)

◈ CONTEXT

The California State University, Fullerton (CSUF), Extended Education Distance Learning Program (known as the DLP) was a collaborative endeavor cosponsored by CSUF Extended Education, the CSUF Department of Foreign Languages and

Literatures' master's in TESOL and ESL certificate programs, and four off-site nonprofit programs: Vietnamese Political Detainees Mutual Association (VPDMA), in Westminster; Service-Employment-Redevelopment (SER)-Jobs for Progress, in Santa Ana; La Vista Adult School, in Fullerton; and Rancho Santiago Community College's Adult Continuing Education (RSCC-ACE) Program.[1]

The DLP began as an interactive, beginning-level ESL course that would prepare mostly Vietnamese and Hispanic students in survival and workplace English and would therefore focus on listening and speaking skills. The ESL course would be nonscripted to save costs,[2] taught in front of a live class in a CSUF television studio classroom, and broadcast to various off-site classrooms. The program's purpose was to enhance already existing English classes or provide classes where none existed before.[3]

The dean of the DLP served as the administrative coordinator of the project in charge of funding, locating off-site sponsors, and directing media center operations. As the ESL specialist in the CSUF Department of Foreign Languages and Literatures, I served as the academic coordinator in charge of curriculum decisions, recruitment and training of faculty, and research. The off-site sponsors generally were in charge of recruitment and retention of students, maintenance of facilities, and, in some cases, compensation of facilitators at their sites.[4] The DLP gradually evolved over the course of three sessions, benefiting from regular feedback and input from administrators and the ESL specialist as well as the television teacher, teacher learner facilitators, sponsors, and students.

◈ DESCRIPTION

Students

Much was learned about the students in the program through a two-page information form or needs assessment (Benhalim, Berces, Dong, & Willoughby, 1993), which was translated into Spanish and Vietnamese and administered to students. Students provided biographical data and their opinions about how many hours a week they spent doing various activities in English (e.g., speaking with U.S. friends, watching television), how much they needed to use English in various situations (e.g., at the supermarket, at the doctor's office), their preferences about class content (e.g., U.S.

---

[1] This latter program was added during the third session only.

[2] To put some perspective on cost, a produced telecourse may cost $250,000–$1,000,000 to produce 18–24 videos. The cost of this project was much less for a number of reasons. First, the university already had contracted certain studio staff (e.g., engineers, camera people), who did not need to be paid additional fees, to provide telecommunications support. Second, the television teacher was not a trained actor who demanded an actors's salary, and she taught live, without scripts. Third, the initial outlay on equipment was about $9,300, but this constituted a reusable cost because the same equipment could be used thereafter. Fourth, teacher learner facilitators, who served as teachers 2 nights a week, were paid salaries commensurate to graduate assistants (versus professional teachers) at the university.

[3] Off-site sponsors cited statistics, such as 20 new Vietnamese immigrants arriving each month for whom there were no English classes available. Also, a large number of new legal residents (through the U.S. amnesty legislation) for whom there were insufficient classes immigrated to Santa Ana.

[4] RSCC (now called Santa Ana College) assigned a regular faculty member who was paid a regular salary (versus a reduced-rate facilitator's salary) to facilitate the class at this site. This faculty member also had been trained in the CSUF MA in TESOL program.

culture, homework), and how much they wanted their children to learn English. They also were asked to rank the importance of reading situations, writing situations, English class activities, and classroom grouping preferences. The form was relatively easy to fill out because many of the items employed a Likert-scale format.

The results of this data collection revealed that students enrolled in the DLP covered a large age span (18–79) and had arrived in the United States between 1961 and 1994. The group was about equally divided between Hispanic (55%) and Vietnamese (45%) students. Most of the students (78.7%) had received at least a primary education in their native country (6 or more years of schooling); however, the majority (76.4%) had completed only 2 years or less of English study. Many students reported having had no hours of English contact with Americans (40.2%) or with anyone else (33.3%). When asked about their desire to learn about North American culture and have their children learn English, however, many indicated that they would like this "much" (79.7%) or "very much" (88.2%).

Classroom Logistics

The program used different types of classroom facilities, from the sparse (the VPDMA office in Westminster) to the well equipped (the showplace classroom at RSCC). Television instruction via telecommunications-based methods was reserved for Tuesday and Thursday evenings, and a live facilitator provided follow-up and reinforcement instruction on Monday and Wednesday evenings from 6:45–8:45 p.m. during the first session and at the preferred time of 7:00–9:00 p.m. during the last two sessions.[5]

During this three-session time period, most of the students received ITI via microwave transmission. However, this was complicated when the RSCC-ACE site, because of logistical difficulties, could only receive the live instruction via cable.[6] The La Vista students received face-to-face instruction in the television studio, but one class at VPDMA received video instruction during Session 2 because of high student demand for classes during an earlier part of the day. See Table 1 for a summary of classroom characteristics at various sites over the three class sessions.

Recruitment, Placement, and Enrollment Procedures

Recruiting students for a nontraditional school setting such as a distance-learning program required extra effort. The DLP was originally advertised through a variety of means (e.g., neighborhood newspapers, radio ads, word of mouth, Job Training Partnership Act referral centers) as a beginning-level class, although students with higher proficiency showed interest in attending simply because of the convenient location of the classes. Nonliterate students (in their first language or second

---

[5] The exception to this was the video class that received video instruction on Monday and Wednesday nights to accommodate the 1-day delay from the time of broadcast to the actual time that the tape could be used.

[6] The fact that RSCC-ACE received the program via cable opened up opportunities for a home viewing audience to see the program. We received only anecdotal comments about the effects of this program on home viewers. They were all positive. In fact, several students enrolled in the program because they or a relative saw the program and inquired about how they could enroll. Other ESL teachers commented to the television teacher and me about how much they enjoyed watching the program as well.

TABLE 1. CLASSROOM CHARACTERISTICS AT DIFFERENT DISTANCE-LEARNING PROGRAM SITES

Session	Weeks	Site	Proficiency Levels	Facilitators	Telecommunications Type
1	16	CSUF/La Vista	1–3 (multilevel)	A	Live studio
		VPDMA	1–3 (multilevel)	B	ITI-microwave
		SER	1	C	ITI-microwave
		SER	2	D	ITI-microwave
		SER	3	E	ITI-microwave
2	10	CSUF/La Vista	1–3 (multilevel)	F	Live studio
		VPDMA	1	B	ITI-microwave
		VPDMA	2	G	ITI-microwave
		VPDMA	1–3 (multilevel)	H	Video
		SER	1	D	ITI-microwave
		SER	2	I	ITI-microwave
		SER	3	J	ITI-microwave
3	10	CSUF/La Vista	1–3 (multilevel)	F/K	Live studio
		VPDMA	1	G/I	ITI-microwave
		VPDMA	2	L/J	ITI-microwave
		SER	1	M/N	ITI-microwave
		SER	2	O	ITI-microwave
		SER	3	P	ITI-microwave
		RSCC-ACE	2	Q	ITI-cable

Note. CSUF = California State University, Fullerton; VPDMA = Vietnamese Political Detainees Mutual Association; SER = Service-Employment-Redevelopment Jobs; RSCC-ACE = Rancho Santiago Community College's Adult Continuing Education; ITI = interactive televised instruction. The letters in the Facilitators column represent the individual facilitators.

language) were encouraged not to enroll. Students were placed into each class according to the RSCC Adult ESL Placement Test, and they mostly scored within three levels: 1 (low beginning), 2 (high beginning), or 3 (low intermediate). Classes at certain sites or times were multilevel, depending on the resources and participants available.

Over three class sessions, the size of the DLP increased from five to seven classes. An average of 262 students enrolled in each of the three sessions (averaging about 37 students a class). The first session lasted 16 weeks (consistent with the CSUF schedule), but this was later reduced to 10 weeks so that the two latter sessions would better accommodate off-campus schedules.

Student Responses to the Program

A key concern of many distance-learning programs is whether students appreciate and learn from them. In this case, classroom observations revealed that students were interested and involved. For example, the class ham in the studio class, a Latin American female, was widely recognized and appreciated at the Vietnamese- and Spanish-speaking sites and thus generated much conversation. Students also learned from each other across sites, as evidenced by the Vietnamese students informing the Latin American students about Tet (the Vietnamese New Year), and the Mexican students teaching others about Cinco de Mayo (a holiday marking the 1862 Mexican victory over the French), as well as other topics. Long, fluent (but sometimes ungrammatical) letters to the television teacher expressed pleasure with the class, as shown in Figure 1.

At the end-of-session graduation party, Vietnamese and Hispanic students mingled and received attractive diplomas of completion. The gifts students bought for the teachers and facilitators showed much appreciation; especially gratifying were the bouquets of flowers purchased for the television teacher by the video class members—and they had never actually met the teacher in person.

◈ DISTINGUISHING FEATURES

Curriculum

The learner-centered curriculum emphasized survival and workplace English skills as identified by the preassessment questionnaire and incorporated a problem-posing component (Auerbach, 1992; Freire, 1981; Wallerstein, 1983a; 1983b) that used students' experiences and ideas as a springboard for discussion. The textbook chosen for Session 1 was *Real-Life English* (Jolly & Robinson, 1988) but was later changed during Sessions 2 and 3 to the more appropriate *Crossroads, Book 2* (Frankel & Fuchs, 1995), which used problem-posing themes.

The television teacher usually prepared lesson plans for one or two units of work, detailing follow-up and reinforcement activities on nontelevision nights and leaving television-night descriptions rather abbreviated because she would be directing instruction on these nights. These plans were distributed through the mail, via the academic coordinator, or among facilitators the week before they would be taught. The plans included important announcements and instructions to facilitators, key dates and topics, names of classroom activities, relevant page numbers in the texts, and supplementary materials and activities.

Teaching in the DLP reflected the full range of communicative and traditional language teaching methods and techniques (e.g., dialogues, drills, dictations, role-plays, games, jazz chants, songs). On television nights, lessons focused on the development of listening and speaking skills, often including several tasks. Typically, the television teacher introduced the first activity of the task for the whole network of learners to complete. Sometimes the studio class demonstrated how it was to be done. This was followed by breakout sessions where each small group at each site worked on the next step of the task (with the help of a facilitator). An "All Sites Practice" instruction graphic reminded the facilitators of what they should do with the class. Finally, the task concluded with a report back to the television teacher and the group as a whole. Direct responses to the television teacher through the

---

Dear _____,

The first thing I want to tell you thank you for teaching us . . . Yesterday I was thinking a lot about your classes and How you teach us, and your classes are so important to me . . . I wanted to tell you something, . . . I hope you never change because it looks that you're a Very good Person . . .

FIGURE 1. Sample Letter to the Television Teacher

microphone were limited to three to five students from any one site; however, all students participated during the breakout sessions.

Managing Class Time on Air

Making the course relevant and interesting to students in this new distance-learning space necessitated a new structuring of class time and a different type of classroom management. First, the television teacher used class names for each of the sites to create a feeling of greater cohesiveness. Students were asked to write letters of introduction to the teacher (who would not be able to see the majority of the students in person because the ITI communication was only one way); some of these were later read on the air so that students across sites would get to know each other.

Another activity with a similar purpose was the program research project, in which the television teacher asked students to bring in forms they had obtained (e.g., medical history forms, job application forms) or pictures, photos, or stories that would be of interest to others. They also were encouraged to continue writing letters to the teacher, who, in turn, incorporated many of these materials into a lesson or displayed them on the television screen.

Differences in the nature of the activities on television nights versus nontelevision nights became more marked as the program went on. Generally, Monday and Wednesday reinforcement nights were reserved for journal writing and textbook and resource book activities because the facilitator could monitor and give feedback on extended writing more easily than the television teacher could. The Tuesday and Thursday television nights tended to include more interactive activities, such as picture stories, dictations, video clips, communicative strategy instruction, idiom practice, music with lyrics, and vocabulary games, to capitalize on the visual nature of the medium and to unite students across phone, microwave, and cable lines.

Less Successful Activities

Open-ended questions as discussion prompts and information gap activities, two activities that would seem to promote communicative interaction, only had limited success in the distance-learning environment. In most ESL classrooms, open-ended questions or referential questions are presumed to effectively generate discussion (Brown, 1994). However, over the air, such questions often would be met with silence. Once the television teacher began naming a particular class to provide the answer, class sessions went much more smoothly.

Where some group members hold certain information and others hold complementary information, information gap activities generally are quite successful in generating discussion among people. However, when each class was provided with different information that was to be shared with other classes over the air, invariably a facilitator from one class had forgotten to complete the photocopying of his or her portion of the activity, causing the whole activity to break down. Games and puzzles such as "concentration" proved much more effective, as the television teacher herself was involved with covering and uncovering hidden information that competing off-sites would try to guess.

Challenges and Roles of the Television Teacher

Television teaching is challenging, and teachers who do it need special training. Although the television teacher had a solid background in TESOL theory and practice with a master's degree in TESOL and several years of teaching experience, she had had no previous experience teaching on television. Her knowledge of the process was largely limited to her own research and written information contained in a training packet designed by the director of the DLP at CSUF (Bentley, 1993). The packet included information about copyright concerns, lesson planning, classroom interaction techniques, and preparation of visuals for the camera.

From the start of the project, the television teacher was optimistic about delivering instruction via distance education, and she approached the task enthusiastically and creatively, emphasizing that the program was a "high-touch, high-tech" program, a program that increased distances between students and the teacher but did not necessarily demand that students lose touch with the teacher.

Overall, the television teacher assumed a different, more expanded role than she usually took in regular classes in the areas of planning, facilitator training, materials design, and supervision.

Planner

Because the program was broadcast on 2 nights with alternate nights labeled as reinforcement nights, the teacher not only wrote lesson plans for the nights she taught on television but also wrote plans for the reinforcement nights that would follow up on television night material.

Facilitator/Trainer

The television teacher helped me (as the academic coordinator) plan and execute various types of preservice training for participating facilitators. This training included a 5-hour orientation at the beginning of the school term, during which facilitators were informed about procedures, materials, methods, and assessment. It also included one or two 2-hour meetings, during which facilitators discussed what was happening at the off-sites, reviewed and discussed pedagogical procedures, and were oriented to the team-teaching approach. After the first session, a 15-minute preclass talk was introduced on television nights to prepare facilitators for tasks and expectations for the evening, as well as any changes in the lesson plans. Because of technical hookup difficulties, these talks did not always ensue as scheduled; however, when they did, they proved very effective in creating a smooth class, as all necessary materials were ready for use.

Materials Designer

Because the two different textbooks that were used did not precisely reflect the goals of the program, the television teacher had to create many new materials that would encourage students' introspection about their own lives and ways they could discuss relevant issues. For instance, the teacher created many original *codes* over the three pilot sessions. A code, according to Wallerstein (1983b), can be a picture, photograph, video clip, dialog, diagram, or other instructional device that encapsulates an issue that is particularly pressing in students' lives. These codes are chosen as a result of the observant teacher listening to the students in order to identify themes or problems (sometimes quite emotional ones) that students are motivated to discuss.

The teacher then leads an inductive discussion, based on the code, in which students name the problem, come to understand it, and possibly solve it. Some of the codes included in this program were original dialog scripts to encourage the use of functional language, found or created video clips related to the students' lives, interesting realia and props, and collected pictures that stimulated discussion among students in the television teacher's class, as well as across sites.

Supervisor of Facilitators

Teaching a distance-learning class with a heavy interactive component, as this one had, necessitated much supervision on the part of the teacher. The teacher had to know the facilitators at each site as well as the teaching conditions of each particular classroom. The demands of the multilevel adult class were increased because now the teacher had several sites to worry about, knowing that sometimes the beginners were straining to understand her, whereas the more advanced students were not challenged at all.

In sum, the television teacher was the key to success in the instructional process. Without a skilled teacher, hundreds of students would have found it difficult to take the course seriously and participate from a distance. Facilitators also would have found it difficult to reinforce materials for an instructor they did not like and respect.

Facilitator Responsibilities, Training, and Roles

Seventeen teacher learners from the certificate and master's programs in TESOL at CSUF facilitated classes during the three sessions. Although we originally had planned that one facilitator would be present in each class all 4 nights a week, we changed this arrangement, as teacher learner schedules did not always permit it. During Session 3, as shown in Table 1, facilitators shared teaching responsibilities with one teacher teaching part of the week and the other teacher teaching the rest. Only a few facilitators carried over from one session to the next. Besides attending facilitator training sessions, facilitators also were required to attend gatherings at the beginning and end (after the first session, only at the end) of the sessions.

The facilitators took on the following roles in the DLP.

Team Teachers

The television teacher encouraged the idea that the facilitators were team teachers with her. For example, on television nights they were to stand in front of the class at three off-sites (or to the sides of the class in the studio) and be prepared to answer questions and direct students in activities, be a catalyst for interaction, and anticipate what the teacher was going to do when she made a suggestion. On the alternate nights, they were to follow up on activities begun or planned by the television teacher. On some occasions, facilitators served as guest presenters in the studio (with substitutes taking their own classes) and gave demonstrations about various topics, such as New York and the Tet festival. The off-site students, who were viewing their everyday facilitator as a movie star of sorts, especially enjoyed these occasions.

Materials Designers

As materials designers, the facilitators adapted the materials planned by the television teacher to the particular level of the students. The television teacher also expected the facilitators to augment the materials to suit student needs. This was especially true in the case of the advanced students, where the materials provided by the television teacher might cover a time period of only 10 or 15 minutes for an advanced group. However, with a little thought and revision, they could be extended to a much longer instructional period by the facilitator.

Teacher Learners

One of the most valuable aspects of this distance-learning model was its ability to provide modeling and supervised teacher training to teacher learners. They learned valuable information about pacing, giving directions, organizing themselves, and planning ahead through observation of the television teacher and trial and error in a real classroom.

Users of Technology

In addition to learning about general principles of teaching, facilitators became acquainted with the use of technology in education. Facilitators learned to hook up the video unit, manipulate the microphones, and communicate with technicians. Quite often a course would not even be delivered on the air because of technical foul-ups or breakdowns. These included such events as Mexican music "magically" superimposed over the television teacher's voice because of improper hookup of phone lines, equipment cords switched and plugged in improperly at the off-sites by other people during the day, burned-out monitors, and malfunctioning microphones. In these cases, facilitators had to assume the role of substitute teacher, think on their feet, and run a class, imperfect as it might be. These sorts of mishaps proved an important way to foster decision-making and spontaneous teaching skills.

Links to Administrators

The facilitators performed a variety of key duties related to administration, depending on the degree of participation by off-site administrators. The facilitators served as representatives of CSUF and its ideals, so they needed to maintain a professional and cooperative relationship at all times. Because of differing assessment requirements at each site, 1 or 2 days might be disrupted because of testing. The facilitators needed to adjust to the particular schedules of each site and also had to observe the different holidays at the sites. At one site, a change in personnel during midsemester disrupted the functioning of the site. In other cases, it was difficult to obtain air conditioning on hot days or desks (versus patio chairs) for students. The facilitators had to take the initiative to make requests as needed.

Counselors

Because of the one-way video/two-way audio configuration of the system, the facilitator played an important role of conveying to the television teacher the needs and desires of the students at the off-sites. When the television teacher would ask a question, the off-site facilitator encouraged a student to use the microphone. The facilitator would assess whether or not the student had answered in a comprehensible way and, if not, would rephrase in standard English the statement containing the incorrect grammar or pronunciation point so that all could understand.

Videotape Facilitator

As noted in Table 1, there was only one teacher (at the VPDMA site during Session 2) who worked entirely with videotapes, rather than with the live broadcast. Like the off-site facilitators, she, too, served as a team teacher, in the sense that she used the television teacher's materials and learned to adapt them to her group although she did not have the benefit of on-line communication with the instructor or the responsibility of enforcing student participation via microphone. She also had to maintain contact with the administrator at a site as well as learn to teach with technology. The video functions were somewhat different, however, with play, rewind, and replay being the most frequent. Students would listen to a segment of the video and if something was not clear, the facilitator could rewind the tape and replay it. Likewise, she could fast-forward the tape during dead air time.

◈ PRACTICAL IDEAS

Tips for the Television Teacher

- Seek training before and during instruction from individuals with experience in television teaching.

- If possible, obtain release time from other assignments or additional compensation for the school term before the project begins to write lesson plans and prepare materials for television nights and nontelevision nights.

- Focus on listening, speaking, and vocabulary activities on television nights and reading, writing, and textbook activities on nontelevision nights.

- Organize 15-minute preclass talks with facilitators to prepare them for the evening activities.

- While teaching, exhibit a warm and caring personality. Smile, use humor, call students by name, thank students for contributions, and collect photos and class assignments for periodic display on camera.

- Organize activities to maximize learning: Give clear directions, involve students in class discussions, be alert to students' verbal and nonverbal cues in the studio classroom, assign names to various sites to reduce confusion, and use a variety of teacher-centered and interactive teaching methods. Be cautious about overusing open-ended questions and information gap activities.

- Individualize instruction as much as possible to students' lives: Use culturally interesting videotapes, music audiotapes, and visual aids to enliven the class. Encourage experiential learning.

- Be prepared to assume and seek compensation for duties beyond teaching (e.g., facilitator training sessions, travel to off-sites on nontelevision nights to visit students and observe facilitators).

Tips for Off-Site Facilitators

- Seek training about equipment and methods before and during instruction.

- Be prepared to instruct students in using the television teacher's materials.

- Be knowledgeable about the subject matter, well organized, and flexible.

- Collect materials and class work when requested by the television teacher.

- Be prepared for technological snags and develop an ability to troubleshoot equipment.

- Cultivate an outgoing personality; motivate students. Be positive and enthusiastic about distance learning. Encourage students to use the new technology (e.g., through use of the microphone, attentive listening, interaction with other students in the program).

- Be a professional representative of the university when interacting with off-site administrators. Be an advocate for students.

Tips for Program Administrators

- Select distance-education sites based on community need and support. Nurture relationships with off-site administrators.

- Recruit ESL students during the first weeks of the school term, using various techniques such as newspaper, radio, and community contacts.

- Ensure adequate funding of the distance-learning program by sharing costs with off-site locations and seeking grants. Charge students minimal fees and utilize teacher learners who are in training to save costs.

- Select an ITI instructor carefully. Expect to pay this person for extra hours performing extra tasks to ensure adequate cohesion to the program.

- Hire clerical staff to maintain attendance and testing records as well as to monitor delivery of course materials from television teacher to facilitators and vice versa.

- Ensure that technological support staff are available for troubleshooting on the evenings that the class is broadcast.

- Budget funds for supplementary textbooks and materials as well as refreshments for a graduation ceremony. Graduation can be held at one of the larger off-sites or on the university campus to allow students from various sites to meet each other and the instructor.

◈ CONCLUSION

The collaborative, personalized nature of this distance-learning program was its greatest success. It synergistically responded to the wants and needs of all participants, and positive relationships were forged among several entities. In an era in which institutions are being requested to share funding and teach collaboratively across levels, this model serves as a relatively low-end technology option that can be replicated successfully in other distance-learning programs.

◈ ACKNOWLEDGMENTS

I would like to thank Carol Ryerson (the television teacher) and my 1993 teacher learners for their collaboration and involvement in the DLP. Without their help, this project would not have been possible.

◈ CONTRIBUTOR

Janet Eyring is a professor and TESOL coordinator in the Department of Foreign Languages and Literatures at California State University, Fullerton, in the United States. She has taught and conducted teacher training in ESL/EFL for the past 22 years in high school, adult school, intensive language programs, and college/ university settings.

CHAPTER 3

Closing the Distance in Adult ESL: Two Approaches to Video-Based Distance Learning

Sylvia Ramirez and K. Lynn Savage

◈ INTRODUCTION

Many adult education programs report waiting lists for their ESL classes. In some programs, learners have had to wait up to 2 years for class instruction. In 1991, there were 1.2 million people enrolled in state-administered ESL programs throughout the United States (U.S. Department of Education, 1991a). According to the Southport Institute for Policy Analysis, this number represents only 15% of adults in the United States who speak a language other than English (Chisman, Wrigley, & Ewen, 1993). The U.S. Department of Education (1991b) estimated that 17.4 million limited-English-speaking adults would be living in the United States by 2000, composing 29% of all new entrants into the labor force. Nevertheless, funding for adult education programs is limited. With this increasing demand for services without increasing resources, adult education ESL programs struggle with how to increase the number of students they can reach.

Limited resources are not the only reason programs do not serve all the adults needing English instruction. Sometimes courses are offered at times or in locations that are inconvenient for learners. Often situations such as work schedules, child care, and other family responsibilities in adults' lives interfere with class attendance. One approach to expanding the numbers served and connecting with this hard-to-reach population is distance learning, an approach chosen by the noncredit division of two community colleges in California.

The two programs in this chapter use the same video-based curriculum and are similar in their goals and the kinds of students they serve. Nevertheless, the two programs take different approaches to delivering instruction. The hybrid approach to distance learning at City College of San Francisco (CCSF) combines group class sessions with individual, video-based home study. In contrast, at drop-in distance-learning centers at MiraCosta College, learners meet with an instructor one on one when they complete each video lesson or at other times as needed. The similarities and differences between these two cases make the comparison especially enlightening by revealing not only common challenges in delivering instruction to distant learners but also possible variations in responding to these challenges.

◈ CONTEXT

The primary purpose of adult ESL programs in the United States is to enable adult learners who are neither fully fluent nor literate in English to become competent in English so that they can function effectively. Most learners in these programs are permanent residents, refugees, immigrants, or immigrant workers. They may range in age from as young as 16 to as old as the late 90s. Their educational backgrounds may consist of little or no schooling to advanced college degrees. One nationality or language group may dominate in some localities, but, in other localities, a class may have 15 or more different nationalities or language groups.

Learners

The programs at CCSF and MiraCosta serve similar types of learners, as illustrated in the following four profiles.

1. José, born in Mexico, has lived in the United States for about 3 years. He enrolled in the distance-learning program because he wants to perform better at his job and get promoted. He has strong speaking skills but has difficulty writing in English. He has never been able to enroll in ESL classes because he has a variable work schedule.

2. Yuko, a very advanced learner from Japan, studied English before coming to the United States. She reads and writes English fairly fluently. She likes to work independently and has never enjoyed the more participatory traditional ESL classrooms. She copies all of the work from the book into a notebook and writes long answers.

3. Dolores, a mother from El Salvador, has been in the United States for more than 20 years. She has always been too busy raising her large family to study English. She wants to communicate better in English. She does not have any place to practice her pronunciation or conversation skills, and she is tired of having her children laugh at her English. Dolores's children often watch the program's videos with her.

4. Mu Ling and Min Ling, both from China, have been in the United States for 5 years. They have very low-level English proficiency, and independent study is very difficult for them. However, their work schedules prevent them from attending traditional ESL classes. Dedicated learners, they replay the videos at least five times a week, copying vocabulary words in their notebooks and practicing the pronunciation of those words with a tape recorder. They are finding ways to succeed in the distance-learning program.

Curriculum

To reach this variety of learners, these two California community college programs use the same set of curriculum materials, *Crossroads Café* (Intelecom, 1996).[1] These

---

[1] Videos were developed by Intelecom, a nonprofit corporation that designs and produces education television series, with four states (California, Florida, Illinois, and New York); the U.S. Department of Education, Office of Vocational and Adult Education; and the U.S. Immigration and Naturalization Service. Print materials were developed by Heinle & Heinle.

materials include 26 half-hour videos. The print materials include *Crossroads Café Worktext A* (Savage, Mooney-Gonzalez, & McMullin, 1996); *Crossroads Café Worktext B* (Savage et al. 1997); *Crossroads Café Photo Stories A* (Savage & Mooney-Gonzalez, 1996); *Crossroads Café Photo Stories B* (Savage & Mooney-Gonzalez, 1997); *Crossroads Café Teacher's Resource Book A* (Minicz, 1997); *Crossroads Café Teacher's Resource Book B* (Minicz, 1997); *Crossroads Café Assessment A* (Minicz, Weddel, Powell, Omori, & Cuomo, 1998); and *Crossroads Café Assessment B* (Minicz et al. 1998). The A book is for video episodes 1–13, and the B book is for video episodes 14–26. There is also one *Crossroads Café Partner Guide* (Minicz, 1997).

The story lines are engaging and relevant for adult ESL learners. The characters in the video episodes are sufficiently diverse in ethnicity, socioeconomic status, educational background, age, gender, and family situation that they appeal to the variety of learners that adult education programs attract. The videos approach language learning with a soap opera-type story line, language at natural speed, and characters with accents.

Approach

Though both programs serve similar kinds of learners and use the same set of curriculum materials, each uses a different approach to their video-based, distance-learning programs. At CCSF, students attend once-a-week class sessions that control the pace and complete 75% of the course work independently. At MiraCosta, learners move through the instructional materials at their own pace and receive assistance from instructors at drop-in, distance-learning centers.

Implementation Issues

Both programs (and many other adult education programs in the United States) face a trio of daunting challenges: prohibitive funding formulas, faculty resistance, and learner recruitment issues.

Funding for most adult education programs in the K–12 system and for noncredit classes in the community college system is based on average daily attendance (ADA), the time students spend in class. This formula does not work for distance-learning programs. Two alternatives to this formula are documentation of actual study time and successful completion of units of study.

Program coordinators who tried but were unable to establish distance-learning programs often mention that the distance-learning classes were too similar in design to traditional classes and appeared to compete for the same learners. When the distance-learning program clearly targeted an underserved population, there was no perceived competition among faculty for learners and, hence, greater support from faculty.

Data from both programs reveal that a large number of enrolled learners are unable to attend traditional ESL classes and that learners most likely to stay with the distance-learning program are learners not enrolled in other classes. Data also indicate that learners who drop out are most likely to do so within the first week or two of the program. These data reinforce the importance of providing orientation for learners who enroll as well as the desirability of targeting different learners for distance-learning programs than those that traditional classes target.

⬦ DESCRIPTION

City College of San Francisco (CCSF)

CCSF, a 2-year community college, serves about 40,000 students a semester, approximately 50% of whom speak English as a second language. The ESL Department serves about 17,000 students each semester in the noncredit division.

The department decided to offer distance learning because

- employed adults who need additional language instruction may not enroll in traditional courses that meet daily, or nightly learners enrolled in the courses that meet 4 nights a week frequently do not attend all 4 nights

- adults, because of other demands in their lives, need flexibility in scheduling study time

The department chose courses that rely heavily on video because

- video can be an engaging medium and is one that most learners are already familiar with and can easily access

- video is an appropriate medium for the development of listening comprehension skills, which all adults need—whether they are at work or interacting with their children's teachers or providers of transportation and health care services

- engaging stories that are relevant to learners' lives may not only entice exhausted adults who have other priorities but also stimulate discussion

The courses are aimed at intermediate-level learners because

- learners who already have a solid base in the target language are the most likely to benefit from independent study

- by providing an alternative delivery system requiring fewer instructional hours, the ESL program might increase the possibility of providing more instructional hours for learners with lower language proficiency, the level where the demand is greatest

The ESL Department at CCSF chose a hybrid approach; that is, the approach incorporates key elements from both distance learning and traditional classroom instruction. As in other distance-learning courses, the learners complete the majority of work outside of class and have access to the instructor through communications channels that do not involve face-to-face interaction (e.g., telephone, voice mail, audiotapes). As with traditional classroom instruction, learners meet on a regular basis with the instructor and other students.

The faculty who developed the course felt strongly that, unlike many distance-learning courses that are content based, a language course is skill based. This hybrid approach had two major objectives:

1. to provide regular opportunities for learners to practice language in a setting where they can get feedback from a trained instructor

2. to place the bulk of work on the learners outside of class time, which is atypical of most noncredit ESL courses

In determining the program design, the course developers looked at the following criteria:

- The technology and delivery system must be appropriate for the goals of the course.

- Learners must have ample opportunity to interact in English in situations that require authentic, meaningful communication.

- Learners must have the opportunity to ask questions and to get regular and ongoing feedback on their use of the language from a qualified ESL professional (California Teachers of English to Speakers of Other Languages, 1995).

The goals of the courses, which have become known as "ESL by TV," are the development of an understanding of English as it is spoken and the development of speaking skills. Video is an appropriate medium for developing listening skills, especially because some researchers maintain that more than half of communication is through nonverbal, rather than verbal, cues. The delivery system, in which 25% of the learning time is with an instructor and other learners, is appropriate for developing speaking skills.

The delivery system provides for authentic communication in three ways:

1. Learners call in their questions to the instructor's voice mail.

2. They discuss the story through in-class activities.

3. Through audiotape and voice mail assignments, they develop their skills in summarizing and expressing and supporting opinions.

Regular class meetings, access to voice mail, and audiotape and voice mail assignments ensure regular and ongoing feedback.

MiraCosta College

MiraCosta, located in the coastal area of North San Diego County, serves approximately 15,000 students in credit and noncredit programs each semester. The noncredit ESL program is the largest of the noncredit programs offered by the college. Eighty-nine percent of the ESL students are Spanish speaking, with the majority coming from Mexico.

A team of ESL faculty at MiraCosta began exploring the possibilities of offering distance learning for the following reasons:

- There are large numbers of learners who are waiting to enroll in evening classes at the largest distance-learning site. There may be as many as 300 learners waiting to begin classes.

- In interviews, many learners describe friends or family members who are unable to attend regular class hours but need English for work, family, and personal communication.

- Because of fiscal constraints, the college encourages all departments to investigate alternative models to serve learners outside a traditional classroom model.

In the fall of 1996, having visited other distance-learning programs,[2] the ESL program at MiraCosta opened three distance-learning centers—one at a community center; a second at an elementary school, which allowed the college to provide services in underserved neighborhoods; and a third at the main noncredit site, which had the largest waiting list. Each center is open for 4 hours a day, with morning, afternoon, and evening hours available among the three centers. An instructor and an instructional aide are always present during distance-learning program hours.

The staff stresses the following benefits of the ESL program:

- Learners may study at any time, from any place, and at their own pace. For example, some learners come every week for a new video; other learners come every 2 weeks. The pattern changes based on learners' needs and their ability to complete the work because of family and work commitments.

- The cost is minimal. For $20, learners may buy or rent a book and video. When learners complete or leave the program, they receive a full refund if they return the video and do not write in the book.

- Learners have an opportunity to receive targeted assistance from an instructor any time during distance-learning program hours.

The staff also has identified some of the difficulties:

- Learners need good study habits, time management skills, and the ability to tolerate some ambiguity as they complete their assignments.

- Learners do not have the opportunity to interact with other learners, as in the traditional classroom. Therefore, they are encouraged to try to form their own learning community among family members and friends.

- Learners with less than high-beginning language proficiency benefit more in traditional ESL classes, which have more aural/oral interaction and increased instructional time. However, if learners say they have no other options and want to try, they are allowed to enroll and usually work with *Crossroads Café Photo Stories* (Savage & Mooney-Gonzalez, 1996) rather than *Crossroads Café Worktext* (Savage et al., 1996).

The distance-learning program is open entry; new learners come any time during the program hours to receive an orientation to the program, receive instructional assistance, or check out new videos. Sometimes a distance-learning center feels like a three-ring circus because several learners, some with small children, arrive at the same time, resulting in a variety of simultaneous activities—some learners checking out new materials, some talking together, some completing *Crossroads Café Worktext* (Savage et al., 1996) assignments, and some doing extra activities. At other times, the centers are quiet, the instructor working with a single learner or waiting for learners to arrive.

---

[2] The two California programs visited were Sequoia Adult School in Redwood City and ABC Adult School in Cerritos. Both programs use several different video courses in their distance-learning programs, including *Learning English* (Los Angeles Unified School District, 1991) and *Putting English to Work* (Los Angeles Unified School District, 1994).

Initially, the college chose to advertise modestly, allowing time for processes related to instruction, record keeping, and materials distribution to be well established. Flyers were distributed to learners on the waiting list and at community centers. This cautious approach paid off as word-of-mouth advertisement brought more than 100 learners to the program in the first year. As successful learners share their program experiences with family and friends, word of mouth continues to be the most common way to market distance learning. The program has operated at capacity the past 3 years, with more than 150 learners served annually.

◈ DISTINGUISHING FEATURES

City College of San Francisco

Use of Technology

Video, voice mail, and audiotapes are used for out-of-class listening and speaking assignments. The videos are crucial for learners to develop their listening skills. The learner usually checks out the video materials from the instructor and provides a $10 deposit to cover the cost of duplicating any unreturned or damaged tapes. The college also airs episodes on its cable channel, and two other local television stations frequently air the shows. Learners are provided schedules for each station airing the show; some choose to tape the program from the broadcast. Learners are expected to watch the video and do the activities in the print materials (which they purchase from the campus book store) outside of class. In-class activities come from the teacher's resource books and from faculty-designed materials.

Out-of-class assignments to develop speaking skills use both voice mail and audiotapes. The campus provides the instructor with a voice mail number, which the students receive in their course syllabus. Students may call the voice mail number with specific issues or questions. They also may call to complete an assignment given by the teacher (e.g., "Call in your answer to one of the questions in 'What do you think?' to the voice mail.").

Other out-of-class assignments for developing speaking skills encourage learners to record story summaries or answers to questions on audiotape. Teachers use the holistic scoring systems suggested in the assessments (Minicz et al., 1998) to provide feedback to learners on these speech samples.

Approach to Administrative Issues

A second distinguishing feature of the CCSF hybrid approach was the process used to solve two management issues:

1.   deciding how many class meeting hours a week to assign to the course

2.   determining a formula for compensation of instructors

The value of noncredit courses is usually based on "seat time"—the number of hours that a class meets. To determine the value of this distance-learning course, the developers estimated the time it would take a learner to complete exercises in the print materials and assumed that each video would be viewed at least two times. Their estimates totaled 9 hours of work outside of class, in addition to the 3 hours weekly in class. Hence, the value assigned to the course is 12 hours a week. The

9 hours completed by learners on their own include viewing the video episode (all view it at least two times and some view it three to six times), completing the activities in the print materials, and completing assignments given by the instructor.

Instructors in noncredit courses normally are compensated for hours that they meet with a class. In determining compensation for instructors in this distance-learning course, the developers estimated, on a weekly basis, the amount of time an instructor would spend with each student outside of class meetings. Through voice mail, they estimated an additional 5 minutes of contact with a student each week. Assuming an enrollment of 24 each section, those 5 minutes create 2 hours of student contact, in addition to the 3 hours of class meetings. Hence, the course is considered a 5-hour-a-week assignment for the instructor.

MiraCosta

Flexible Program Design

ESL faculty guessed that distance learners might require greater flexibility than learners enrolled in traditional classes. Nevertheless, the faculty felt strongly that this flexibility must feature opportunities for learners to interact with an instructor. They felt confident that the strong curriculum and opportunities to replay videos at home would allow for less frequent, but still meaningful, instructor/learner interaction.

Targeting Learners

MiraCosta's primary reason for developing a distance-learning program was to serve learners on waiting lists and those unwilling or unable to attend traditional ESL classes. Therefore, only learners not enrolled in traditional ESL classes were eligible to enroll. When distance learners have an opportunity to join traditional classes, they must choose between continuing in the distance-learning program and joining the ESL class.

Staffing

A small team reviewed the curriculum and then planned for and implemented the distance-learning program. Team members had been involved in planning other successful innovations, and they worked well together. An integral part of the instructional distance-learning team is the instructional aide. The aide manages the extensive paperwork, checks out videos and books, orients new learners to the program, and provides assistance for learners waiting to meet with the instructor.

Videos and Book Rentals

The program team decided to implement a video checkout program with the option to rent materials. Under this program, learners pay a $5 deposit and borrow the videos, one at a time. Learners may also rent or buy the book for an additional $15. If they return a book that has not been written in, they receive a full refund. The decision to rent books solved many problems, including (a) maintaining federal guidelines of having available books for learners; (b) encouraging the sale of books without setting up difficult money handling situations, particularly at off-site locations; and (c) covering the cost of lost or damaged videos. Even though learners may rent the book, more than 80% elect to buy it.

There have been two interesting results from the materials distribution process. The first is the low number of lost or damaged videos. Even when learners move, friends or family members return the videos. The second was the initial concern from some learners about the affordability of the materials. Apparently many immigrants had already invested hundreds of dollars in commercial video language products sold in their neighborhoods. They had not been successful with these products and wondered about the quality of materials they could obtain so reasonably. Most were pleasantly surprised with the materials and the program.

◈ PRACTICAL IDEAS

A major strength of ESL distance-learning programs is the ability to offer learning at any time, from any place, and at any pace to individuals who have been unable to access traditional ESL classes. However, learners in these programs may be unprepared for independent study and may feel isolated. Solutions developed by practitioners of the two approaches described in this chapter include developing forms to reinforce independent learning and using activities to build community in a distance-learning program.

Support Independent Learning With Special Forms

This section highlights forms that support and promote independent work among language learners. Several samples can be found in the appendixes to this chapter. The forms are prototypes now available with *On Common Ground Teacher's Resource Book: Distance Learning Edition* (Ramirez & Savage, 1999). (The *On Common Ground* series is another distance-learning program.)

Goal Setting Form

On this form (Appendix A), learners identify their goals for studying English and prioritize the areas of language that are most important for them. It is a tool for learners to begin the self-assessment process. Instructors review the form on a regular basis with learners to be sure the information continues to address their changing needs and abilities.

Weekly Study Schedule Plan

A grid showing days of the week and times of day, this form (Appendix B) helps learners plan for their study outside of class. Learners indicate which days and hours they plan to study and what activities they will do during each of those time periods.

Learner Log

The learner log (Appendix C) provides a system for learners to record when they studied and for how long and to reflect on that study. It also provides questions that help learners prepare for their next class or individual meetings with an instructor. Programs use this documentation of at-home study hours for reporting purposes. Instructors use the information to determine study patterns of their learners. If learners do not do well on a unit, it may be a result of their study patterns—too much time in one session or not enough sessions. Learners who are not doing well with activities may need guidance about how often and how long to study.

Date	Comments
1/1/99	*Socorro struggles with pronunciation. She made a list of words that she had trouble pronouncing with her family, and we worked on the correct pronunciation. SR*
1/18/99	*Today Socorro worked with another student who was studying the same video. She seemed to enjoy the opportunity to assist the other student, and was able to practice her pronunciation. She seemed more confident about her English. JB*

FIGURE 1. Sample Entries From a Learner Progress Form

Learner Progress Form

This form provides a system for instructors to document conversations with learners, the progress of learners toward their stated goals, and other information that promotes learner success. The form is especially critical for subsequent sessions when instructors rotate among sites, such as in MiraCosta's program. The completed form can also become a part of the learner's portfolio. Figure 1 shows example entries from a Learner Progress Form.

Build Community Among Learners

The traditional classroom provides a natural setting to build community among learners and a safe environment to promote and reinforce language learning. In contrast, learners in a distance-learning program have few opportunities to participate in community-building activities.

Instructors might use the following activities to promote community:

- Have learners exchange photos with each other or post photos of learners in the program.
- Request permission to exchange assignments among learners.
- Provide a phone number with voice mail so that learners can call for assistance.
- Have learners with access to e-mail exchange e-mail addresses.
- Have learners exchange phone numbers to collaborate with each other.
- Make regular phone calls to check learners' progress.
- Provide certificates for successful completion of assigned work.

◈ CONCLUSION

Although there is widespread awareness of the extraordinary amount of unmet need for ESL instruction, distance learning is not common in adult education programs. Nevertheless, both CCSF and MiraCosta have found that an engaging video-based course for distance learning appeals to adult learners and effectively develops their language skills. However, until funders provide funding formulas that recognize distance learning and programs provide clear delineation between distance learners and classroom learners, there will be barriers to the successful implementation of distance learning in adult education. More important, learners such as those profiled in this chapter (José, Yuko, Dolores, Mu Ling, and Min Ling) will remain distanced from opportunities to achieve their employment, family, and personal communication goals.

◈ CONTRIBUTORS

Sylvia Ramirez is a professor at MiraCosta and coordinates the large noncredit program. She has more than 20 years of experience teaching all levels of ESL. She developed the ESL distance-learning program at MiraCosta and teaches in the program.

K. Lynn Savage is an instructor at CCSF, where she started the distance-learning program in the noncredit division for the ESL Department. She was a coauthor of the print materials for the *Crossroads Café* series and coauthored, with Ramirez, *On Common Ground Teacher's Resource Book: Distance Learning Edition* (1999).

◈ APPENDIX A: GOAL SETTING FORM

Instructions: Complete the left side of this form before you begin the course. Complete the right side of the form after you complete *Worktext A*.

Name: _____   Date: _____

1. Why are you taking this course?
   - ❑ to help my children
   - ❑ to communicate when I shop, etc.
   - ❑ for work
   - ❑ to become a citizen
   - ❑ to get more education
   - ❑ Other: _____

2. Why did you choose a distance-learning course?
   - ❑ My job makes it difficult to go to class.
   - ❑ I need to be home with my family.
   - ❑ I don't have transportation to class.
   - ❑ I like to learn on my own.
   - ❑ Learning by television is easier.
   - ❑ Other: _____

3. What do you need the most help with? *Check only one.*
   - ❑ Listening
   - ❑ Speaking
   - ❑ Reading
   - ❑ Writing

4. Which areas of English language development are most important to you? *Check only two.*
   - ❑ Spelling
   - ❑ Grammar
   - ❑ Pronunciation
   - ❑ Idioms
   - ❑ Vocabulary
   - ❑ Other: _____

5. What do you like best about studying in the distance-learning program?

   _____

   _____

   _____

   _____

   _____

6. Where have you made the most progress?

   _____

   _____

   _____

   _____

   _____

7. Where do you need additional help?

   _____

   _____

   _____

   _____

   _____

◈ APPENDIX B: WEEKLY STUDY SCHEDULE PLAN

Instructions: Develop a study plan. For every 3 hours in class, plan to study about 9 hours outside of class watching the episode, doing the activities in your book, and working with a partner.

Example   *9–11 a.m. Do "Before You Watch" exercises in* Worktext, *watch video, do "After You Watch" exercises in* Worktext, *and check answers.*

	Morning	Afternoon	Evening
Sunday			
Monday			
Tuesday			
Wednesday			
Thursday			
Friday			
Saturday			

◈ APPENDIX C: LEARNER LOG

Instructions: Complete this form for each episode and *Worktext* unit. If you spend more than one week on a unit, use another form.

Name: _____   Date: _____

Unit: _____   Name of Episode: _____

Number of Times Watched: _____

Day/Date	Time (hours: minutes)	Comments
Sunday		
Monday		
Tuesday		
Wednesday		
Thursday		
Friday		
Saturday		

Write answers to these questions.

1. What words did you learn in this episode?
2. What else did you learn in this episode?
3. What questions do you have about this episode?

Think about these questions before you meet with your instructor.

1. Which activity was the most difficult for you? Why?
2. Which activity do you want to review together? Why?
3. What is one new idea you learned in this unit?

CHAPTER 4

"Show the Baby," the Wave, and 1,000 Thanks: Three Reasons to Teach via Satellite Television and the Internet

Christine Uber Grosse

INTRODUCTION

Has one of your students ever e-mailed you about being a proud parent, then scanned and sent you a picture of the new baby? One of my distance-learning students did. When I asked his permission to put the picture up on satellite television for 116 students all over Mexico to see, he wrote back: "Show the baby." And I did.

Have your students ever shouted "la ola! la ola!" (the wave! the wave!) at the end of class, and then done the wave[1] for you 2,000 miles away over satellite television? At the end of my first satellite class, I watched my students doing the wave and did the wave back to them. They laughed as we went off the air.

Have you ever gotten an e-mail from a student with the subject "1,000 thanks" 1 month after the class ends, in appreciation for your class? One of my distance-learning students sent me that e-mail.

Experiences like these await you when you accept the challenge of teaching via distance learning. Distance learning holds great rewards and challenges for the instructor and learner. It also carries some risks. If done properly, teaching at a distance can promote a special closeness and sense of community. Interactive satellite television and the Internet allow you to reach beyond the boundaries of the traditional classroom, breaking down the old walls of time and space. They permit access to new learners and resources and can also build strong learning communities. Distance learning of this type is changing the texture of our educational system in some very positive ways.

CONTEXT

This chapter discusses a class called English Business Communication for Executives that I taught via distance learning in the fall of 1998. The class consisted of 116

---

[1] People typically "do the wave" at U.S. sporting events to cheer for their teams. They stand up, one after the other in rapid succession, raising both arms up and down at the same time, which looks like a wave of motion to the team in the field.

Mexican executives in their first semester in the new Master of International Management for Latin America (MIMLA) degree program, jointly offered by Thunderbird, the American Graduate School of International Management, and the Instituto Tecnologico de Estudios Superiores de Monterrey (ITESM). I taught from Thunderbird's main campus in Glendale, Arizona, whereas my students lived, worked, and took the class in Mexico City, Monterrey, and Guadalajara in Mexico. The MIMLA students were excited about being part of the new joint master's degree program. They welcomed the opportunity to participate, without having to leave family or job, in a degree program from an international business master's program that *U.S. News & World Report* (1998) ranked first in the United States.

The class was taught via satellite television on seven Saturdays in the fall of 1998 and over the Internet using a Web-based discussion board (an electronic tool on the Internet that facilitated communication among participants) and e-mail. The interactive satellite classes lasted 2 hours and 40 minutes every other Saturday afternoon. As the instructor, I saw, heard, and interacted with 60 students in the Monterrey class with two-way video. Monterrey is the main campus of ITESM's Virtual University, which has 29 campuses throughout Mexico. The other students attended the satellite sessions at three sites: Guadalajara (6 students), Campus Ciudad de Mexico (CCM) and Campus Estado de Mexico (CEM) (50 students) in Mexico City. These groups had one-way video connections and were not seen on interactive television. Instead, they watched me in Glendale and the class in Monterrey on a television screen and sent me comments and questions during class via e-mail. A faculty facilitator at each location took roll and led discussion groups with the students for an hour after class. The five facilitators sent me reports via e-mail after each satellite class.

We posted announcements and homework assignments as well as students' photos and biographical data on the Web board. The Web board supported class discussion threads as well as a chat room, which we used for office hours. Thunderbird used the Web board software for just one semester, until it developed its own intranet called My Thunderbird.

The MIMLA students took three courses their first semester. My business communication course was Thunderbird's first venture in distance learning for credit. Thunderbird's partner, the Virtual University of ITESM, has extensive experience in distance learning in Mexico.

Designing the curriculum for the course took place over a period of time. It was based on a course in advanced business communication that Professor Bill King and I developed for our international students at Thunderbird in fulfillment of the English language requirement. Table 1 describes the curriculum development history.

◈ DESCRIPTION

The English Business Communication for Executives course satisfied the first half of a four-credit language requirement for the MIMLA degree. All students (regardless of English proficiency) were required to take the class in fulfillment of Thunderbird's foreign language requirement. The levels of language ability in the course ranged from native and near-native ability (about 25 students) to advanced (about 80 students) to high intermediate (about 11 students). Although the course satisfied the language requirement, course content focused on business communication rather than English language instruction. Seven graduate student assistants worked with me

TABLE 1. COURSE DESIGN STEPS FOR ENGLISH BUSINESS COMMUNICATION FOR EXECUTIVES

1. Fall/spring 1997–1998	Teach English Business Communication to Thunderbird students in computer lab
2. Summer 1998	Collect materials for Internet-based class
3. Fall 1998	Spend one course release time designing 50-page detailed on-line syllabus
4. Spring 1999	Receive notice that Master of International Management for Latin America (MIMLA) program postponed until Fall 1999 because of lack of students
5. August 1999	MIMLA program has 117 students; receive approval to proceed
6. August 1999	Request course be divided into several sections; request denied; trim syllabus to 11 pages; learn Web board technology
7. September 1999	Select seven graduate assistants; build team; teach first class

to provide English language feedback and correction on written work and tutoring in grammar as needed. Six of the seven assistants worked as neighborhood managers, which are described later in this chapter.

Course Description

The three main instructional objectives were

1. business communication skills
2. technological expertise
3. entrepreneurship

English language skills were taught indirectly within this context, in keeping with principles of content-based instruction and writing across the curriculum.

Instructional Materials

We used the same text for this class as in the traditional Thunderbird English business communication class: *Basic Business Communication* (Lesikar, Pettit, & Flatley, 1999). This text is designed for native speakers of English rather than ESL learners.

Program Outline

The five goals of the course were to

1. develop more effective English business communication skills
2. use interpersonal skills to promote cross-cultural understanding
3. improve knowledge of English vocabulary, pronunciation, grammar, and structure

4. build a more solid understanding of the role of communication in entrepreneurship

5. apply technology to build communication skills

◈ DISTINGUISHING FEATURES

Teamwork

Working as a team rather than an individual is one of the biggest differences between traditional and distance-learning courses and one of the greatest challenges. The team for a satellite television and Internet-based course consists of the learners, instructor(s), instructional support staff, technicians, and program administrators. Each member of the team plays a vital role in the course's success.

Learners

My 116 students were executives working full-time jobs in Mexico, employed by more than 80 corporations such as Citibank, Vitro, Cemex, Aeromexico, Ford, Avantel, Lucent, and Andersen Consulting. Most of the students were Mexican, complemented by a few Americans, Germans, Brazilians, and Panamanians. They were more mature than my traditional students at Thunderbird.

When the class began, I was nervous about many aspects of the course. First, it was Thunderbird's opening venture in distance learning. Would the technical systems work? We had to get several new systems in place just as the course took off running. It got off to a shaky start as we worked out some bugs.

Second, I tried not to be overwhelmed by the number of students in the class, the number of sites, and the distance between us. How could I teach so many when my normal class size was 10 students? How effective could the course be using technology?

Third, how would the Mexican executives like the course? I had heard that they, like most executives, would be busy, competent individuals with a low tolerance for irrelevant materials and learning activities. Others who had taught executives at a distance told me that the students would expect a response to questions and comments via e-mail within 24 hours. Could I deliver?

Fourth, what difference would the cross-cultural factors have on my teaching? How would the largely Mexican student body receive my teaching? Would I offend people unknowingly?

Fifth, I was afraid that technology would dilute the effectiveness of my teaching. How could I convey the information and lead the activities when I was thousands of miles away, relying on television, e-mail, and a Web board I had never used before?

Finally, I worried whether I could overcome the two biggest problems a friend had encountered in a 2-year, on-line specialist degree program offered to 200 teachers in Florida:

1. changes faculty made in the syllabus and course requirements during the semester

2. technical problems and questions students had that were not resolved quickly

Learning from her experience, I resolved to plan my syllabus carefully at the outset and avoid changes later on. I realized that this would be difficult, not knowing how much I could cover at a distance with both unfamiliar technology and a new type of student.

My friend also pointed out that her classmates became frustrated when the technology did not work properly. I understood this problem because the learners depended on technology to receive instruction, post homework, communicate with one another, and review assignments. When the technology fails, it puts up obstacles that the students are helpless to resolve without assistance. Therefore, I paid attention to the urgent need for excellent and speedy technical support for the students in a distance-learning class. As my course represented Thunderbird's first venture into distance learning, I had no way to know what our technical support would be like.

Instructor(s)

Teaching via distance places new demands on instructors in terms of putting in the time and effort required, planning and organizing the course, managing and working as part of the team, understanding the technology, and working through the complexity of course design and electronic delivery systems. Designing a course for television delivery or over the Internet requires rethinking teaching methodologies to match the medium's opportunities and limitations. Interactive television lends itself to visual and emotional tools, whereas computers promote networking, interaction, and the exchange of ideas. These media also affect teaching style. The importance of voice and appearance is magnified on television and takes on much more importance than in the regular classroom.

Fortunately, I had experience teaching on live public television in Florida in sessions broadcast to 30,000 teachers who were fulfilling a training mandate for content-based instruction for language minority students. Even with this experience, I was nervous before each interactive satellite session with the Mexican students. Once the session started, I relaxed and enjoyed the interaction with the students, the challenge of making the session interesting and fun, and the edginess of keeping all the pieces of the class going for 2 hours and 40 minutes.

Neighborhood Managers

I was concerned about how I would provide prompt responses to 116 students' e-mail messages and personalized feedback on English language issues in their homework. With permission from my chair, I hired seven graduate assistants to help me provide feedback to the students. The assistants were critical to the success of the course.

We divided the 116 students into six "neighborhoods" and assigned one graduate assistant to each as a neighborhood manager. The seventh assistant handled the e-mail from the classes in Mexico City and Guadalajara during the Saturday satellite television sessions. He responded to some of the comments that came in during class, screened all the questions, and sent many to me via a television monitor that I could see in the studio.

We named the neighborhoods after places near and dear to several of the instructional staff members and me (e.g., Charleston, Durango, Jackson Hole, Miami, Omaha, San Francisco). I wanted to give the students a sense of community and the opportunity to interact with a smaller body of students within their groups.

The neighborhood managers, instructional support person, and I met for 1–2 hours weekly for 2 months. During these sessions, we worked on how to use the Web board, the revision tools in Microsoft Word (Microsoft, 2001), e-mail, and ways to give feedback to students on homework. We brainstormed about the problems we encountered and ways to address them. The meetings helped us provide mutual support during the difficult start-up period. Together, we learned how to provide electronic feedback on writing. Through our work, we learned that the one-on-one interaction that e-mail encourages is a very effective instructional tool.

I was impressed with the sensitive, caring comments that the graduate assistants made on their Mexican colleagues' writing. In our sessions, we worked on (a) how much correction to make, (b) types of comments, (c) what to correct, and (d) what errors to let go. In training the neighborhood managers to respond to written work, I instructed them to use their judgment to indicate the more important errors in student work, following the belief that students learn more from focusing on and correcting a few selected errors on each assignment.

We also addressed the importance of meeting deadlines and providing timely feedback. The workload was tremendous, and sometimes the graduate assistants had trouble getting the assignments back in time. Because the next batch of homework rolled in every 2 weeks, it was essential to keep the deadlines we established together on providing feedback. We agreed to do half of the corrections within a week and the second half by the second week. We established an e-mail procedure that automatically channeled the students' e-mail messages to their neighborhood manager and me and provided immediate acknowledgment of receipt of the e-mail messages.

One of the technical problems we faced and never overcame was that e-mail messages sent to students on certain systems would at times bounce back as undeliverable. This was frustrating and time consuming.

Faculty Facilitators

The MIMLA program design required 2 hours and 40 minutes of satellite television instruction every other Saturday throughout the semester, followed by 1 hour of on-site instruction delivered by a faculty facilitator. I worked with five ESL professionals who served as faculty facilitators for the sites in Monterrey, Mexico City, and Guadalajara. After each satellite session, they sent me a report about how the satellite class was received by their students, an attendance roster, and what they did in their session. I prepared general lesson plans as guidelines for their seven sessions. These evolved over time in response to shared feedback and their excellent suggestions.

Instructional Support Staff and Technicians

The MIMLA team consisted of a graphic artist, producer, computer technician, instructional designer, telephone specialist, two camera operators, and two MIMLA staff members. The team was competent and worked well together, although it took several weeks to develop a good working relationship. In addition, the team interacted with the ITESM Virtual University technicians in Mexico, who were encouraging, supportive, and helpful.

Administrators

Administrative support is critical to the success of the distance-learning effort. It is especially difficult to know precisely what support is needed when starting up a program. But as the course gains momentum and the instructor needs help, the administrators who provide the resources make all the difference. Administrative support helps to ensure a high-quality, adequately supported effort that serves the students well without burning out the instructor. The instructor needs to build a strong working relationship with all administrators involved with the program.

Technology

The technology we used challenged me from the first day until the end of the course. We used interactive satellite television for formal class instruction and the Internet-based Web board for posting and reviewing homework and class announcements, and for holding chats during office hours. In addition, we used e-mail extensively for sending messages, homework, and feedback and correction on homework.

Web Board

Our class was the first at Thunderbird to use a Web board, which students accessed with a password. There we posted announcements, student assignments, and discussion threads, and held virtual office hours in a weekly chat session. I held virtual office hours in the evenings for 1–2 hours. With up to 10 students in the chat room at once, discussion was lively. Students joined in the live discussion from three or four cities in Mexico. If I began the chat session tired, I quickly became energized with the real-time discussion with my students. Each chat session brightened my day. It was exciting to exchange ideas, ask one another questions, and get instant feedback during the chat sessions. Virtual office hours are an unusual experience. With the conversation written instead of spoken, participants have more time to think about a response.

I created areas on the Web board where students could post their work on various assignments. Each assignment area was subdivided into the neighborhoods described previously, with about 20 students in each neighborhood. Students could go into any neighborhood to view other students' comments and work.

E-Mail

The lifeline of the course was e-mail. I spent hundreds of hours on e-mail writing to my 116 students. At the end of the course, I had written about 3,000 e-mail messages, judging from the number in the "sent" mailbox. On bad days, I would be up until 1 a.m. or rise at 4 a.m. to respond to e-mail. Often, I started at 5 a.m. and worked until my hand took the shape of a claw and I could type no more. I knew that my students worked as hard as I did and that they appreciated the comments. One Mexican executive with a Master of Business Administration (MBA) degree from New York University said that the feedback he received from our course was better than any he had received during his entire MBA program.

Satellite Television

These satellite television sessions required extensive advance preparation. Although every minute on television needs to be planned in advance, the teacher must remain flexible and have an alternative lesson plan as a backup in case the technology fails or the unexpected happens. For example, we lost the audio connection with Monterrey for about 20 minutes one Saturday when I had planned an activity based on interaction with those students. I had to switch to another activity until the sound came back on.

The lesson plan/schedule for the third class appears in Table 2, showing various activities and time allotted for each.

The television production manager needed this schedule so that he and his crew could follow me closely and know the order of the class and timing for the break. The graphic artist also needed the schedule for the slides she prepared.

Face to Face

In a study I conducted of distance-learning MBA programs (Grosse, 1999), the program administrators emphasized the importance of some face-to-face meetings with the distance students to establish a connection or bond with the students. Preferably, this should take place the first week of class. In the case of the MIMLA students, they came to Thunderbird for an orientation week in August, and I met with them for just 15 minutes.

TABLE 2. TYPICAL SCHEDULE FOR SATELLITE TELEVISION INTERACTIVE CLASS

English Business Communication Class, Session 3	Time	Slides
1. Introduction/Today's Topics Slide	2 minutes	1 slide
2. Assignment 2 Review	15 minutes	6 slides (includes student slides, ELMO display)
3. Web Board Review	10 minutes	1 slide (access the Web board)
4. Neighborhood Manager	5 minutes	1 slide
5. Guest Speaker–Professor of Entrepreneurship	45 minutes	1–3 slides
BREAK		15 minutes
6. Chapter 6 Indirectness in Bad-News Messages	15 minutes	13 slides
7. EBC Entrepreneurs Speak	15 minutes	1 slide/intro (live from Monterrey class)
8. Chapter 7 Persuasion and Sales Messages	20 minutes	12 slides
9. Doing E-Business	10 minutes	1 slide
10. Assignment 3	10 minutes	1 slide
11. Summary	5 minutes	1 slide
12. Thank You		1 slide
Total	168 minutes	(3 minutes over)

I vividly remembered what the other distance-learning MBA program adminis-trators had said about the importance of an early face-to-face meeting with the distance students. I saw this as an opportunity to meet my students before we launched on this exciting new venture. I was determined to see as many of them as possible, and, apparently, even those 15 minutes mattered, as several of the students referred to those moments later as making a lasting impression on them.

Another face-to-face encounter occurred during the last class, when I taught the last Saturday satellite class from CCM. CCM was one of the two Mexico City campuses that viewed the broadcast by television with an e-mail connection for interaction. I had never seen these students but knew them well from their writing. It was an emotional experience to be with them live after working closely together for months.

I also went to CEM to meet the 15 students there during the break in their Friday night accounting class. I wished they could have joined the other Mexico City campus for the Saturday session, but the classroom was too small for the classes to join. Going there made me realize how much I missed being with the students physically. When I went back to teaching my regular Thunderbird students in the spring, I was happy to meet with them face to face.

In the Class

I used many different types of activities, most of which related to the entrepreneur-ship project. For one assignment, the students created their own companies, working in small groups. The students completed a preclass assignment called "About You" (see Figure 1). Their responses provided me with useful information on their English language backgrounds and how they used English on the job.

About You

Please answer the following questions about yourself, and send me your responses by e-mail:

1. How did you learn English (e.g., family, education, work, travel, living abroad)?

2. What are your strengths in English? Where do you most need to improve (e.g., grammar, speaking, listening, reading, writing, vocabulary, pronunciation)?

3. How do you use English on your job? Tell me how you use English on a typical workday.
    Whom do you usually speak with in English? For what purposes?
    Do you speak English over the phone or face to face?
    What do you read in English at work?
    Describe the e-mail messages, faxes, letters, memos, or reports that you write in English at work.

4. How do you use English outside of work?
    How often do you watch English television programs and movies?
    Do you listen to songs or radio programs in English?

5. What are your goals for this course? What do you expect to learn?

FIGURE 1. Sample Preclass Assignment

◈ PRACTICAL IDEAS

Work as a Team Member

The biggest difference between distance learning and traditional instruction is the necessity for teamwork in course design and delivery. Teaching via distance requires a team effort because many people are involved in the instructional design and delivery of the course. In a traditional course, the instructor has the chief, if not sole, responsibility for the class. However, with electronic delivery systems, the instructor depends on technology and technicians for course delivery. As a result, distance learning requires close teamwork and collaboration between academic and technical personnel. Consequently, the instructor must build a strong working relationship with the team members and develop mutual respect. The success of the course hinges on the smooth functioning of the team.

Get to Know Your Students, Personalize the Class, and Build Community

My biggest frustration with teaching at a distance was not knowing my students' faces. This was especially frustrating when I saw them on satellite television. To overcome this problem, the face-to-face meetings were crucial. In addition, name signs for each student were helpful. We also created a "Meet Your Neighbors" section on the Web board, where we posted the students' pictures accompanied by their biographical data.

Through on-line communication, the instructor can get to know students as individuals. Because of extensive communication through e-mail and the Web board, I eventually got to know the 116 students better than I normally know the 20 students I teach face to face at Thunderbird. I considered every e-mail message an opportunity to personally reach each student and personalize the class, and every interaction with the students a good way to model the communication lessons taught in the course. To get to know one another better, the class posted press releases they had written as an assignment on the Web board. The press releases contained interesting information about the students' backgrounds, education, work experience, and personal goals.

We personalized the class as much as possible by incorporating student work and recognizing special efforts on assignments, interesting e-mail, and jokes. We showed videos, student slides, scanned pictures, sales material, and corporate Web sites they developed for e-business for the companies they created in the course. Several students volunteered to make presentations on their companies.

To personalize the first class, I brought in a list of the Monterrey students and called on them by name. Class members then passed the microphone around to the identified student, with the camera focusing on the student. Technology made it easy to see and hear students in the back row of the high-tech Monterrey classroom, much easier than if they had been in a large auditorium face to face with the instructor. To further personalize the class, we took a few minutes in each satellite session to celebrate weddings, births, birthdays, Halloween, and Thanksgiving.

The MIMLA team and I tried hard to build a sense of community and unity among our students using the Web board, e-mail, and television. Each session, I invited one or two of the neighborhood managers to talk briefly about the

Subject: 1,000 THANKS

I really miss your class. You not only teach a business communication class, but also how beautiful it is to do what you like. I learned a lot from you . . . . All your cheerful comments in every assignment, no matter how many students you might have. You share with us your family, your treasures, your humor . . . .

FIGURE 2. Thank-You E-Mail

neighborhood, recognizing student work and personal facts. Our graphic artist created a slide in honor of each neighborhood.

Set a Class Size Limit (and Get Help for Teaching Larger Classes)

Would I teach this course again? Yes, if I could make certain major changes. I would not accept a class of 116 students again, unless I could divide the class into groups of 20 with an ESL professional in charge of each group. The ESL instructor would read and grade the assignments for the group. I declined to teach the next section of the course (with 130 students); however, the instructor now in charge of the course has four professors helping, each with responsibility for grading and responding to the writing of 33 students.

◈ CONCLUSION

I learned a great deal from my experience with English Business Communication for Executives. I found this distance-learning project to be risky, difficult, at times overwhelming, and the most rewarding professional development experience of my 26 years in education.

Working with the students and the MIMLA team was the highlight of the course. The students were exceptional. They worked as hard as I did, and we developed mutual respect. I felt their appreciation throughout the course, especially when it ended. One executive sent me one of the nicest e-mail messages I have ever received. Part of her message appears in Figure 2.

I hope that this chapter will help colleagues design and implement an effective and professionally rewarding distance-learning course. I cannot emphasize enough the importance of teamwork to the success of a course. Mutual respect, flexibility, planning, cooperation, and a sense of humor go far in ensuring the success of a satellite television, Internet-based course.

◈ CONTRIBUTOR

Christine Uber Grosse is a professor of modern languages at Thunderbird, The American Graduate School of International Management, in Glendale, Arizona, in the United States, where she enjoys using technology to teach business communication to international students. She recently served on TESOL's Professional Development Committee as leader of the Electronic Education and Technology Group.

CHAPTER 5

Make It a Conference Call: An English Conversation Course by Telephone in South Korea

Robert J. Dickey

◈ INTRODUCTION

Our "telephone class" at Miryang National University in South Korea enabled students to complete an English conversation classroom course when they were no longer able to attend classroom sessions. For these false beginning- to low intermediate-level students, their English conversation course, focusing on listening and speaking skills, was the only contact most of them had with English instruction throughout their university studies. Leaving school at midsemester for career-entry jobs, the students were able to continue their studies in this one-semester, 3-hour-a-week course via telephone conference calls, meeting three times each week in the late evening from their homes. I selected telephone technology because I did not have access to high-speed, quality Internet service or knowledge of any other type of audio discussions. In addition, many students would have been unable to participate in any high-tech computer/multimedia synchronous communications. No one, including me, looked forward to class at 11 p.m., but the students gave high marks to the telephone course nonetheless.

◈ CONTEXT

English Teaching and Learning in South Korea

South Korea is widely recognized around the world as one of Asia's newly developed economic powers. Despite the economic crisis of 1997–1998 and the long climb back to prosperity, the general environment for English study at a university is unchanged. Higher scores on the Test of English in International Communication (TOEIC) and similar grammar-based and listening comprehension exams are critical to success with preferred employers. Even those students who claim to hate English can be found studying grammar and vocabulary books as well as sample tests and listening to model listening comprehension exams. On the other hand, few students actively study or prepare for their English conversation course. Many students view conversation skills as irrelevant to gaining that all-important first job in a society still largely oriented to a philosophy of lifetime employment. Private language study schools are filled in the evenings with young business professionals who are studying conversation to fulfill their actual job duties, but this seems a lifetime away to students.

Before entering the university, most Korean students have studied English for 4–6 years in middle and high school. Recently, English instruction has begun in elementary schools as well, but this will not affect universities until the year 2006. Instructors in middle and high schools typically employ the grammar-translation method. Generally, university students are first introduced to communicative methods, if at all, in courses titled English Conversation, taught by native speakers of English, with 35–50 students in a classroom.

Students typically have weak reading comprehension skills and, although they may have fairly extensive vocabularies, they likely are unable to recognize those words when spoken. Their writing skills are poor, with frequent errors in grammar: Students study to recognize errors (a test-taking technique), not to compose. Speaking skills are often nonexistent beyond the phrases and dialogues memorized in high school. Cultural aspects of communication are largely unknown.

Traditionally, most classes in Korean universities are composed of students from only one major. This was the case in Miryang, except when classes were too small or when a few students needed to make up a course. Depending on each department's curriculum, an English conversation course may be offered in the first, second, third, or fourth year of study.

Foreign language study is a relatively recent phenomenon in Korea. It was not until after U.S. forces came to Korea in 1945 that ordinary citizens recognized English as a distinct language. According to Dustheimer and Gillett (1999), prior to Peace Corps language teachers joining university staffs during the 1960s and 1970s, the few English teachers in Korea were primarily missionaries who mostly taught at church-sponsored schools. In the late 1970s, a wave of professional teachers began arriving, who were largely employed at universities and the business conglomerates' own language centers. Since the late 1980s, native speakers of English have been found all over Korea, hired by the blossoming private language school industry. The legal standard for these teachers, based on eligibility for a "teacher's visa," is graduation from a 4-year university in any major. English conversation classes have become a hobby for housewives and older adults, a kind of child care for 2- to 5-year-olds and middle school students, and required professional development for those involved in business. Conversation classes, however, are still dreaded by the majority of university students because they are perceived as unimportant and difficult.

The Korean environment demonstrates a fascination with and a high level of activity in computer-based multimedia instruction. At the same time, it suffers from an underdeveloped nationwide and neighborhood-level telecommunications infrastructure, though high-speed Internet service is now becoming available in many neighborhoods. This combination of characteristics encourages study of languages through interactive multimedia CD-ROMs and Internet Web sites but does not allow many students to maintain the high-speed connection necessary for Internet audio in their homes (using a modem and standard telephone lines). Further, few students have computers with microphones that would allow them to speak to others over the Internet. As the teacher, I, too, was challenged by these technological shortcomings in the development of the telephone course.

Miryang University

The site of the telephone course, Miryang University, is a remote, small city school and a polytechnic with a focus on agricultural and industrial technologies. The university requires only one semester (3 lecture hours a week) of English conversation. Part-time Korean instructors who are neither fluent in English nor interested in teaching conversational skills usually teach this course. There is no English department or major. With few exceptions, the course becomes a grammar and reading comprehension course, though sometimes listening comprehension is included to help students prepare for the TOEIC exam. As the first foreign, native-English-speaking instructor ever hired at Miryang, I helped to shift courses toward oral communicative skills, at least for the 40% of English courses I taught or shared. The telephone class was an outgrowth of those changes. The term *team teaching* is not used here because it is rare for Korean instructors to be interested in coordinating lessons beyond asking the students, "What pages did you do with the other teacher last session?"

Miryang students typically have a self-image problem. The school is one of the lowest ranked in a nation that is compulsive about building ranked lists. Most students at Miryang failed in their attempts to enter a midlevel university. Nearly half of all students commute daily by train or bus from large cities 45 minutes away; the other half are residents of the rural mountain valley who probably could not enter higher rated universities because small-town high schools are considered inferior. As a national university, tuition is cheaper, and some students need to work on the family farms. Other students qualify for university admission only through affirmative action credits based on rural schooling or single-parent backgrounds. Miryang students are well aware that they are considered substandard university students in Korea and, as faculty and parental expectations are lower and students have no history of high scholastic achievement, they generally put little effort into studies. The cumulative effect is unmotivated students who believe they have no chance for top-level jobs and faculty who reward mediocre performance with top grades to enhance the prospects of graduates gaining employment at small to medium-sized corporations.

Teaching via Telephone

When discussing teaching via telephone, confusion often arises because various writers use terms with different or overlapping definitions. A few clarifying definitions are therefore appropriate. Parker and Monson (1980) have identified four types of teaching by telephone:

1. *Telelecture*: an outside expert enters a formal classroom via telephone

2. *Teleteaching*: a homebound person attends a class via speakerphones in the classroom and at home; the homebound student listens in on the class and may occasionally contribute to the class activity

3. *Teletutoring*: a tutor provides one-on-one or small-group instruction to a student who is studying outside a formal class

4. *Telephone-based instruction*: a teacher instructs a group of geographically disparate students over the telephone (the form utilized in the course discussed in this chapter)

Frequently, the term *teleconferencing* may be used in the literature when discussing telephone conference calls, satellite communications systems, and dedicated communications systems. Teleconferencing involves conferencing (i.e., shared discussions) via some sort of telecommunications, which may include all of the previous types of teaching by telephone, as well as one-way or two-way radio (e.g., shortwave radio) or television broadcasts. Also possible are on-line, synchronous (live) computer communications that may include text, audio, and video; viewing of videotapes or television with simultaneous audio communication under one of the teleconferencing modes listed above; or videoconferences via microwave or satellite links. For this class, simplicity and expense were critical issues, so I chose telephone conference calling.

In telephone conference calling, participants use an existing public telephone system to communicate with other participants, using their personal telephones by means of a *telephone bridge*. This bridge connects the various parties together in a single call. A bridge may be provided by the public telephone system, a private communications business, a corporate or university telephone system, or other telephone merging systems (including holding several telephone handsets close together).

◈ DESCRIPTION

When I was teaching at Miryang, 10 senior students in one department left school shortly after midterm exams in their final semester to begin their professional careers in cities that were 1–7 hours away from school. As this department's senior practicum occurs at midsemester and preparation for the event is quite demanding, classroom instruction within that department generally is completed at that time. Other than within this department, it is unusual for professors to abandon instruction in this manner (and, in fact, not officially allowed in any case). On the other hand, in Korea, it is not unusual for students to abandon their classes at any time during their senior year to begin work, and instructors are expected to make special allowances in such cases. I, however, was determined to have students complete my course. Many of the Korean faculty at this university seemed not to understand why I even bothered with this unpaid special course, particularly when I paid for the conference calls. Looking back, I, too, wonder at my enthusiasm. Nevertheless, it is entirely consistent for a foreign professor, brought in to introduce Western academic ideas, to find a way to realize his or her ideals while respecting the local educational constraints; I could not just fail the students. And allowing them to pass with good grades, without doing the work, would have told all university students that this foreign professor's course was no different and should therefore be treated with the same lack of concern.

The 35 students in this class included a mix of seniors from this early-ending department and 10 seniors from another department. I learned of the students' impending departure only while taking attendance in the classroom, 1 week before these students expected to complete their studies. In shock, I hurriedly announced that students who remained in the area would continue to attend the regularly scheduled class meetings (the traditional group) and that studies would continue via telephone for students unable to attend those sessions. The students were surprised and not happy with this announcement. Several of the students were already out of town, and those who had not left yet rushed to me after the class asking questions such as "What?" "Why?" and "How?", along with statements such as "It's impossible!" and "But I'm finished!" Ultimately, 10 students, all from the early-ending department, were included in the teleconferencing method of instruction. These students did not volunteer for these lessons; they were coerced by the threat of an incomplete grade, which would automatically change to a failing grade after one semester.

The initial attempts to obtain telephone conference call service in Korea were not encouraging. The university's telephone facility for conference calls was limited to a maximum of three outside lines. Private, commercial teleconferencing services were not found. I eventually selected "Dial 101" service through Korea Telecom, the major telephone utility in Korea. Under this service, a maximum of nine students, plus the instructor, could be joined in a teleconference. Fortunately, on no evening were all 10 students available for instruction, so the potential crisis of leaving 1 student unconnected never came to pass.

Although this was a straightforward commercial service, it was complicated because I could not communicate effectively with the 101 operator. Each evening of class, I dialed 101 on my home telephone at approximately 10:58 p.m. The conference call operator made connections from a list of student names and telephone numbers submitted earlier by a Korean-speaking university staff member. This list was submitted by voice, as Dial 101 had no facilities for fax reception of a list. After making the connections, the operator activated the conference call between 11:02 p.m. and 11:14 p.m., except on two occasions when I was somehow disconnected and had to start over. On these evenings, classes began a little later. Unfortunately, not all students were successfully connected each night, and there were times when students were disconnected during the session. There were several causes: Call-waiting might influence a student to leave the conference connection and then not be able to return, or other family members needed to use the telephone.

One serious limitation of this system was that students not connected at the beginning of each session could not be added after the operator handed the call over to the instructor; there was no dial-in service. Similarly, once students were disconnected, they could not reenter the conference call.

The telephone instruction occurred 3 nights each week and lasted for $5\frac{1}{2}$ weeks into the examination week. Concurrently, the remaining students maintained the original teaching schedule, meeting on campus with me in a traditional face-to-face classroom, 2 course hours a week. Most of the telephone group participants missed the semester's 9th and 10th weeks of instruction while I arranged the technical aspects of teleconferencing. There was no option; these students had already left the area. To make up for the lost sessions, the telephone group met twice during final exams week (whereas the traditional group met just once), for a total of 15 telephone class sessions. By the end of the course, the telephone group had met with me for the same number of sessions as the traditional classroom group. These telephone meetings, however, were of shorter duration. Additionally, the telephone group had no contact with the Korean instructor during the final 7 weeks of the semester.

To begin the telephone course, I held an orientation on the weekend before the course began for those who could travel back to the school. The point was to stress the necessity of being ready to answer the phone and begin class at 11:00 p.m. The final examination schedule was announced for this group—the same day as for the traditional group—and failure to complete this course would result in an F and failure to graduate. The students were saddened to see that I was fully serious. I could see that they had doubts of their ability to keep up with the students in the traditional classroom group, as well as reluctance to continue after they had thought their university studies were complete.

The final examinations in my English conversation classes were nearly identical in each of many class sections, extending over several years. These exams consisted of a listening comprehension component and a 3-minute, face-to-face interview requiring short answers to 12 simple questions. The common final exam made it possible to conduct a comparative study of the two groups after the course had been completed. As discussed below, the telephone teaching method resulted in comparable final exam results.

In general, the teleconferencing session consisted of the group session, pair work, and my follow-up with one, two, or three individual students. As explained to the students in the initial orientation, students were responsible for participating in the phone class from 11:00 p.m. until 11:55 p.m. I anticipated that group instruction and discussion would continue until approximately 11:35 p.m., at which time the conference call would terminate, and students would contact their partner via a conventional telephone call for 10 minutes of pair work. Partners changed each session. After that 10-minute period had passed, I, too, used ordinary telephone service to call a few students and check their work and also do one-on-one remedial work. For the most part, this plan was realized. Of course, depending on the unit, some group sessions ran longer and some shorter.

During the phone sessions, many of the students seemed to enjoy the class, as evident from the postgrading survey results. The late evening hour of the class sessions, based on when the students and I were available, occasionally impaired the liveliness of the sessions; the most popular answer to the question "What will you do after this class?" was "I will go to sleep."

◈ DISTINGUISHING FEATURES

This telephone class was not designed with much foresight; it was a last-minute activity with students who would have preferred not to take this course at all, especially not in the late evenings via the telephone. In truth, one of my goals for the telephone course was merely to have the students benefit from the practice time identified in the school curriculum for the English conversation course. The use of a telephone conference call was a leap of faith. In a previous business career, I had used such technology for lectures and business discussions, but that had been done in the United States with fellow professionals. The overseas teaching environment presented a host of challenges to overcome.

Standing in front of a classroom of students who had just informed me that nearly one third of them would not be there the following week, I made the on-the-spot decision to teach by telephone without looking at any published research on this medium of instruction; I had no idea if it even existed. Following that class session, I raced to my computer, attempting to survey the literature on foreign language instruction by telephone but found no information. Research in this line continued through the months during and following the course. I found little. A response from an inquiry to the executive director of the Association for Educational Communications and Technology was revealing:

> Sounds like you have been doing distance learning at almost its most basic level. I really don't know of anyone else who has conducted a class in this manner, although it must have happened someplace at sometime. I just don't have any idea where to suggest you look. (S. Zenor, personal communication, December 15, 1997)

In my various inquiries, largely conducted via e-mail, I occasionally received messages along the lines of "Oh yes, we did that years ago. We don't seem to have those records anymore." Realizing that I was on my own, but with the decision already announced, I pushed forward even when those in the teaching community questioned why I bothered.

The telephone group continued with the same course book used with all of my English conversation courses. This course book was designed to maximize student interaction by emphasizing listening skills and information sharing in initial sessions and requiring pair work and small-group discussions for task completion. There was no significant change in the syllabus. In fact, my aim was for the telephone class to emulate, as much as possible, the remaining students studying in the traditional classroom environment, as the two groups would take the final exams together.

As I had taught this course before, I could anticipate some trouble spots. I made a few lesson substitutions and mailed conference call students supplemental materials during the 4th week of teleconferencing (e.g., color photocopies of photographs used as discussion points, a simplified "Locations and Directions" unit).

The course did not further develop students' reading and writing skills; that was not part of the curriculum. However, an instructor could easily add such a component by using mail or fax transmissions of students' work.

The students in this course had studied together throughout their university careers, were comfortable with one another, and were an effervescent group in the classroom. After four or five teleconferencing sessions, a similar mood prevailed over the telephone, except when the material became too difficult for the teleconference environment. At such a time, the students became silent and would not participate. It became a teacher-centered, lecture-format course for the remainder of the evening. It might be difficult to establish such a well-bonded group exclusively through the telephone, even if students had chosen this teaching medium of their own volition.

This telephone group met more often with me (three times a week) than their traditional classroom peers did. Thus, despite losing several weeks of lessons while the technological logistics were being resolved and despite that the contact hours were somewhat shorter over the phone, the group ended the semester with the same number of contact hours as the native-English-speaking instructor, though less course hours overall.

◈ PRACTICAL IDEAS

Teaching by telephone was an ear-opening experience: As the teacher, I learned as much as my students. Here are a few suggestions that might benefit other teachers in similar situations.

Develop Special Activities and Materials for the Telephone

With time and forethought, I would have changed the instructional materials to improve the quality of discussions. For example, in the regular classroom, I generally prefer not to use a bilingual approach for vocabulary issues, utilizing instead an active visual presentation model, which is not viable over the telephone. More attention is required to minimize lexical challenges when students cannot see the teacher, and better course book illustrations would assist greatly in this area. In addition, for telephone discussions, each discussion item and sentence needs to be clearly identifiable so that students can find it easily when the teacher refers to it. Unlike the classroom, there are no chalkboard illustrations to help students orient themselves. Along the same lines, Korean students of English consistently find certain content areas in English difficult (e.g., locations and directions). Students generally lack confidence in this content area and require more group work before pair work becomes effective. The telephone exacerbates problems of confidence because students cannot just lean over a desk to help each other. For telephone teaching, simplified activities need to be developed for troublesome content areas to reflect this weakened student support system.

Some other activities, which typically are moderately difficult but enjoyed by the students in the traditional classroom, are much more challenging over the telephone. Musical dictation or dictogloss is one example. Working with "I'll Be There" (Jackson; *The Best of Michael Jackson*) was much more difficult over the telephone because we could not use a chalkboard to present the progress of the dictation; students had to listen for the answers.

On the other hand, teacher-centered activities with simple and complete materials for the students were generally successful over the telephone. The challenge was to find ways to make the activity more conversational, requiring more productive skills from the students. Students also seemed to enjoy and become more involved in repetitive exercises, such as tongue twisters for pronunciation.

Orient Students to the Technology

An orientation to the technology's limitations might have been a wise investment of time. Group discussion activities were generally not very effective because of the lack of consideration for the limitations of basic telephone service: Only one voice can be transmitted at a time. The first voice eliminates all others, so even the quiet whispers of a student trying to memorize a word can overpower the teacher's instructions or another student's answers. A teleconferencing guide should be made available to students before the course to facilitate more active group discussions. Of course, in a telephone class of longer duration, students would most likely become more accustomed to the telephone environment, and an instructor would face fewer of these difficulties.

Interestingly, technology was sometimes more a foe than a friend. Call waiting and other advanced telephone services were a hindrance in telephone teaching. Whenever one student received an outside call during a class session, everyone could hear the notification tones, and it was unclear who was being called. Worse still, parties were sometimes dropped from the conference call when responding to the other call.

Arrange Opportunities for Pair Work

It was extremely frustrating that I could do one-on-one work only at the end of the session. This meant that students had little chance to practice repaired language/ pronunciation. In many cases, this situation could be avoided. A school or business with a high-tech communications system (a telephone bridge) could probably arrange for the instructor or bridge operator to match up calls for pair work, and the instructor could monitor and enter these conversations. Following pair work, the class could be reconvened for final work. Only in such a technological environment could a teleconferencing English conversation class be considered a full-fledged equivalent to a traditional face-to-face course. Another, slightly less desirable, option would be to convene a second conference call immediately after the pair work had been completed. This option would only be effective if the second conference call could be set up quickly and easily, with the students calling in to the bridge as they completed their pair work assignment. The disadvantage is that a second call would not allow for instructor monitoring and would require all students to wait until the last pair completed their work and called in again.

Share Expenses When Feasible

Sharing costs is an important consideration. Distance between the callers was an important aspect of the total bill for conference call telephone services. In my own case, I had no method for cost sharing, so I paid a substantial fee for the conference calls. Sharing considerations should include not only the teleconferencing but also the pair work and instructor follow-ups, as well as faxing and teacher-student conferences. The system used in this study required all expenses to be borne by the originating caller, which was me. If students had been able to call into the telephone bridge, instead of waiting for the call to come to them, most issues of disconnections and phone charges would have been resolved. Such systems are widely available in North America.

◈ CONCLUSION

Despite the numerous difficulties encountered, the class was a success. Several months after the course's completion (and posting of final grades), a Korean-speaking university staff member conducted a telephone survey to ascertain the students' assessment of the teleconferencing instructional method for English language study. From the students' perspective, the telephone class was a success: 87.5% of the respondents voiced approval in terms of usefulness, 85.7% said they enjoyed the course, and 75% thought the course should be repeated for other students. Based on a comparison of learning between the telephone class and their traditional class peers, using the midterm exam as a pretest and the final examination as a posttest, the levels of growth in the two groups were roughly equivalent. Even if the telephone class students were extraordinary, the literature in the field of distance learning and telephone-based instruction indicates that their results are not unusual (Russell, 1999).

Whether the telephone group students were more motivated in a quasi-tutorial environment is worth considering. The special circumstances of this small group (generally six to nine students each session) allowed a different type of instructor-student interaction during the instructional period. On the other hand, there was virtually no student-instructor contact before or after the instructional period each day. The question of whether these variables affected the outcome is left unanswered in this study. Nevertheless, it would seem likely that the smaller group instruction in the teleconferencing environment enhanced learning. Naturally, if the traditional classroom contained a similar number of students, those students' motivational levels might increase comparably.

Continuing education in English for public school teachers in non-English-speaking countries is one promising application of this technology. Many Korean public school teachers have a strong knowledge base in English but little opportunity to practice speaking and listening. As working professionals, these teachers have little time or energy left at the day's end to travel long distances and attend an English conversation course. Using telephones, however, small groups of teachers could discuss topics of interest, with or without the involvement of a tutor who is more proficient in spoken English. This would be particularly effective in groups who have existing ties (e.g., former university classmates) or as follow-up practice for classmates from the elementary school teachers' English training programs.

In summary, teaching via telephone conference calling is a widely available, yet generally overlooked, medium of distance education. Despite the lack of visual instructional support, it provides a significant opportunity for students to benefit from a professional language teacher and their own peer support system. When blended with pair work, it offers many of the advantages of the communicative approach. Because it does not require a large start-up cost on the part of the students or instructor, teaching by telephone merits consideration for any English language learning, distance education program.

◈ CONTRIBUTOR

Robert J. Dickey has been teaching in Korea since 1994 and currently is an assistant professor of English in the School of Foreign Language and Tourism at Kyongju University. He is active in Korea TESOL, and his research interests include professional ethics and learning supplements that do not require high technology or great expense.

CHAPTER 6

Using the World Wide Web as a Resource for Models and Interaction in a Writing Course

Janet Raskin

◈ INTRODUCTION

It is late on a hot summer night. An Israeli businessman sits down at his computer. He is attending class with a retired Brazilian pilot who is enjoying a cool winter evening. They chat about world population with a teacher in Germany and a translator in Venezuela. They do not talk; they type. They have never met in person but it does not matter. They are enrolled in an Internet school called *Englishtown*.

The Internet offers a wealth of authentic reading material on topics that are of high interest to ESOL students. In 1997, I took advantage of this content explosion and began developing an on-line writing course called *EnglishLive*. This case study traces the development of the course during its first 10 months (January–October 1998) and examines how the materials were developed and used with students in a truly global classroom.

◈ CONTEXT

I developed the course for a commercial Web site, *Englishtown.com* (http://www.englishtown.com). It began under the name *NetWriting* and was offered as a noncredit writing course for adult and young adult learners with an intermediate or higher level of English. Guidelines and sample reading at the registration page of the Web site helped potential students gauge whether the course was within their ability. The registration form included a text field for a writing sample. This allowed me to informally assess the student's writing ability in English.

Students enrolled for a variable period of time—from a minimum of 4 weeks to a maximum of 16 weeks. New students were allowed to enter a class every 2 weeks. In the 10-month period of this case study, most students enrolled for 4 weeks. A smaller number enrolled for 8 or 12 weeks. I taught one class of 6–12 students each week and had approximately 70 students during the period discussed in this chapter.

EnglishLive students included a wide span of abilities, ages, occupations, and nationalities. Abilities ranged from beginners, who reported that they had never studied English formally but had picked it up by surfing the Internet, to very advanced. Only one student was a native English speaker who wanted to improve her writing skills. There was only one class running for most of this 10-month period, so students at varying levels worked together.

The majority of the students were in their late 20s to late 40s. The youngest was 15; the oldest students were in their 60s. Because none of the participants could see one another, students often did not know the age of the person with whom they were corresponding.

Although enrollment changed every 2 weeks, there was, generally speaking, an equal mix of European and South American students and a smaller number of North American and Asian students. EnglishLive participants have been Arab, Argentinian, Brazilian, Colombian, Danish, French, French Canadian, German, Israeli, Italian, Japanese, Korean, Mexican, Polish, Spanish, Swedish, Swiss, Taiwanese, Thai, and Venezuelan. Most resided in their home countries, but a few were living in the United States or Canada. Their occupations included high school and university students, engineers, doctors, pilots, health care professionals, landscapers, architects, house-wives, translators, and educators.

Students took the class for a variety of reasons. Most said they wanted to improve their writing skills by expanding their vocabulary and learning how to organize their work or use grammar correctly in context. Without exception, students wanted a teacher to correct their writing. Some students took the class to maintain their English skills, whereas others simply enjoyed socializing on the Internet. Students who traveled frequently for business said that they wanted a convenient way to take a class. Other students, such as high school students and retirees, reported that they were learning to use their computers and the Internet. They wanted to study English while acquiring computer skills.

❖ DESCRIPTION

The course consisted of 16 one-week units based on general interest topics, such as current events, science, business, travel, animals, sports, literature, and art. Because new students entered every 2 weeks, the lessons were designed as independent modules. Lessons did not build on one another from one week to the next in a linear fashion but, rather, addressed specific topics and writing problems.

Each week, the students were e-mailed a study guide that included the URL of a Web site and study materials to help them understand the reading. After working through the study guide, students wrote approximately 150–300 words on the topic. The writing took different forms, such as letters, recipes, speeches, résumés, and personal narratives.

A typical study guide contained eight parts:

1. introduction

2. preview of vocabulary

3. Web site URL and instructions about what parts to read

4. reading comprehension questions (answers were e-mailed separately)

5. chat preparation

6. prewriting questions

7. organization of the writing assignment

8. peer review instructions

The introduction presented the topic and set an objective to be accomplished in a week's time. An example of an objective might be: "After reading about clothing at this Web site, you will write your own fashion review." To preview words, I instructed students to go to the Web site and do the vocabulary tasks in the study guide. These tasks included matching, cloze, and short-answer exercises.

The study guide next led students to visit a Web site (sometimes two) and outlined the reading that was required. After working through the Web site readings, students could check their comprehension with questions in the study guide. Some guides included grammar exercises in addition to vocabulary and reading comprehension.

Students could attend an optional 1-hour chat session every week. It was helpful for me, as a teacher, to structure the chat sessions, which are discussed in depth later in this chapter. I found that I needed to clearly outline the nature of the discussion. Therefore, I included a special section in the study guides that listed questions to think about. Providing structure and vocabulary in advance of the chat session helped students prepare for an hour of fast thinking and typing.

The prewriting questions in the guide's next part directed the students to look at the topic in light of their own experiences. Did they have strong opinions about the topic? Did they have experiences similar to those of the creators of the Web site? What could they draw from their lives and write about?

With an idea for a story, letter, recipe, or other writing task, students then went on to the organization section. Step-by-step examples helped students organize and write their ideas in the style being explored that week. For example, the recipe guide explained the use of the imperative and referred to examples at the Web site. The current events guide gave examples of the informal writing style of a letter of opinion. The résumé guide gave tips on the style expected in a U.S. résumé.

Students wrote a first draft for a peer assigned as a partner. Partners were expected to e-mail one another feedback on their writing and help one another clarify their ideas. More important, partners motivated one another to write; this contributed to a sense of community. Pairings changed each week to allow interaction with different students during the course.

After editing their first drafts with the help of peer review, students sent their second drafts to me for correction. They received comments on organization, style, vocabulary, and grammar in addition to highlighted errors to correct.

◈ DISTINGUISHING FEATURES

The biggest challenge in distance learning is to supply the elements of human contact and community that are inherent in a face-to-face learning situation. I attempted to do this by including a weekly chat, asking students to collaborate with their peers via e-mail, and giving students corrections and comments on their homework.

Weekly Chat

The highlight of the week for many students, and certainly for me, was the weekly chat. A chat room is a Web site where people called *chatters* log on in real time (e.g., 12 p.m. in New York, 6 p.m. in Paris, 2 a.m. in Tokyo). This is also known as *synchronous chat*. When one chatter types a message in a text field and sends it (usually with the enter key), the message will appear on the screen of all the chatters logged into the site at that moment. The message automatically appears with the name the sender used when logging onto the site, as shown in the following example.

Henri:	Hi Paula. Are you new this week?
Janet enters:	Hello everyone.
Henri:	Hi Janet.
Paula:	Henri, where are you from? Hi Janet.
Paula:	Yes, this is my first week.

Messages appear at varying speeds depending on computer speed, type of Internet connection, how busy the Internet is, and the length of the message being transmitted. Some messages appear within seconds; others take several minutes. For this reason, a chat does not always flow like a face-to-face conversation. The order in which questions and answers appear is not always consecutive, and sometimes there is confusion about which answer belongs to which question. The word *chat* confused some of my students, who thought that they would hear actual conversation via their computer. At that time, Internet chat of this sort signified written conversation only.

I invited students to come to a private chat room once a week for 1 hour to discuss the Web site topic. Three chat times scattered throughout the day made it possible for students in all time zones to attend. There was no question that the chat was a social event, because some of the conventions of conversation persisted in chat communication. Invariably, people said hello, followed by "How are you?" and "What do you do?" Questions such as "How is the weather?", "Are you male or female?", and "How old are you?" were not unusual. Socializing is an important aspect of the chat, and I always allowed time at the beginning for small talk. The small talk consumed time, however, and I soon learned to get into the discussion as quickly as possible.

To structure the chat, I listed questions in the study guide that allowed students to prepare some of the vocabulary they needed beforehand. Chats took place several days after students received their study guides.

The chat was the time to get inspiration for the weekly writing assignment. At the beginning of the discussion, it was not unusual for students to report that they did not know what to write about. In the process of chatting, students told stories, recalled experiences, and asked one another questions until ideas gelled. I recall a chat when an Italian student said that she had not done her homework (a travel story) because she had never done anything adventurous. It turned out that she had taken a vacation to Zanzibar. The other curious chatters asked her many questions about her trip, and the student answered with wonderful details. At the end of the chat, she typed in that she knew what she would write about and, subsequently, wrote a story containing rich details about her vacation.

Handling corrections in the chat was a bit of a puzzle when I first started. I tried not to interrupt the flow of communication with corrections, yet students asked for them. I settled on this system: If a student used a word that did not make sense or used grammar that was confusing, I typed in, "Can you explain that in a different way?" When students typed in sentences that contained common mistakes, I put the correction in parentheses and continued the conversation, as shown in the following example.

Student A: What means "simmer"?
Teacher: (What does simmer mean?) It means to cook something in
              water, just below 100°C.

Unfortunately, the written response in the EnglishLive chat room is as ephemeral as the spoken word. Once the dialogue moves off the screen, it is gone forever. Although I used the "save screen" function, the text documents with the saved screens were blank when I opened them.

Peer Review

I designed EnglishLive to reflect a process approach to writing. It seemed natural to adapt the peer discussion portion of the process to a written review by e-mail. The study guide listed the names and e-mail addresses of students who should work in pairs or groups of three during the week. I instructed students to paste their first drafts into an e-mail message to send to their partners for feedback. Partners were responsible for asking for clarifications as needed. Students sent copies of their first draft and comments to me as well. Here is an example of a written peer review between Maria, a Polish student living in the United States, and her partner, Luiz, in Brazil.

> Dar Maria; I'm sending you the firt homework about Pets. I had difficult because I dont have pets. I would like if you help me with my homework. sincerely,
> Luiz
>
> PET STORY (first draft)
> I have never buy any animals but I would like to have a dog. I prefer a stray dog and midle size dog.; I found a dog when I was treeking in a mountain in Pirenpolis . . . This dog is stray, midle size , with brown coat. It lives in a far or field near to Pirenpolis; I Didn't give name and brought the dog to my house because, I'm living in an apartament . . . Sometimes I come back to Pirenopolis and meet with the dog during my treeking.

Maria responded:

> Luiz;
> I think, Is a greate story about that dog, just add some details; emotion, how you feel when you see or not see the DOG. Do you think about him often? Do you take something for him when you go to see him? How he greats you?) . . . Why don't you name him? Looks like you have a good friend in that Dog.

Luiz incorporates Maria's suggestions:

> Hi Maria,
> Thanks for your letter. . . I commited a big mistake, I forgot the emotion, but, I attempted again.
>
> PET STORY (second draft)
> I have never buy any animals but I would like to have a dog. I prefer a stray dog and midle size dog. I found a dog when I was treeking in a mountain in Pirenpolis . . . This dog is stray, midle size , with brown coat. He lives in a field near to Pirenpolis . . . I named the dog "Hairy" because he lives in the mountain called Hairy. Sometimes I come back to Pirenopolis and meet with Hairy during my treeking. he is energetic and happy. It likes to dally with the

other animals (birds and lizards). He sometimes dropped in a rain puddle and rivers . . . When I was going out to the town the farewell is unhappy. He get up and put his two front paws in my breast, following run away. In that time I think, I will cant see Hairy again.

Peer review usually did not focus on grammar correction, though partner feedback sometimes pointed out grammar errors as the source of their confusion with a piece of writing. Jesús, in Spain, gave feedback on grammar to one of his partners in Brazil, who wrote about Romario, a pet bird, using the second person *you* and *your* instead of the third person *it* and *its*. Jesús wrote:

> I'm sending my commentary about your "Romario." I don't know why you write "Your arrived in my . . ." "Your calour is all yellow," "your cage." If I were you I write "It arrived . . . its color . . . its cage."

Not all students felt capable of critiquing a classmate's work, especially when a beginning student was working with an advanced student. In general, I tried to pair advanced students with advanced or intermediate students and high-beginning students with intermediate students. Each week I formed new peer groups so that students worked with others at levels slightly higher or lower than their own. This did not always work out, and in some cases, I gave the higher level student feedback on the homework.

Peer review provided motivation. There is an audience waiting to read what has been written, and, further, the audience expects the writing within a week's time. It is difficult to find the discipline to write, but sometimes a little pressure from a writing partner is just what is needed. Writing for a partner, not the teacher, takes some of the stress out of the task. The first draft can be considered an experiment, which allows the writer the freedom to try new language.

Peer review did not always work. There were times when partners did not e-mail feedback to one another. On those occasions, I reviewed first drafts of homework. I found that groups of three made more sense for an on-line course. If one student was away on business during the week, the other students still had a partner.

Electronic Error Correction

Through postings on the *TESLCA-L*[1] electronic discussion list, I found a way to make electronic corrections using software already installed on most computers. Holmes (1996) wrote about his system of marking texts by highlighting errors and using proofreading marks, whereas Bowers (1997) explained how to use Netscape tables and mail to send responses on student writing, a system in which anyone with a browser could receive the table and see the corrections.

I used Netscape Gold 3.0 (1996), which allowed me to create a two-column table with students' work on the left side and my comments on the right. I marked errors in the students' work with bold letters, strike-through, underlining, and superscript proofreading marks. On the right side of the text, I made comments or

---

[1] To subscribe to the branch list TESLCA-L, you must first be a member of the main list, TESL-L. To join TESL-L and TESLCA-L simultaneously, send an e-mail message to listserv@cunyvm.cuny.edu. Leave the subject line blank. In the body of the message, on the first line, type SUB TESL-L yourfirstname yourlastname (e.g., SUB TESL-L Jane Doe). On the second line, type SUB TESLCA-L.

suggestions for vocabulary. The Netscape table was attached to an e-mail message and sent to the student for correction.

When students received the homework from me, they had to review their work and make the necessary corrections using the proofreading marks and comments. Only after students corrected their work did I consider the writing finished. I gave students a guide to the proofreading marks at the beginning of the course (e.g., SP: spelling; NS: new sentence [create two sentences from one long one]; WW: wrong word; WO: word order). See Figure 1 for a sample homework correction.

Making electronic corrections with Netscape tables was an easy and reliable system. With a little bit of experimenting, I figured out how to make my comments in the right column move into position alongside the homework text in the left column. Students could easily see the errors and the comments. I suggested that they place their homework document on half of the screen and the Netscape table on the other half. They could then type the corrections on their document while looking at my comments. Students e-mailed their corrections, and I checked to see that they understood the writing problems I had corrected. In some cases, students sent back near perfect work. In other cases, I needed to e-mail the student with more explanations.

One of the disadvantages of working with Netscape tables was that it was labor intensive. I spent 20–45 minutes correcting each homework assignment. Highlighting text, inserting superscripts, and typing on both sides of the table required a lot of mouse work. It was very hard on the wrist. An ergonomic keyboard, a wrist splint, and a mouse controlled by finger movement would have helped. The screen also flickered as it refreshed while typing, deleting, or inserting superscripts, making it tiring for the eyes. I made a habit of looking away from the monitor as I typed. This electronic correction system worked well for the small number of students I had each week (an average of seven), but it would probably not be practical for large classes.

◈ PRACTICAL IDEAS

Whether you are teaching on-line or in the classroom, a good Web site can supplement your curriculum and liven up a course. Nevertheless, appropriate sites do not appear magically. I averaged 2–3 hours of surfing, reading, and comparing sites before finding one I would use. Then, I spent more time developing supportive guidance and instructional activities. Based on my experience, here are six hints for finding and using an appropriate Web site.

Narrow Your Focus

Finding an appropriate site may take hours of surfing or a matter of minutes. To speed up the process, I narrowed my focus as much as possible.

Utilize Web Resources

A faster and more efficient way to find sites is to get reviews from educational organizations, such as Pacific Bell's *BlueWeb'n Update* (2000). Free subscriptions are available at http://www.kn.pacbell.com/wired/bluewebn/. *BlueWeb'n* e-mails a list of recommended Web sites weekly. Subjects include social studies, computer technology, language arts, math, and science. *Classroom Connect* (http://www.classroom.com)

Student's Homework	*Homework Correction*
In the **shade** of Ben Nevis	shade = shadow. These are two different words in English. "Shadow" also implies that a large, important thing exists next to which there is a small or unimportant thing in its shadow.
Four years ago I travelled ___the first time **of** my life to an English speaking country. We Ossis (**so are the East Germans**^{WO} called here) only had the right to travel abroad for two years, **but naturally not instantly the money to realize all our dreams right then**^{WW} . So you may imagine what it meant to me when I was finally able to travel by car to **Scottland**^{SP}. Only two years before we would not even have dared to think of it	travelled for the first time in my life (prepositions) as the East Germans are . . . You have two interesting ideas here that are connected in time. This is what I interpret. "We . . . had gotten the right to travel two years before, but naturally we had no money to instantly realize our dream of traveling." (Past perfect is in the first clause; the past tense is in the second, showing chronology.)
When you're driving along the empty winding roads it seems as if the mountains never **ended**... While I was fascinated by what I saw my poor daughter **got serious stomach trouble because she felt/got (difference??) sick in the car like in a roller coaster.** So we had to stop at the first house we saw in order to get some water and to clean her clothes . . . Here we experienced the proverbial Scottish hospitality: my^C daughter could **lay**^{WW} down and have a nap while I was getting some **hot strong** tea and ~~was (necessary to repead?)~~ talking with **the nice old Lady.** You will never guess what her name was! Her first name was Hazel and her last name Nut. **Having** a cat sitting on her shoulder Mrs. "Hazelnut" told me the eventful story of her life until my little girl woke up and we could continue the tour . . .	"ended" should be "end." You have "are driving," so continue with the present tense. got carsick (poor thing!) You can simply use that expression—everyone knows that feeling. capitalize "my." lay (to place something on a surface) vs. lie (to recline your body) strong, hot tea—There is actually specific order for adjectives. nice old lady—This sounds a bit negative, though you don't mean it that way at all. "elderly lady of the house" or "elderly hostess" sounds better. With a cat sitting on her shoulder,

Note. WO = wrong order; WW = wrong word; SP = spelling; C = capitalize.

FIGURE 1. Excerpts of a Homework Correction for a Travel Tale

also reviews sites and gives recommendations. The sites are generally for native speakers of English in K–12, but some sites can be easily adapted for adult and young adult ESOL students.

Tips on interesting Web sites also come from educators who have set up Web pages with links to content-rich Web sites, including *Leslie Opp-Beckman's Homepage*

OPPortunities in English to Speakers of Other Languages (Opp-Beckman, 2000) at http://darkwing.uoregon.edu/~leslieob/index.html.

Be Selective and Use Predetermined Criteria

It pays to be picky about a Web site. At a good site, the content holds the students' interest and the layout or style makes the content comprehensible. I had three criteria for choosing Web sites for the EnglishLive course.

First, good Web sites deal with a topic in an interactive way. There were many sites that offered information about health and fitness, for example, but I looked for sites that gave visitors a chance to answer questions or make decisions about the material presented. My favorite finds were sites with quizzes, surveys, or message boards that invited visitors to e-mail their comments. Some science sites suggested simple experiments and gave details on how to perform them. Some sites had QuickTime (Apple, n.d.) movies to watch. Interactivity is a key factor when students work independently.

The second criterion for selecting a Web site was its linguistic appropriateness for intermediate to advanced-level ESOL students. After 10 years of working with students at this reading level, I often could predict the language problems they would encounter. I rejected sites that had long, difficult texts and no pictures. Sites with many short texts presented with clear pictures were my first choice. I also found many sites that had glossaries, a wonderful bonus. Whenever I had a choice of sites, I opted for ones that had less detailed explanations, easier vocabulary, and shorter sentences. However, I sometimes had to compromise. With sites that were particularly interesting but so long that most students might get frustrated or bored, I selected only parts of the text for the weekly reading assignment.

Finally, in almost every Web site, I looked for texts that would serve as models for a particular writing style or skill. Recipe sites, for example, showed the use of the imperative in giving instructions. Interactive message boards provided examples of an informal letter writing style. Sites about animals had detailed descriptions and were great for students to model descriptive writing.

Investigate Sites Thoroughly

Finding a site is only half the job of using it in a class; not all pages in a Web site will fit the lesson. The site must be thoroughly investigated and previewed, including testing all links and determining how long it will take to download pages with pictures on the computer you will be using.

Beware of Changes in Sites

Two drawbacks to using content readings from the Internet are that Web sites go down and messages on bulletin boards change. There is no guarantee that the reading material will remain the same or that the author will maintain the site. It is best to have an alternative site on the topic as a backup and be ready to adapt materials as needed. In the period of this writing course, 2 of the 20 sites I used were taken down. One way to avoid this problem is to use sites sponsored by relatively stable organizations (e.g., museums, libraries, corporations) rather than individuals. It is wise to visit a site at least once every 2 months to make sure it is still up.

Support Site-Related Activities

Assigning content from a Web site is no different from assigning a reading from a newspaper or magazine. Time must be spent on developing self-directed study materials, role-plays, vocabulary exercises, or discussion guides that pertain to the Web site. Whether the site will be used for group work in the classroom or as an independent activity, materials must be prepared to direct students to the language-learning goal.

Look for Publication Possibilities

I strongly favor using Web sites that accept submissions from visitors. Message boards on new sites, such as CNN (http://www.cnn.com), accept postings. Some travel sites accept stories about vacation spots. The possibility of having work published was a motivating factor for a student from Argentina, whose recipe for potato pie had been accepted by a recipe Web site.

◈ CONCLUSION

As the teacher of this on-line course, I never failed to be amazed that I worked in a global classroom. Three years ago, I could not conceive of teaching students living in other countries from a computer in my home. I would not have believed that we would read articles in electronic form, much less converse with one another by typing at the same time. Yet the extraordinary is now commonplace. It is possible to find interesting content readings on the World Wide Web and incorporate them into classroom and on-line courses. These readings can be developed into a complete course when self-study materials are written for them, or they can form the basis of supplementary material in the classroom. When all you need is a computer, a modem, and an e-mail account, the opportunity is too good to pass up.

◈ CONTRIBUTOR

Janet Raskin is currently an on-line course developer for Pearson Education. In addition to her on-line work, she has developed CD-ROMs for Heinle & Heinle and EF Education, including the award-winning *Escape From Planet Arizona* (EF English First, 1995).

CHAPTER 7

Teaching Tomorrow's Class Today: English by Telephone and Computer From Hawaii to Tonga

Brent A. Green, Kory J. Collier, and Norman Evans

◈ INTRODUCTION

Consider the vastness of the Pacific Ocean. A 5-hour flight from San Francisco, California, leaves a traveler in the Hawaiian Islands and less than a third of the way across the Pacific. Another flight 7 hours from Hawaii in a southwesterly direction takes our traveler across the equator, over the international date line, and into tomorrow in Tonga, the only remaining kingdom in the Pacific. Beyond Tonga lie 5 more hours of open ocean before the traveler makes it to Sydney, Australia.

Throughout history, the Pacific Ocean has been a formidable barrier to warriors, merchants, discoverers, travelers, and, now, English teachers. In 1996, instructors in the English as an International Language (EIL) program at Brigham Young University Hawaii (BYU-Hawaii) embarked on an attempt to cross this barrier when they instituted a distance-learning project for teaching English from Hawaii to students in Tonga via telephone lines and computer connections using real-time interactions.

◈ CONTEXT

BYU-Hawaii, a small, 4-year liberal arts university with 2,300 students, is dedicated to educating students from the Pacific Basin and Asian Rim countries. BYU-Hawaii is not only small but also remote. In addition to being 2,400 miles from the U.S. mainland, its rural location on the north shore of Oahu is approximately a 1-hour drive from Honolulu.

Most of the 2,300 students at BYU-Hawaii come from Hawaii; the U.S. mainland; the Asian Rim countries; most of the major islands in the Pacific; and many smaller, more remote island nations. In lesser numbers, students from many other regions of the world push the total number of countries represented to more than 50. Nearly 30% of the students enrolled at BYU-Hawaii come from countries where English is not widely spoken.

One of the consequences of this great cultural and linguistic diversity is the need for a strong English language program. At any given time, 30% of the students on campus have been or are enrolled in the EIL program. Today it is the second largest department on campus in terms of total enrollment. All of the students in EIL classes are academically integrated into the university. Students receive university credit for their language study and can begin enrolling in general education and major classes once they have reached the advanced levels of EIL study.

Our EIL program has grown and developed over the years to meet the changing nature of the university. Perhaps the best example of this is the pair of in-country programs operated in Samoa and Tonga from which the distance-learning program in Tonga got its start.

For more than 30 years, the Church of Jesus Christ of Latter-Day Saints has operated two large primary and secondary school systems in the independent nations of Samoa (formerly called Western Samoa) and Tonga. Most of the Tongans and Samoans who come to BYU-Hawaii come from these two school systems. One of the challenges BYU-Hawaii faced in admitting students from the South Pacific was that many of them had limited opportunities to improve their English skills beyond an intermediate level in their home countries. The result of this was that most students would have to spend a full year or more at BYU-Hawaii increasing their English skills. The expense for this extra year in Hawaii was economically demanding not only on BYU-Hawaii's resources but also on the students and their families.

In 1990, BYU-Hawaii decided to open EIL programs in Tonga and Samoa to reduce the time students spent at BYU-Hawaii studying English and, ultimately, shorten their time to graduation. Students from these island nations were expected to reach an advanced level of English proficiency while still in their country. This allowed them to study English while living in a far less demanding economy and within a culturally familiar environment. With all the housing and school facilities already in place, it seemed like an economically sound move to make. However, Tonga and Samoa could not provide trained ESL teachers with experience in BYU-Hawaii's EIL program. Therefore, BYU-Hawaii's EIL program sent its teachers to the South Pacific on 1-year assignments to teach and direct the in-country programs.

After 7 years of operating the in-country programs, BYU-Hawaii reached an unforeseen obstacle—the pool of teachers who could or would accept a South Pacific assignment had dried up. Without trained teachers to run the programs, the options were few and, in some cases, bleak. By 1996, BYU-Hawaii was considering five options for Tonga:

1. Close completely.

2. Close temporarily.

3. Provide local teachers with ESL training.

4. Restructure the program so that local teachers without ESL training could run it.

5. Develop a distance-learning program that used a local teacher as a site coordinator working in conjunction with an EIL teacher at BYU-Hawaii.

The distance-learning idea was the most radical, yet most widely accepted, of the five options. Within weeks of its proposal, BYU-Hawaii approved the proposal and began preliminary work on the distance-learning model.

◈ DESCRIPTION

Once BYU-Hawaii approved the distance-learning model, a distance-learning team was assembled and work began on program implementation. The team consisted of the two EIL lecturers who would be teaching the distance-learning courses, a computer and technology expert, and the BYU-Hawaii EIL program administrator. The team met weekly for 3 months to work out the preliminary details of the distance-learning program. They decided what teaching media would be used, what equipment would be required, and how the responsibilities would be divided. After a careful examination of the existing infrastructure and access to technology, such as computers, modems, phone lines, and the Internet, the team decided that the best approach would be to use real-time audio classes and data transfers over an existing remote-access computer network system.

At the time of the team's initial planning, the only Internet access in Tonga was at one school. As the church school was not part of the government system, it was very difficult to get permission to use the government school's Internet service. Therefore, the team ruled out the Internet as a possible medium for teaching and transferring data and information. Fortunately, the school did have several international phone lines that would allow a remote connection from one computer to another or to a computer network. Although BYU-Hawaii had Internet access and a campus network, at that time, remote access was not available. Because of time and schedule differences (discussed later in this chapter), a full-time remote connection to the distance-learning teachers' computers was not feasible. The team decided that the best way to handle this situation was to set up two mail boxes on an administrative network in Sydney, Australia: one mail box for Tonga and one for Hawaii. Tongan school administrators were already using this network, which was set up to accept remote access.

The teleconferencing equipment for the audio class (a Polycom Sound Station EX with two extension microphones for the classroom and a headset for the distance-learning teachers) was purchased early in the planning stages. Because none of the distance-learning team had ever been involved in a distance-learning course, the team gave a few pilot classes with the audio equipment to gain some understanding of the dynamics of an audio class. During these pilot classes, the team worked out several technological glitches and gained a clearer view of what audio classes required from a pedagogical perspective. In one of the pilot classes, for example, the team observed that students needed more interaction than was considered acceptable in a traditional class setting. In short, the students were having a hard time staying focused. This observation helped the distance-learning teachers recognize the importance of classroom interaction using this mode of delivery.

Of course, preparing for this distance-learning venture required more than merely setting up the telecommunications systems. In the semester leading up to the distance-learning program's implementation, BYU-Hawaii gave the distance-learning teachers release time to prepare distance-learning materials. In addition, the teachers were assigned to teach courses that mirrored the courses that they would later teach from a distance in terms of texts and objectives.

The Tonga distance-learning program began in January 1997 and continued for 2 years. A detailed description of the essential elements of the program follows.

Schedules

The distance-learning school year consisted of two 13-week semesters and one 9-week term for a total of 35 weeks of instruction. This schedule followed BYU-Hawaii's semester and term schedules as closely as possible, with a little adaptation to meet the high school's schedules in Tonga. Adjustments had to be made so that our site coordinator, who was required to teach two high school classes in addition to her site coordinator responsibilities, would be able to fit her daily rotating high school classes into our distance-learning schedule and also allow her time off for holidays and school breaks, which were usually different from BYU-Hawaii's breaks. Also, because Tonga was 23 hours ahead of Hawaii, the distance-learning teachers did not teach on their Friday (Saturday in Tonga), and the students did not have an audio class on their Monday (Sunday in Hawaii).

Students met daily in class for 3–4 hours of reading, writing, and grammar instruction and had 3–4 hours of lab work. This allowed them to do their homework in the classroom and write their major assignments on the computers. Lab time in the schedule represented, for the most part, an open lab; students were free to come and go as they pleased during that time. Grammar audio classes were held Tuesdays and Thursdays; writing audio classes were held Wednesdays and Fridays. Each audio class was 45–50 minutes long. In addition, students had a distance lecture for listening practice every other Wednesday. Table 1 illustrates how the rotating schedules, time changes, and class and lab times worked out.

TABLE 1. 1998 WINTER SEMESTER DAILY SCHEDULE FOR ENGLISH AS AN INTERNATIONAL LANGUAGE (EIL) PROGRAM IN TONGA

Monday (Sunday)	Writing 8:35– 9:20 a.m.	Grammar 9:25– 10:10 a.m.	Lab 10:25– 11:50 a.m.	Reading 12:00– 12:45 p.m.	Lab 12:45– 3:45 p.m.
Tuesday (Monday)	Reading 8:35– 9:40 a.m.	Lab 9:45– 11:20 a.m.	Writing 11:30 a.m.– 12:15 p.m.	Grammar 1:00– 1:45 p.m.	Institute 1:50– 2:35 p.m.
Wednesday (Tuesday)	Lab 8:35– 10:20 a.m.	Reading 10:30– 11:40 a.m.	Writing 11:45 a.m.– 12:30 p.m.	Grammar 1:00– 1:45 p.m.	Listening 1:50– 2:30 p.m.
Thursday (Wednesday)	Lab 8:35– 9:50 a.m.	Reading 10:00– 11:10 a.m.	Grammar 11:15 a.m.– 12:00 p.m.	Writing 12:10– 12:55 p.m.	Institute 1:15– 2:00 p.m.
Friday (Thursday)	Reading 9:00– 10:10 a.m.	Grammar 10:15– 11:00 a.m.	Writing 11:05– 11:50 a.m.	Lab 11:55 a.m.– 3:45 p.m.	

Audio Classes

Grammar	Tuesdays and Thursdays (Mondays and Wednesdays)
Writing	Wednesdays and Fridays (Tuesdays and Thursdays)
Listening	Lectures every other Wednesday (Tuesday)

Note. Days inside parentheses indicate the day in Hawaii. All session times in Hawaii were 23 hours earlier than their corresponding times in Tonga.

Curriculum

The primary objective of the distance-learning program was to help students learn more English in Tonga to reduce the time they spent studying English at BYU-Hawaii. Specifically, our goal was to get students to reach at least the advanced level of English proficiency before transferring to BYU-Hawaii. The distance-learning curriculum, including specific course objectives, closely followed BYU-Hawaii's intermediate-level EIL curriculum. Having a curriculum already in place made it much easier for the distance-learning teachers to plan lesson materials and class activities. Without these, it would have taken much longer to fully develop an English program that would have met the needs of its students.

Travel

Travel became an important aspect of the distance-learning program. The distance-learning teacher traveled to Tonga three times a year. During this time, he met and got to know students firsthand before returning to Hawaii, where he taught for the next 9–12 weeks from his office. In addition, he administered exams, such as semester or term finals and oral interviews to the distance-learning students as well as an English proficiency exam to both the distance-learning students and others who were interested in attending BYU-Hawaii. The distance-learning teacher's time in Tonga also was used to coordinate grades with the site coordinator as well as to plan and coordinate the following enrollment period's syllabus. In addition, the distance-learning teacher usually brought with him the next semester or term's textbooks, coordinated budgets and other administrative responsibilities with Tongan administrators; hand-carried student visa documents and other BYU-Hawaii admissions documents; and worked out technological problems. A 1-week stay in Tonga was usually sufficient to complete all these tasks.

Division of Responsibilities

During each semester or term of the distance-learning program, one of the two distance-learning teachers was released from teaching all but one class at BYU-Hawaii so that he could plan and oversee the teaching and testing of reading, writing, and grammar for the Tonga program. He provided feedback for most of the students' written work and taught two writing and two grammar audio classes each week. The other distance-learning teacher kept a full load of classes at BYU-Hawaii but planned and oversaw the teaching and testing components of the listening course, including the biweekly lecture.

In addition to carrying out writing and grammar class activities that she sometimes helped plan during the non-audio class days, the site coordinator taught the reading courses and helped the distance-learning teachers in a number of important ways. First, she became the eyes and ears of the distance-learning teachers during the audio classes. She determined when students were confused, encouraged the students to speak up so that the distance-learning teacher could hear, and wrote (or directed students to write) information on the chalkboard. Moreover, she set up and took down the audio equipment after each audio class, recorded attendance, prepared overhead transparencies, scheduled rooms, and publicized important dates.

Audio Classes

The audio classes were held in the site coordinator's usual classroom, which, in addition to the necessary phone and electrical outlets, had the advantage of being set apart from the other classrooms in the school. Because of its location, the traffic of the high school students and faculty (which can be very disruptive in the tropics where open-louvered windows and open doors are the norm) was avoided. This made the audio classes much easier to conduct.

When conducting classes from their offices at BYU-Hawaii, the distance-learning teachers initiated the calls. They used a headset and had the phone codes that allowed them to access an international line. Schedules and "Do Not Disturb" signs were placed outside the office doors in advance so that the audio classes could proceed with few interruptions. On a few occasions, the site coordinator would phone the distance-learning teacher from the classroom (the equipment had the capability of sending and receiving calls). This happened, however, only when connections from Hawaii were not clear.

Before each audio class, the teacher set up the audio equipment by placing the main unit on a desk in the middle of the room and extending the external microphones across to two desks, one on each side of the main unit. The students situated their desks around the main unit and microphones (see Figure 1).

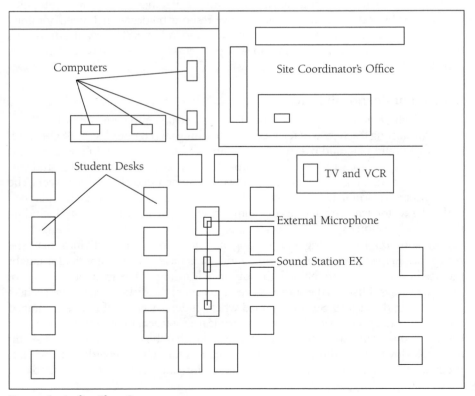

FIGURE 1. Audio Class Setup

Data Transfer

Regular homework assignments were checked by the site coordinator at the beginning of each class and reviewed by the distance-learning teacher during the audio classes or the site coordinator on non-audio class days. Students completed all of their major assignments on the four computers situated at the back of the classroom, as shown in Figure 1. When students did their writing assignments or took tests, they saved their work on a disk and gave it to the site coordinator. She attached these documents to an e-mail message to the distance-learning teacher and sent it to the Hawaii mailbox in Sydney. When she dialed the Sydney network, all of the returned and marked assignments were automatically sent to her computer through her Tonga mailbox. She then printed off the marked papers and gave them to the students, who often were required to make computer-generated revisions and send them back to the distance-learning teacher in Hawaii. Using a system of marks created by the distance-learning teachers, the teachers gave all writing feedback on the electronic documents themselves.

◈ DISTINGUISHING FEATURES

Although our program was successful in terms of helping students meet our objectives, it was hardly cutting edge in the technological sense. Our mode of delivery through real-time audio courses and use of computer-generated writing assignments and feedback have been a part of English language teaching for a number of years. Likewise, the distance-learning teachers used well-known ESL teaching practices. Perhaps the most distinguishing aspects of the Tonga distance-learning program arose from the challenges that we faced in the areas of scheduling and technology and how we dealt with them.

Technology Challenges

One of our technological challenges was the use of different types of computer operating systems. The school in Tonga used computers running the Microsoft Windows operating system; the distance-learning teachers in Hawaii had Macintosh computers. Fortunately, this was not as difficult a problem as first thought. The Macintosh computers could easily translate the Windows-produced documents sent from Tonga, and the distance-learning teachers would simply save their handouts, tests, and other Macintosh-produced teaching materials in Windows format before sending them to Tonga. There were times, however, when a test or handout that the distance-learning teachers created on their Macintosh machines would not translate when it reached Tonga. In those cases, the distance-learning teacher would fax the information. Although the translating process did take a little time, a certain automation was developed. Translating became a small, routine part of the whole transfer process.

Another technological problem occurred during the audio classes. For reasons that are still unclear, when it rained heavily in Tonga, the telephone connection would buzz. Students would have a difficult time hearing the distance-learning teacher, and often the classes would be cut short. The solution was to always have detailed lesson plans available for the site coordinator so that she could finish up the audio class and give out the homework assignments when disconnections occurred.

Scheduling Challenges

Scheduling proved to be somewhat of a challenge for the distance-learning teachers and the site coordinator. It often took creative juggling to work around the rotating high school classes and special class hours on sports days and assemblies when students were let out early. Fortunately, the Tongan students were out of high school, were enrolled solely in the EIL courses, and were told that they needed to plan on being at school for the whole day. This certainly helped with the class scheduling and indirectly gave students time to study and complete homework in an environment that was more conducive to learning. None of the students owned their own computers and, because of home responsibilities, rarely had time to complete their homework after they left school for the day.

The high school's holidays and calendar were often different from BYU-Hawaii's holidays and calendar. Distance-learning teachers often gave up their Hawaii holidays so that they could hold their audio classes. It was much easier for the distance-learning teachers to adapt their schedules than it was for the site coordinator and students. This, however, did not always go over well with the distance-learning teachers, who wanted to share U.S. and Hawaii holidays with their families. Of course, these teachers were off when Tonga had a holiday or a school break, and Tonga seemed to have more holidays than Hawaii. The only difference was that the distance-learning teachers were not always completely off for the day because they still had teaching obligations on the Hawaii campus.

Because the school year in Tonga begins in January and ends in November, the distance-learning teachers often had to work through BYU-Hawaii school breaks and cut their summer vacation short by a couple of weeks so that they could fit in the required 35 weeks of course work. Again, this was a bit of a sacrifice for the teachers, but they were compensated with a lighter load once the distance-learning course finished in early November.

◈ PRACTICAL IDEAS

Most of our practical suggestions are related to two broad types of interaction—live and computer.

Create Opportunities for Teachers to Meet Students Face to Face

To enhance live interactions among those involved in the program, the distance-learning teachers traveled to Tonga. Though it added to each semester's expenses, this trip was considered necessary for a variety of reasons, not the least of which was allowing the teacher and students to meet. Remembering their teacher as a real, live person later helped the students overcome the feeling that they were not being taught by a disembodied voice, and the teacher similarly benefited from getting to know the students in person before having to teach them for a whole semester. Seeing the classroom environment before the start of the first semester was also helpful to the teachers, who later had to visualize what was happening there.

Keep Interaction Levels High Through Special Protocols

Maintaining a high level of interaction during the audio class was essential for language learning but quite challenging at first. The distance-learning teachers quickly learned that certain classroom protocols needed to be established for this interaction to be successful. The teachers needed to direct questions to specific individuals or groups. General questions to the whole class did not go well because there were either many responses or none at all. When several of the students responded at once, it was almost impossible for the teacher to pick out individual voices. As the courses progressed, the teachers and students learned the protocols and the audio classes improved considerably.

Devise a System to Track Student Participation and Groupings

We discovered that it was difficult to keep track of who had participated during the audio sessions, and we needed some type of system that could tell us who was speaking, who had already participated, and what individuals were paired or grouped together. One teacher found that by laminating a large piece of poster board, taping it to the wall in his office, and then creating name cards for each student, he could manipulate their names on the board as they participated or worked in pairs or groups. If students were absent, he simply left the cards off the board or put them aside.

Select a Capable Site Coordinator

Another key to overcoming the program's challenges was the selection of a very capable teacher at the school in Tonga to serve as a site coordinator. The site coordinator acted as the distance-learning teacher's eyes, hands, and sometimes ears during the audio classes. She taught classes on her own when the distance-learning teacher was unable to, whether because of time constraints or the international date line. She was also in charge of sending out and receiving data and preparing materials for the classes.

Get the Site Coordinator to Facilitate Live Interactions

The foremost way to facilitate live teacher-student interactions in our distance-learning classes was to use the site coordinator who was with the students during the audio classes. This arrangement was a central part of our approach.

Although teaching over the phone was at first considered a challenge to the live interactions of the class, it was soon discovered that this arrangement also enhanced the students' ability to interact in certain ways. Most Tongan ESL students are culturally conditioned to be somewhat shy about speaking up in class. At the beginning of each semester, most comments or questions by the students had to be repeated by the site coordinator because they were spoken too quietly to be heard by the distance-learning teacher over the phone. At the end of each semester, however, it was surprising to see how well the students had learned to speak up and project their voices, and the site coordinator had to serve as a go-between far less often.

Develop a System for Labeling Computer Files

Computer interactions were also an important part of our Tongan distance-learning program; many student essays, other assignments, teacher feedback, and correspondence between the distance-learning teacher and the site coordinator were continually being sent back and forth between Tonga and BYU-Hawaii as computer data.

Because of the volume of student work being sent back and forth by computer, everyone involved followed a strict system of naming files to avoid confusion. The computers that the students and the site coordinator were using in Tonga required that file names be no more than eight characters long with a three-character extension, but this was enough to include all necessary identification. The first part of the file name was an abbreviation of the type of assignment, such as OCE for an out-of-class essay, followed by a number to distinguish a particular assignment from earlier and later ones of the same type. The extension (after the period) of each file name was the student's initials, to which the distance-learning teacher added a "C" if the assignment had been corrected (marked and given a score with comments added). A file named OCE#8.STC, then, was the eighth out-of-class essay by Sam Tati, which the distance-learning teacher was now returning with feedback.

Systematize Procedures for Providing Feedback on Students' Writing

Marking essays and other assignments on computer was an interesting challenge for teachers who previously had always used a red pen for that task. One of the distance-learning teachers decided to use bold type as a substitute for red ink (and asked the students not to use bold type themselves). This allowed the students to zero in on the comments, suggestions, and corrections made by their teacher and not confuse that feedback with their own typing.

The task of adding that feedback electronically was at first awkward and tedious enough to be a bit daunting, but it got easier with time and was facilitated considerably by utilizing macros. For example, one macro highlighted an entire essay and changed its font to a larger size. This made the essay easier to read and mark. Another macro made it easy for the teacher to make a longer comment as a numbered footnote at the bottom of the student's essay, with a corresponding number in superscript at the particular point in the essay that the comment referred to.

One of our teachers had never used macros and was barely even aware of them before becoming involved in the distance-learning program. After processing just one batch of essays from Tonga, however, he was motivated to spend about 4 hours learning how to use macros and set up ones that would aid him on future batches. His 4-hour investment was returned to him many times over in the course of one semester and made providing feedback on the essays far less tedious and much more pleasant.

Do Not Rule Out Visual Media When Teaching via Audio Channels

One final practical idea that emerged from this program was that the distance-learning teacher could use visual media, provided that he could have at least a rough copy to refer to while teaching. The several lectures that were given each semester for listening practice were on a wide variety of topics and often made use of detailed color transparencies on the overhead projector. Before sending the original audiovisual materials for each lecture to Tonga (numbered and prearranged in the correct order), the teacher who gave these lectures made rough black-and-white photocopies of the transparencies. Though they were not nearly as nice as the originals, they were good enough for him to use while he talked about them, as he was already familiar with the original copies being shown by the site coordinator to the students.

One lecture even involved a short video. The distance-learning teacher kept the original videotape in Hawaii and sent a good copy of it to Tonga. He arranged for a

VCR and television to be set up near his desk before the lecture. At the appropriate point in the lecture, he had the site coordinator hit the play button in Tonga and simultaneously did the same in his office. As the video played in both locations, the distance-learning teacher could comment on what the students were seeing, knowing exactly when they were seeing it. This procedure worked surprisingly well and was repeated on other occasions.

◈ CONCLUSION

This distance-learning program linked teachers in a place that was quite remote geographically (Laie, Hawaii) over a great distance (thousands of miles of Pacific Ocean) to students in a place that was even more remote (rural Tonga) and that offered limited and occasionally unreliable technological options. The challenge of this teaching connection was deepened by the fact that the schools in the two locations were divided by different day-to-day and month-to-month schedules and did not even share the same calendar day. Given these challenges, it was apparent that telephone connections would be the best technological option.

The intensity of listening comprehension practice was an incidental but valuable benefit of teaching over the phone. More than one observer of the distance-learning class commented that the students had really concentrated on understanding what their teacher was saying. This concentration was necessary to make up for not having a teacher that they could clearly hear and see, but it also produced a level of concentration that ESL listening teachers would love to get their students to exercise under normal, non-distance-teaching circumstances. The progress that the students in the distance-learning program made in understanding their teacher over the teleconferencing equipment left them feeling confident about their ability to understand professors in their classrooms when they began their studies at BYU-Hawaii.

Being taught in Tonga by a teacher who was actually at BYU-Hawaii also helped the students feel more connected to the university that they were looking forward to attending. Under the old system, students and teachers sometimes grappled with the feeling of being disconnected from the university. The distance-learning approach actually helped the students feel less distant.

Although this distance-learning program may not have blazed new technological or methodological trails, we feel it does show that considerable obstacles of distance, limited technology, and scheduling problems can be successfully overcome. The very people who piloted and conducted this program initially entertained some doubt that it would measure up to the usual system of sending a teacher to Tonga for a year. Although a few aspects were inevitably weaker, the distance-learning program proved to have some strengths all its own.

The English language preparation that our students have received in the distance-learning program is comparable to that of the previous Tongan students who studied in a conventional classroom arrangement. Most of our distance-learning students have arrived on campus as much as a year ahead of where they would have been in their English language proficiency without the distance-learning program. That is not bad, considering that their teachers were always a day behind them.

◈ CONTRIBUTORS

Brent A. Green, a senior EIL lecturer at BYU-Hawaii, in Laie, Hawaii, in the United States, directs the EIL program at the Church College of Western Samoa. He has taught ESL in Hawaii, the Marshall Islands, Tonga, and Utah, and EFL in Taiwan.

Kory J. Collier is a senior lecturer in the EIL program at BYU-Hawaii. Two and a half of his 10 years with the EIL program were spent directing and teaching the Samoa EIL program.

Norman Evans is the former director of the EIL program at BYU-Hawaii, where he is a faculty member of the Languages and Linguistics Division.

CHAPTER 8

An Academic Writing Course in Cyberspace

David Catterick

◈ INTRODUCTION

One of the major catalysts of change in higher education in recent years has been the World Wide Web. From humble beginnings as a vehicle for collaborative research just 15 years ago, the Web has burgeoned into a vast network of users across the world. Though for most of the past decade its use in higher education generally has been limited to the transmission of information from one user to another, more recently, computer applications such as bulletin boards, chat rooms, whiteboards (an area on a display screen in which multiple users can write or draw), and conferencing have allowed interactivity that has paved the way for Web-based instruction and Web-enhanced language learning (WELL).[1]

WebCT (Worldwide Web Course Tools) (2000) is just one example of a piece of software that integrates various applications, such as chat and whiteboard, into one convenient package. Users access the software via a standard browser that provides a familiar, nonthreatening user environment. WebCT was designed at the University of British Columbia for delivery of distance and flexible learning courses and has become an extremely popular package. Institutions across the world are now adopting WebCT to teach courses as diverse as town planning and electrical engineering.

This chapter describes the use of WebCT in the context of an English for academic purposes (EAP) writing course, provides reasons for choosing WebCT, describes some of the triumphs and challenges of using the software in the course, and, finally, offers suggestions for future utilization of the technology.

◈ CONTEXT

The Writing Up Research (WUR) course is a 6-week, 12-hour thesis-writing course offered to international graduate students at the University of Dundee, Scotland. It is a noncredit course designed to be an adjunct to the weekly 2 hours of EAP teaching offered to all international students through the English Support Programme. WUR covers the writing of structures (e.g., abstracts, conclusions) as well as writing skills

---

[1] WELL is a United Kingdom-based e-mail discussion list and Web site (http://www.well.ac.uk/menu.html) designed to promote the use of technology in language teaching.

(e.g., paraphrasing, referencing) and is one of the most oversubscribed courses run by the Centre for Applied Language Studies (CALS).

Students tend to apply to join the course for one of two reasons: They have been counseled to do so by their departmental supervisor or they themselves feel they need it. Staffing and resource issues mean the department can currently offer only two WUR courses each year, which has made a rigorous, by-merit-only selection procedure essential. The criteria used in the selection process are as follows:

- attendance at weekly noncredit English Support Programme courses
- supervisor's permission/recommendation for the student to attend the course
- proof that the student will be starting to write a thesis/dissertation in the current calendar year

The biggest problem in finalizing the class list from applicants who meet these criteria has always been to find a suitable slot in the schedule to run the class. Because the students come from various departments across the university, there are, invariably, scheduling conflicts that make it difficult to find a convenient 2-hour slot for WUR each week. Even when a slot is found, it is frequently the case that, due to other, often last-minute, commitments, not all students are able to attend every week. This ongoing problem led to the need for a creative solution, one that an on-line learning environment, accessible 24 hours a day, seemed to provide.

◈ DESCRIPTION

WUR Course Overview

The WUR course is based on two complementary approaches to academic writing:

1. process
2. product

In terms of process, the course emphasizes the stages involved in writing a thesis or dissertation, from the prewriting stage to editing and submitting the final draft. The product element is brought out by an emphasis on structures within the thesis, such as outline, abstracts, introductions, and bibliographies. This dual focus creates a somewhat dense and demanding course, but it also provides a thorough one, as can be seen from the course outline in Figure 1.

In the traditional, classroom-based WUR course, classes are held on Thursday afternoons. The 2-hour sessions are a mixture of teacher-fronted instruction and group-oriented, task-based activities. In Week 5, for example, the teacher begins the session by eliciting the nature and purpose of abstracts. Aspects such as genre, purpose, readership, and length are all discussed. Students are then placed in groups, handed a sample thesis abstract, and asked to identify the different types of information provided by the writer. The information identified forms the basis of the next task that requires students, again in groups, to reorganize a collection of jumbled sentences from another abstract. The teacher then points out variations in verb tense in the sample abstracts and highlights useful phrases that signal the beginning of each section.

In the second hour, the class moves on to a discussion of the specific language needed for describing figures (e.g., charts, graphs, tables). The teacher begins this

Week (mode)	Writing Products	Writing Skills
1 (Classroom)	Outline	• Deciding on a thesis
2 (WebCT)	Introduction	• Using discourse markers
3 (Classroom)	Body/development	• Paraphrasing
		• Synthesizing
		• Avoiding plagiarism
4 (WebCT)	Conclusion	• Quoting
5 (WebCT)	Abstract	• Describing and citing nonlinear information
6 (Classroom)	References and acknowledgments	• Editing

FIGURE 1. Course Outline for Writing Up Research (WUR)

phase of the class by handing out a sample line graph. Students are asked to interpret the line graph and identify the most significant points on the line (usually peaks and troughs or sections with particularly marked variations). The teacher then elicits the language used to describe trends in terms of adjective/noun (e.g., *a sharp increase*) and adverb/verb constructions (e.g., *to rapidly decline*). Finally, the students write a description of the trends in a second sample graph.

All the materials used in the course are produced in-house, though the approach to teaching is no doubt similar to approaches used in similar programs in other parts of the world.

Origins of WebCT for the WUR Course

In September 1998, I learned about WebCT through a message posted on TESL-L.[2] At the WebCT's Web site (http://about.webct.com), interested parties had the chance to evaluate the software by setting up their own free sample course. Following a brief evaluation, I became convinced of the software's potential for creating distance-learning programs. It also seemed suited to partly solving a more pressing need, namely, the long-standing scheduling problems of the WUR course. With permission from the CALS director, I began preparing a WebCT version of the WUR course to begin in February 1999.

To manage the change as efficiently as possible, it was suggested that the course be multimode; that is, rather than running all the WUR sessions via WebCT, the software would be used for only three of the six sessions: Weeks 2, 4, and 5 of the course. The University of Dundee, like so many other institutions around the world, had been experimenting with WebCT (on an informal basis) and was therefore able to provide access to the software on the university's UNIX server. With the help of the university's Information Technology (IT) Services in creating the course directory, and following the purchase of user licenses, the process of designing the course began.

---

[2] TESL-L is a free, electronic discussion list that focuses on issues of interest to ESOL teachers. See instructions for joining on page 66.

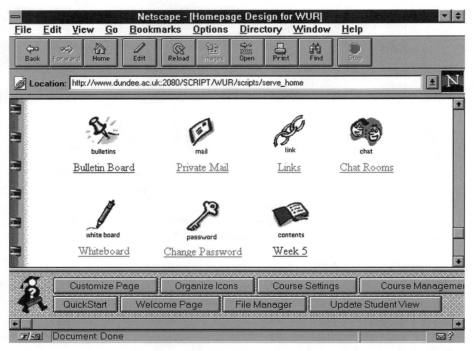

FIGURE 2. Instructor's View of WebCT

Design of the WebCT WUR Course

WebCT provides two separate interfaces, one for the instructor and one for the student. The instructor interface includes a split screen with help functions and buttons at the bottom of the screen to aid in the configuration of the WebCT pages. To instructors with no previous experience with WebCT, this is a great boon, but for those already familiar with hypertext markup language (HTML) editing, the endless row of buttons can seem a little unintuitive and can be more of a hindrance than a help.

As Figure 2 shows, the software's various features are accessed via labeled icons provided by WebCT. A student wanting to access the whiteboard, for example, simply has to double-click on the whiteboard icon, which, in turn, loads that facility. Cosmetic changes to the page's appearance are also possible by clicking on buttons to add text and change the background.

In addition to customizing the overall layout of the pages, the instructor also has to set up student accounts by deciding on a username and password for every course participant. This information is needed to gain access to the course through WebCT's password protection system.

With the pages customized for the WUR course, my next step was to convert the course materials from the word-processed format in which they were written to HTML codes. Although more recent versions of word-processing programs allow for a straightforward conversion, the program I used did not support HTML. Consequently, I needed to copy and paste the text into a basic HTML editor to create a file in HTML format. In the standard WUR course, the teacher distributed the course materials in class, and students had the chance to seek clarification and have their answers instantly corrected. This immediate interaction was clearly absent in the on-line materials; therefore, I incorporated tasks with built-in answers into the course materials. These on-line tasks took two forms:

1. tasks with an anchor link to the answers further down the page

2. tasks designed to have solutions that could be e-mailed to me for grading

Figure 3 illustrates an example of the second type of task. In this task, students first read a humorous article from a tabloid-style newspaper and then wrote an abstract based on the research it described. They sent their completed abstracts to me via e-mail. These were then used as source material in the review at the beginning of Week 6.

Once I had edited the course material files, I needed to upload them to the university server. Though for normal Web pages this can sometimes be problematic, in WebCT this procedure is once again a matter of clicking a button. With all the pages customized, student accounts set up, and all course materials uploaded, the software is ready to use.

Start of the WUR Course

The course's first week was classroom based; the only change from the standard format was to allow 15 minutes toward the session's end to demonstrate WebCT. Instructions for logging on to WebCT, including personalized usernames and passwords, were also handed out to the students. I encouraged the seven students taking the course to try logging on as soon as possible to allow enough time to solve any problems that might arise.

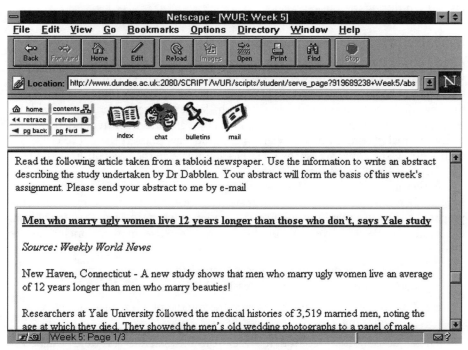

FIGURE 3. Sample Course Materials With On-Line Activity for Abstract Writing

◈ DISTINGUISHING FEATURES

Perhaps the most distinctive feature of this academic writing course was its use of WebCT. This use had many different dimensions that deserve explanation and comment.

Student Tasks on WebCT

Students were asked to do two tasks with WebCT. First, they were required to view the course materials and complete the on-line tasks early in the week. Second, they were asked to log on for about an hour during the normal scheduled session between 2:00 p.m. and 4:00 p.m. on Thursday afternoons. For both tasks, students logged on from a variety of different locations, some from computers in the university computing labs and others from computers in their offices or in their homes.

Student Tracking and Follow-Up

WebCT has a student-tracking facility that indicates when students log on and off the system and which facilities they access. I was interested to see that one student chose to work on the on-line tasks each Sunday afternoon, not a time I would expect to be very popular. On a few occasions, the student-tracking facility indicated that by Thursday morning, some students had still not logged on to view the materials. I then sent those students an e-mail suggesting they log on if they wanted to get the most out of the on-line discussion later that day. At first, students seemed surprised that the instructor had access to this sort of information, but, despite the Big Brother overtones, it provided some of them with the impetus they needed to complete the tasks, even during the busiest weeks.

Synchronous Discussion Session

After viewing the course materials and completing the on-line tasks earlier in the week, students logged on between 2:00 p.m. and 4:00 p.m. on Thursday afternoons. One student had a lecture between 2:00 p.m. and 3:00 p.m. and therefore could join the chat discussion for only the last hour. In Week 4, one student was unable to attend because she attended a workshop given by a guest lecturer in her department. In the normal classroom-based WUR, she would have missed the entire class, but with WebCT, she could access the materials, complete all the tasks on-line, and read the chat logs to see what was discussed.

Earlier in the day of the chat discussion, I posted five questions on the WebCT bulletin board related to the week's materials. Reading the questions and being prepared to discuss them on-line was the students' first task once they logged on. Questions for Week 2 were about the use of discourse markers, including the following:

- What type of discourse marker is "hence" (e.g., addition, cause and result, comparison and contrast, concession)?

- Can discourse markers be used in the middle of a sentence as well as at the beginning?

These questions followed from the week's on-line materials and were designed to focus the on-line discussion (through the WebCT chat facility) and mirror the usual interactive classroom dynamic. Chat enables a logged-on user to send text messages in real time to other users who are also logged on. The messages can be read instantly and replied to by everyone in the chat room, with the software keeping a log of the entire discussion.

Errors in Students' Chat Discussion Writing

The use of the chat facility highlighted a major difference in interactions between students and teacher in the classroom-based WUR class and the WebCT WUR class. In the classroom-based WUR sessions, interaction was oral. In chat sessions, the entire discussion was through the written medium. Apart from slowing down the discussion significantly, the fact that chat was completely text based highlighted the students' grammatical errors that usually go unnoticed or uncommented on in speech. To compound the error issue, the speed with which students were expected to write seemed to foster problems of accuracy. As a result, tolerance for errors became a matter of some debate in the CALS Department. The department decided on a policy in which grammatical errors in chat discourse would be

- tolerated to the same degree as in spoken discourse
- viewed as less significant than the overall message
- used in the final session on editing skills for analyzing the differences between typo, slip, and error

Chat Discourse Characteristics

One source of interest was the actual quality of the chat discussion. I had feared that it might be difficult to start the discussion and that it would take a great deal of instructor input to maintain the momentum. As it happened, discourse seemed quite natural, and the quality of the questions asked and the answers given was particularly high. Here are a few excerpts from the chat logs, followed by comments on certain aspects of each.

Excerpt 1

(Week 2: First session to use chat facility)

Omar:	Hi
Warat:	Hello Omar.
Warakorn:	hi omar
Omar:	let me introduce myself
Omar:	I am civil engineering studing doing PhD
Omar:	studing = student
Warat:	Nice to meet you. I'm doing Computer Aided Architectural Design. MSc.
Warakorn:	I am studying MSc in energy
Omar:	nice to meet you all
Warakorn:	nice to meet u too

Excerpt 1 shows the very first dialogue on chat. As in the first class in any course, students take time to introduce themselves. In this excerpt, the interaction was completely spontaneous and the instructor was not even logged on at this point. In terms of the previous discussion on errors, notice the use of the lower case (a standard feature of the chat genre) and the absence of the indefinite article in two of the messages.

Excerpt 2

(Week 4)

Instructor:	Did everyone understand the task about synthesis in this week's work? Why is synthesis so useful?
Katerina:	It is used to connect 2 texts and transfer the logic from one to the next?
Warat:	And conclude both of them into a single idea.
Instructor:	Yes, correct. To show the logical relationship between the two texts and put them into a single expression.
Instructor:	What was the relationship between the two paraphrases on the topic of secularism I gave you in this week's materials? Explain how you know.
Katerina:	The first one seems to contradict the 2nd one. The 1st one is the rational approach where "supernatural" have no place
Instructor:	So, if it is contrast, what sort of a discourse marker would you use?
Katerina:	however?
Katerina:	On the other hand
Warat:	Whereas?
Instructor:	Oh dear!! I must be a terrible teacher! What is the difference between a marker like "whereas" and a marker like "however"?
Warat:	One is contradiction while another is concession?
Warakorn:	they are different meanings
Instructor:	Good! I'm not the world's worst teacher after all!
Virginia:	I am sorry, I just can't think as quick as everyone today. It must be the cold!

In Excerpt 2, we see the way students cooperate to arrive at a correct answer. In the third line of the excerpt, Warat elaborates on Katerina's answer. Later on, three different students focus on correct use of discourse markers for two paraphrases they were asked to synthesize as part of an on-line activity in the week's materials. In discourse terms, this log could easily have been taken from a classroom-based recording.

Excerpt 3

(Week 5)

Instructor:	Would anyone like to make a start by answering one of this week's questions or asking a question of your own?
Warakorn:	both table and graph are figures
Katerina:	When we write X (1985) said . . . . do we have to write (1985:22) at the end of the quotation too?
Instructor:	Let's deal with Katerina's question first. Does anyone have an answer?
Warakorn:	I think you have to write because the author might state that words in different year of publishing.
Instructor:	Thanks Warakorn. Does anyone else agree?
Amy:	I only write year..i.e (1985)
Instructor:	OK. Who's right and why?

Instructor:	The year does indicate when it is published. But why might the page number be important?
Virginia:	I think if it is a statement, the page number may be useful for the reader to refer back to it.
Instructor:	Yes, Virginia. It's for the benefit of the reader.
Katerina:	hoe does the reader know which book to look into if you only state the date and page number?
Instructor:	Ah! Good question, Katerina. Can anyone answer that one?
Warakorn:	you can find in bibliography

In Excerpt 3, we see Katerina asking a very pertinent follow-up question. The question seems to indicate her confusion over the purpose of a bibliography, a topic that is dealt with in Week 6 of the course. Once again, students seem eager to be involved in the discussion and work together to arrive at the answer.

It can be noted from the chat log excerpts that the on-line discussions are highly planned and teacher directed. Though there is obviously some scope for social discourse as there would be in any classroom context, the chat session during the 2 hours runs according to a fixed purpose and agenda, with the pace being maintained in order to cover as many questions as possible in the time students are on-line. In fact, though students were only required to spend 1 hour on-line, in practice, most students remained logged on for the 2 hours.

Flexible Access

WebCT is useful not just for distance learning but also for flexible learning. In terms of distance learning, WebCT enables students from anywhere in the world to log on to the WebCT system with nothing more than a Web browser and a password. Institutions, therefore, can market courses to a much wider range of clients and can save on the cost of resources, such as copying and room bookings. Although this was not my main reason for running the WUR course via WebCT, it was nevertheless a background issue that the CALS Department will consider in the future. I chose WebCT because it provided greater flexibility so that students could schedule their own time for completing the course work. Interestingly, the student feedback made no mention of the value of this flexibility, perhaps because it was simply taken for granted.

❖ PRACTICAL IDEAS

As the first WebCT version of the WUR course was a trial, student feedback was especially important. My suggestions in this section are based on the information provided by the comprehensive feedback forms returned by the students at the end of the course. I have organized these suggestions into a number of categories, starting with the broadest and most theoretical and ending with the most specific and practical.

Recognize the Limitations of the Software and Use it Accordingly

WebCT, for all its user-friendliness and robustness, is still a limited piece of software. In terms of English language teaching, its biggest limitation is undoubtedly the fact that it is essentially text based and lacks full multimedia support. Although the software does allow small sound and video files to be uploaded and made accessible to students, the result is a far cry from synchronous, streaming multimedia that would be invaluable for language teaching. I was aware of this limitation while still evaluating the package, and this was a factor in choosing to pilot WebCT in a writing course. It is to be hoped that, in the future, advances in technology will allow for full multimedia integration in packages such as WebCT. Some teachers may prefer to delay using WebCT-style packages until the technology has developed enough to accommodate multimedia capability.

Allow Time and Resources for Initial Setup and Continuing Operation

As with so many things using technology, the initial time investment is quite considerable. It took me approximately 15 hours to evaluate WebCT, upload all the course materials, and set up student accounts. As this was a new project and not viewed by the CALS Department as part of my regular assigned duties, neither finances nor support staff time could be provided. Such, of course, would be the case in many institutions. However, I strongly recommend that teachers seek out as much support, both in terms of finance and staff hours, as possible.

The course also put a strain on the department's computing facilities. During the design phase, I discovered that the 3-year-old computer in my office could not cope with the demands of the whiteboard. I had planned to use the whiteboard for collaborative writing in Week 4 but had to change my plans because it was difficult to get access to a Windows NT (New Technology) machine. Though the students seemed to have fewer problems accessing a suitable computer, this was clearly a resource issue. Anyone wishing to use a WebCT-style package needs access to a high-end Pentium or Macintosh computer running a 32-bit operating system.

Do Not Be Intimidated by the Technology

Some teachers feel that they would not have the technological know-how to set up a course like this. The reality is that, for anyone with a basic knowledge of how to use a Web browser, designing a course on WebCT is very simple. Customizing the WebCT pages and setting up accounts are simply a matter of button clicking. Of course, if resources allow, a person with an IT background might take over setting up the course so that the teacher is left only the responsibility of designing the materials and actually running the course.

Use the Full Range of WebCT Features

WebCT has a fully integrated student assessment and management system. This enables the teacher to create on-line quizzes and multiple choice-style tests, the scores of which are automatically added to student records. As the WUR course is noncredit, I chose not to use this feature of WebCT, but it would seem to be an essential feature of any for-credit, distance-learning course. WebCT also allows for links to outside sites. This was used to a limited extent in the WebCT course by providing a link to a comprehensive grammar site on the Web and a link to the department's own on-line study links page. With the wealth of information available on the Web, this feature could be used to great effect.

◈ CONCLUSION

A frequently asked question when talking about distance-learning courses is "Isn't a classroom-based, face-to-face contact course always better?" Feedback comments from students seemed divided on this issue. Although many students enjoyed their experiences using WebCT, others were somewhat less enthusiastic:

> I like the use of classroom-based teaching as well as using WebCT. This was new for me. However, more class-based teaching may have been slightly more helpful.

> I suggest having all the course documents written on the Web site with more details or even links to go back to overtime I need them. I suggest having a long term chat room.

My own feeling is that Web-based instruction is a very effective substitute for face-to-face teaching when basic geography or scheduling precludes it. In terms of a student's overall performance on the WUR course, the course work submitted was of an equally high standard as the course work from previous classroom-based WUR courses. This may have been because students spent up to an hour extra on the course in the weeks when the course was via WebCT. None of the students commented on this extra time investment in their feedback.

Student feedback about the course also seemed to suggest that the trial of WebCT was an overall success. General comments about the usefulness and effectiveness of the course were no different from previous years, indicating that the change in mode of delivery did not detract from the general opinions about the course:

> This course was useful because it helped me identify my problems, particularly in my introduction.

> It was very useful in terms of showing how to organise our writing (dissertation or not!). Information obtained was applicable to all smaller pieces of course work during the term.

> It was very useful to understand the structure of the research paper before, or even during, writing. There would be less problem and less time needed in writing a research paper if students know what should/should not be in it.

As a result of the trial's general success, the CALS Department has decided to offer more courses via WebCT in the future. This is partly in recognition of the time already invested in WebCT but also to allow for the flexibility in course scheduling that a package such as WebCT brings. At the time of my writing this chapter, discussions are under way with a Finnish institution to sell the WUR course as a distance-learning package. In the meantime, the search is underway for software that will more effectively integrate multimedia. Though this will put even more strain on computing facilities in the department, it is seen as a vital next step in the further development of more varied on-line English language courses. With the department profiting financially from the sale of any distance-learning programs, it is hoped that more funds can be allocated to pay for the staffing and training costs essential to the development of these programs.

There are, however, a couple of caveats about implementing such a program as this. First, as stated earlier, the text-based nature of WebCT makes it ideally suited to a writing course. I would like to see an enhanced multimedia capability before I would opt to pilot it with other English language teaching courses (Catterick, 2000). In addition, the students' language proficiency must be considered. In the case of my WUR course, I used WebCT with high-intermediate language learners. It would clearly be less appropriate for learners who lack confidence in their communications skills in the second language and are therefore intimidated by the chat function.

With organizations such as TeleEducation NB, a distance-learning network in the Canadian province of New Brunswick, reporting an exponential rise in the number of courses being offered on-line around the world, the future of on-line education seems secure. I trust this chapter has shown that there is no reason why on-line English language courses cannot be part of the distance-learning trend.

◈ CONTRIBUTOR

David Catterick is a lecturer in EFL at the University of Dundee, Scotland. He has taught in various universities in China and the United Kingdom and holds an MEd in TESOL from the University of Manchester. His research interests include Web-enhanced language learning, teacher education, and EAP.

PART 2

Preparing ESOL Teachers at a Distance

CHAPTER 9

Making Distance Learning Dynamic: The Evolution of the TelESOL Web-Based Teacher Education Program

Joyce W. Nutta

◈ INTRODUCTION

Some educators maintain that distance education is a poor substitute for traditional, on-campus classes. Others assert that courses that impart facts and develop declarative knowledge are the only type that can be taught from a distance. However, a new vision of distance learning is emerging, using the inherent properties of information communications technologies to support learning from a different paradigm: the constructivist model. This chapter describes the evolution of the TelESOL program, a distance-learning, Web-based training program in TESOL, from its initial conceptualization based on traditional distance-learning courses (first generation), to its eventual development into an interactive course (second generation), to its current status based on a constructivist and collaborative learning model (third generation) using asynchronous Web-based instruction.

◈ CONTEXT

In 1990, as a result of a lawsuit filed by advocacy groups for parents of limited English proficient (LEP) children, K–12 teachers throughout Florida were required to complete training in TESOL. Many different programs emerged to meet the overwhelming training demand created by the state mandate, including courses delivered through traditional means as well as through television broadcasts, videotapes, and workbooks. Small counties that lacked resources to hire trainers and the crowded professional and personal schedules of teachers affected by the new requirement presented daunting challenges. Clearly, innovative and creative solutions in the spirit of the legislation were needed to meet these challenges in order for teachers to provide appropriate instruction and services for LEP students. At the same time that TESOL training began to be offered throughout Florida, the College of Education at the University of South Florida began Learn From a Distance (LFAD), a distance-learning program. The LFAD program began by offering four e-mail courses in instructional technology (IT). Participants in this program completed individual assignments and sent the results to the course instructor who, in turn, provided individual feedback via e-mail. Because the topics of these courses lent themselves to mastering a technological skill (e.g., programming languages, authoring tools), the courses did not emphasize participant-to-participant interaction. The classes were correspondence courses accelerated by e-mail and organized according to what I call *first-generation distance learning*. These first-generation courses employed a programmed instruction model, with participants completing the self-paced readings and assignments and sending them to the instructor via e-mail. The instructor responded by e-mail to indicate whether the activities were completed correctly, and no other type of interaction or exposure to various media occurred.

In 1995, the LFAD program asked a colleague and me, as faculty in the Foreign/ Second Language Education (FSLE) program, to develop e-mail courses that would help teachers meet the Florida TESOL training requirements. As a first step, we enrolled in the IT distance-learning courses to experience them from the learner's perspective. Realizing that TESOL training courses would not be successful if they were based on the same format as the other e-mail courses, we then spent an additional semester designing two interactive TESOL training courses that attempted to overcome the disadvantages of distance learning.

We determined that the design of the first-generation model led to specific problems that had to be addressed in the development of the TESOL courses. First of all, attrition was high. Because no deadlines were enforced, many participants dropped the courses or requested an incomplete grade. In addition, the amount of e-mail that the instructor had to read and respond to was unmanageable, leading to problems in record keeping and providing adequate feedback. Another challenge was to structure the TESOL courses to achieve their purpose: to prepare participants to teach nonnative speakers. This entailed going beyond simply exposing them to concepts and skills. The courses needed a practical emphasis as well as an instructional approach that modeled the type of teaching expected of the future teachers.

◈ DESCRIPTION

Second-Generation Distance Learning: An Interactive Approach

We had many concerns as we considered how to design the TelESOL courses. How could we conduct practical, hands-on courses through distance learning? In addition, we had to address many smaller, yet no less significant, issues. How could we create a learning community and foster interaction among participants? How could we ensure comprehension of all assignments and avoid confusion? How could we evaluate participants fairly, holding them to the same course objectives and standards as an on-campus course? At this point, questions regarding basic teaching effectiveness and instructional design guided our efforts, not any specific overarching educational philosophy.

Using principles of instructional design (see Smith & Ragan, 1999, for a good introduction to instructional design), we analyzed the learning context, the learners, and the learning task. We determined that we needed undergraduate and graduate courses that provided a general overview of the main issues affecting LEP students' academic success, so we began to develop two courses from the same basic set of objectives. We designed the undergraduate course as an overview of best practices for teaching ESOL students who have been mainstreamed. The graduate course was designed to expand the objectives of the undergraduate course by emphasizing second language acquisition (SLA) research and theory as well as global education.

We discovered a number of important considerations. First, there was a need for distance-learning TESOL training throughout Florida. Second, many of the learners who would enroll in the TelESOL courses were teachers with family responsibilities that precluded weekly class attendance or teachers who lived in remote areas or in counties that lacked resources to provide on-site training. Lastly, the learning tasks included the development of knowledge, skills, and dispositions that would enable participants to teach mainstreamed LEP students more effectively.

The next step was to develop the instructional strategy. How would we organize the materials, deliver the instruction, and manage the courses? Having decided that the courses would emphasize reflection, interaction, and field experiences, we developed a self-contained instructional packet with carefully designed activities and related readings that would serve as the core of instruction as an all-inclusive packet could minimize the potential for confusion, especially for undergraduates.

The course packet comprised seven modules, each of which included readings, reading questions, and activities. The reading topics spanned methods, curriculum, assessment, culture, and SLA. Often controversial and thought provoking, the readings gave a practical and theoretical basis for the activities, which included a case study. We developed corresponding open-ended questions for reflection for each of the seven modules and divided the activities into two types: those that would be completed in class if it were conducted on campus, and those that involved working with an individual LEP student (referred to as the *case study activities*). We included many interactive activities, such as a role-play in which each team member participated from the perspective of a different decision maker (e.g., classroom teacher, ESOL specialist, counselor) in a discussion of whether to promote an LEP student or refer him or her to special education. The case study activities applied each module's topic to an individual LEP student, requiring participants to complete a cultural interview with the LEP student and his or her parents, or just with the parents; assess the student's level of English language proficiency; and create, teach, and evaluate a lesson specific to the student's needs.

Because we required participants to submit in writing every reading question response and activity that they would have discussed in an on-campus class, we did not grade all assignments. Just as an instructor cannot give individual feedback and grades for every small group discussion, so it is with distance-learning courses that use e-mail as a medium of discussion. Some assignments could be assessed in a pass/fail approach, but others should be evaluated carefully and assigned points. We compiled the case study activities, as well as other selected activities, in the course portfolio, which the participants submitted at the final class meeting.

In trying to set the course context, clarify course objectives and expectations, and create camaraderie within and among the teams (groups of 6–10 classmates established at the beginning of the course), we developed a mandatory, face-to-face, orientation session. This session included a hands-on demonstration of a lesson emphasizing comprehensible instruction; a step-by-step explanation of how the course operated; and a number of different team-building activities, including taking digital photographs of each team and giving each member a copy to post by his or her computer. In addition to the orientation session, we offered two optional face-to-face sessions emphasizing experiential and hands-on learning for extra credit for participants who preferred to have more contact in person. At the end of each course, there was a closing session during which participants presented information on their projects and gave a portrayal of their case study students and what they learned from them.

Employing aspects of the first-generation courses (e.g., e-mail as the primary means of communication), the TelESOL courses then incorporated participant-to-participant interaction by requiring learners to send their work to their team members as well as to the instructor. This involved establishing regular and strict deadlines for submission of work. We required participants to comment biweekly on each other's work and reflections and engage in collaborative activities.

Figure 1 explains the organization of course content and participant interaction patterns.

When the course was first offered, I was unsure of what to expect. During my orientation session for the class of 35, I emphasized the pilot nature of the first course. Dubbing the participants *pioneers,* I cautioned them that problems could occur and that I wanted to offset their confusion and possible frustration by being constantly accessible to them. The participants knew exactly who the needs assessment indicated they would be—classroom teachers from around the state, parents and parents-to-be, and many others with a diversity of life experiences.

To illustrate, a participant named Bernice enrolled in the TelESOL course as well as in a different course that I taught on campus. Bernice was an older learner who returned to school after raising five children and ending an abusive marriage. Her appearance was in sharp contrast to that of the typical students on campus. She wore homemade clothes, and her face and hands were worn by having spent her life taking care of others. Her speech revealed her Appalachian upbringing. In the on-campus course, the younger learners marginalized Bernice. When she spoke up in class, classmates rolled their eyes and interrupted her. It was not long before she became reticent and withdrawn. In the distance-learning course, however, Bernice used her skillful storytelling to keep her team members enthralled. As part of a course project, she began to volunteer in a migrant camp and used her creative skills to start a crafts project to teach migrant women English. Every week she wrote stories about her classes, and her teammates praised her copiously for her skills as a teacher and a writer. They voted her star of the team and asked that her stories be sent to every team. It was becoming clear to me that distance learning was not just a substitute for a real class but that it had inherent qualities that might better meet the needs of certain learners than traditional on-campus courses.

Changing Attitudes

I observed that participants were comprehending and applying the course content and that they were developing appropriate knowledge and skills. Nevertheless, I wondered whether a distance-learning course could affect another important issue: participant attitudes. It was not enough that the teachers would learn how to instruct LEP students; they also needed to empathize with and be an advocate for them. Was this too much to ask of a distance-learning course?

One event gave the first indication that the course could change participants' attitudes toward LEP students. As the team members communicated regularly with one another, I was astonished by their insightful and supportive feedback to one

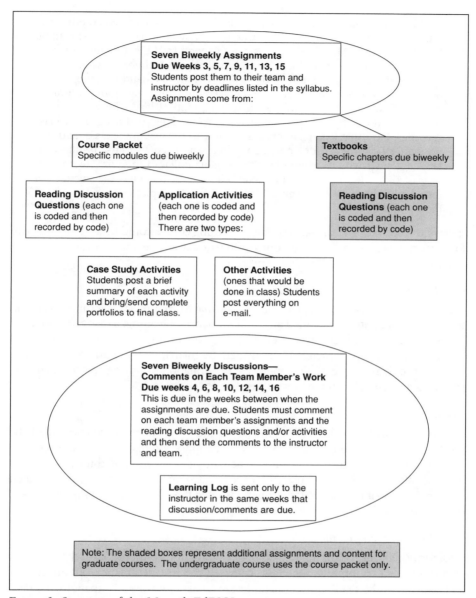

FIGURE 1. Structure of the 16-week TelESOL courses

another. Reading their comments was affirming and inspiring and, most of the time, I felt I could not have said it better myself. A math teacher named Bob had begun his correspondence by stating that he thought that if a family immigrates to the United States, they should learn English before leaving home. Many of his teammates gently nudged him into considering other perspectives, as did the course readings, activities, and I. After about 6 weeks, I was amazed to read his comments:

> At this point, I have read Module III activities . . . I just received an 8th grade transfer student, Lalo, from Texas this week. Word apparently is spreading fast that being in Mr. _____'s class is good for LEP students like him. He's in my homeroom and first period math class. Additional Hispanic LEP students are asking to be in my homeroom. On the one hand it's flattering, on the other it's a real challenge. I've plugged him into my "group within a group." That is, my case study student, Luz, kind of leads the way steering others around campus to the language aides and helps during math class activities. I ask that Lalo take quizzes along with the rest of the class, and that no matter how things turn out, he try his best. Then I discuss results with language aides who re-administer the same or similar exam/quiz, etc. to him. At least I can show a "before" and "after" effect/grade that gives me a better feel for whether he is really learning what is taught (Dr. J please jump in and tell me if I'm doing this right or not!) . . .

It was now becoming clear that a distance-learning course could be as transformative for participants as an on-campus course. Only now was I beginning to see the power of an interactive distance-learning approach.

Challenges

During the first semester, I kept a reflective journal to identify areas for improvement. Problems I encountered included an overabundance of reading; a massive amount of record keeping; and an overwhelming role as a timekeeper, taskmaster, and cheerleader to keep participants motivated to turn in their work on time. The primary problem for the participants was the limitation of relying solely on reading materials and e-mail as the media of instruction.

Attrition

In contrast with the high level of attrition in the first-generation courses, all of the participants completed the class. My efforts at supporting retention were successful, but it was taxing and time-consuming. The participants appreciated my accessibility and indicated that this compensated for the few assignments that were not explained as clearly as possible. The course evaluations rated the effectiveness of the class as 4.8 on a 5-point scale.

Additional Developments

I used my reflections, the participants' questions during the pilot, and the course evaluation data to improve the class. I revised the instructions for certain unclear assignments in the reading packet and began to explore ways of expanding beyond print for conveying information. Along with my colleague in the FSLE department, I was awarded a $7,500 grant to develop videos and CD-ROMs for the courses as well as to create five additional courses that would compose the courses required for ESOL certification in Florida. While developing these enhancements, we created the third-generation approach to distance learning.

Third-Generation Distance Learning: The Dynamic Distance-Learning Approach

In the course of developing and refining the seven teacher preparation classes, the TelESOL program made two major changes to the second-generation model. It adopted a constructivist approach in all courses and incorporated a variety of media into the instruction. Constructivism is

> a theory about knowledge and learning. Drawing on a synthesis of current work in cognitive psychology, philosophy, and anthropology, the theory defines knowledge as temporary, developmental, socially and culturally mediated, and thus, non-objective. Learning from this perspective is understood as a self-regulated process of resolving inner cognitive conflicts that often become apparent through concrete experience, collaborative discourse, and reflection. (Brooks & Brooks, 1993, p. vii)

As we became more immersed in the emerging research and theory on computer-mediated distance learning, we became convinced that its properties not only accommodate but also actually facilitate the development of a constructivist learning environment (Nutta & Feyten, 1999). Contrary to the widely held notion of technology at the service of pedagogy (and not vice versa), we were discovering a more dynamic and reciprocal relationship between the two. In other words, pedagogy shapes the use of instructional technology and, yes, instructional technology can and should shape the use of pedagogy. There are certain aspects of learning that virtual instruction can support better than classroom instruction, and we gave these components of the course a priority.

Cooperative Teams

Whereas the first-generation model considered learners as independent individuals who must sink or swim in the course according to their own degree of motivation and discipline, and the second-generation model considered the learners as coparticipants who looked to the instructor for enforcement of discipline and motivational support, the third-generation model views the participants from a different perspective. Borrowing notions from constructivist learning theory and collaborative learning, the third-generation courses place responsibility for completion of course objectives on the participants as members of a cooperative team. Each participant chooses a particular cooperative role, either as record keeper, phone-tree coordinator/encourager, summarizer, classroom mentor, technology mentor, Webmaster, or course veteran mentor. Group members send all work to each person on the team as well as to the instructor; every role requires regular reports to the instructor. Each team member shares responsibility for the success of the group, creating what cooperative learning specialist Kagan (1994) terms *positive interdependence*. Through the establishment of the cooperative roles, participants now take more responsibility for their learning while freeing the instructor to intervene when truly necessary.

The following list outlines the cooperative roles and their responsibilities:
Record keeper (RK): Required for each team

- Fax biweekly reports to course instructor (CI).
- Call or e-mail phone-tree coordinator/encourager if anyone is late or needs encouragement.
- E-mail CI if there are any problems (e.g., late submissions, misunderstandings).

Phone-tree coordinator/encourager (PTC): Required for each team

- Call all group members when CI requests (e.g., for reminders, special opportunities).

- Monitor group members' work for problems (e.g., misunderstandings).

- Call individual group members if work is late or has problems (based on notification from the RK or your own monitoring).

- Help keep e-mail discussion positive and inclusive.

- E-mail CI weekly, noting all special contact (specific to your role as encourager) with participants (e.g., phone, e-mail) and the results of your action (if no contact needed, just send brief e-mail to instructor indicating that none was necessary)

- If all members complete all course requirements on time, you receive a prize at the last class.

Summarizer: Required for each team

- Write a biweekly one-paragraph summary of participant reading reflections.

- Write a biweekly one-paragraph summary of participant activities (either end-of-the-chapter activities or course packet activities or both).

- Write a biweekly one-paragraph summary of group discussions.

- E-mail the three summaries to CI and Webmaster (WM) by the biweekly deadlines.

Classroom mentor: One or more each semester

- Invite participants from all groups to your classroom and help them complete classroom-based activities.

- Be available to meet or talk on the phone with participants who need assistance in areas in which you are experienced (e.g., lesson planning).

- Submit a monthly report to CI listing each contact—who, when, what, how/where (e.g., by phone, in person, by e-mail) and the result of your action.

- Contribute monthly insights (one paragraph of tips and suggestions) from the classroom to the Web site; submit to the WM and CI.

Technology mentor: One or more each semester

- Be available to meet or talk on the phone with participants who need assistance.

- Help participants with their equipment/software problems (home visits if necessary).

- Help participants find alternatives to their own equipment if needed.

- Submit a monthly report to CI listing each contact—who, when, what, how/where (e.g., by phone, in person, by e-mail) and the result of your action.

- Contribute monthly insights (one paragraph of tips and suggestions) to the Web site; submit to the WM and CI.

Webmaster (WM): One or more each semester

- Update Web site (e.g., scan photographs, add ESOL links, incorporate participant suggestions).
- Edit biweekly summaries from each group.
- Post edited summaries every other Wednesday.

Course veteran mentor: One or more each semester

- Must have taken one of the seven courses previously.
- Answer all course procedural questions (by phone and e-mail) and contact instructor if unsure about an answer.
- Write a monthly newsletter including teaching tips, current events, and participant spotlight (information provided by CI). Submit the camera-ready newsletter by the deadline listed in the monthly course calendar.

Collaborative Learning

Working within the constructivist framework, we also incorporated principles of collaborative learning. Sheridan, Byrne, & Quina (1989) define collaborative learning as

> a pedagogical style which emphasizes cooperative efforts among participants, faculty, and administrators. Rooted in the belief that knowledge is inherently social in nature, it stresses common inquiry as the basic learning process. (p. 49)

We incorporated contract grading, individual learning contracts, and project-based learning. The contract grading set minimum requirements and standards (with clear guidelines and samples of exemplary work) for a grade of C or B and allowed participants to attain an A by completing a variety of projects, most of which were service oriented. For example, some participatns worked together on creating a curriculum for LEP children enrolled at a charter school at a homeless shelter. Another participant created a weekly bilingual section of a local newspaper focusing on the migrant community. Other participants have created Web sites, developed videos and training manuals, created materials or research reports for the course Web site, and developed a multicultural cookbook with adult ESOL students. Participants may also check out commercial videotapes on teaching techniques and other ESOL issues, write a review, and create and teach a lesson for each video. Another option is to complete a key pal project with an Israeli EFL student. For this, participants are paired with EFL students at Tel-Aviv University, and they both read and discuss two articles in English on cross-cultural communication. Then they select questions from a list of possible cultural interview items and exchange answers weekly. Depending on the EFL key pal's preference, the TelESOL participants may correct certain messages in English and explain English rhetoric and style.

A folder is kept on each participant, and once participants have completed one type of project, such as a local service project, they must choose a different type of project (e.g., videos, the Israeli key pal project). This ensures a breadth of experiences in completing the five courses required for certification. As five new graduate courses were added, we chose two textbooks and assigned different segments of the course packet for each course. We created assignments to correspond with the chapters in the textbooks and divided the chapter contents into seven sections to fit the instructional cycle. The additional courses are as follows:

- Instructional Methods and Strategies for Teaching ESOL Students
- Promoting Communication and Understanding in a Culturally Diverse Classroom
- Language Principles, Acquisition, and Skills for Teaching ESOL Students
- Instructional Materials Development and Modification for Teaching ESOL Students
- Assessment and Progress Management for Teaching ESOL Students

Mixed-Media Course Delivery

The other element of third-generation distance learning is mixed-media course delivery. Rather than the exclusive use of e-mail for interaction and instruction, the third-generation courses have expanded to a mixed core of media as well as a number of choices for enhancement.

To expand the variety of media, we created many enhancements, including developing videotapes of real classroom footage illustrating the topics of each module of the course packet. Also, I videotaped an overview of each module's objectives and an explanation of its assignments. The course packet was put on CD-ROM as well as on the library reserve's Web page. A Web page (Chaney, n.d.) was created for the course with numerous resources and links. We piloted integrated Web-based course software (WebCT [Worldwide Web Course Tools], 2000), including a requirement for a synchronous group chat for a virtual role-play that required participants to assume one of five roles (e.g., classroom teacher, ESOL teacher, school psychologist) and come to a consensus about whether to promote ESOL students or recommend that they be placed in special education.

❖ DISTINGUISHING FEATURES

The combination of the distinctive TelESOL program features led us to create the term *dynamic distance learning* to describe our model. This model has seven basic principles.

1. Constructivist Approach: Emphasizing Reflective Learning and Authentic Assessment. This approach encourages participants to take more responsibility for their learning, guiding them to access, evaluate, critique, synthesize, and apply information. In addition, it enables them to monitor their own and their team members' comprehension of a topic and allows them to demonstrate this mastery in authentic and applied ways.

2. High Level of Interaction Among Participants and Between the Participants and the Instructor. Participants approach the course content in various ways, actively constructing their own meaning through discussion with one another and the instructor. Many active learning techniques (e.g., role-plays) are modified for synchronous or asynchronous distance learning.

3. Facilitative and Supportive High-Touch/High-Tech Communicative Focus. Priority is given to developing and nurturing facilitative communication skills. This is accomplished by creating a regular requirement for intra-team communication and promoting an encouraging tone of dialogue and constructive critique. The instructor communicates regularly to the entire group formally (through presenting information and expressing opinions on pertinent issues) and informally (through highlighting participants' accomplishments and sending other types of good news) and to individuals (through the learning log and feedback on selected assignments). In addition, the course Web site and newsletter increases interteam communication and exchange. Cross-cultural communication is a focus of the case study and special projects (e.g., the Israeli key pal project).

4. Learning Communities, Cooperative/Collaborative Learning, and Team Responsibility for Course Management and Completion. An esprit de corps develops among team members to support each member's achievement. Each person plays a crucial role on the team, and the positive interdependence created by this structure pushes individuals to do their best work and to submit it on time out of consideration for the others. If a member's work is missing, it affects the whole team's discussion, and participants are very respectful of this responsibility.

5. Mixed Media for Content Delivery and Interaction. A variety of videos (both commercially produced and amateur footage of local classrooms and the instructor's presentations and demonstrations) are available, and newer technologies, such as videoconferencing, are being piloted as an ancillary option. A planned addition is the development of courseware (especially for the Language Principles course) to be used with the textbooks.

6. Participant-Assisted Renewal and Updating of Course Content. The course Web site is the main locus of this evolving knowledge base. As part of the individual contracts, participants create annotated lists of pertinent Web sites that are linked to the class home page, develop and upload reviews of research (e.g., formal papers, overhead presentations) on topics of interest, and post practical or instructional materials they have developed.

7. Site-Based Field Experiences: The Case Study Activities. This feature provides a local context for the course content, connecting the readings and activities with classroom practice. Two major benefits of the field experiences are (a) involving participants in the content through real experiences and (b) enriching group communication and learning through the discussion of different field experiences conducted in diverse settings throughout the world.

Each of these principles takes full advantage of the inherent properties of current communication and instructional technologies as well as the diverse contributions of participants from different locations, contexts, and perspectives. We are now beginning to pilot this model with other faculty for application in distance-learning courses in other subject areas.

⊛ PRACTICAL IDEAS

Participant interaction is the most crucial feature of the TelESOL courses. Having participants share their work with each other deepens their understanding of the content, motivates them to submit their best work on time, and exposes them to a wide variety of perspectives and experiences. Setting up the team structure is simple and straightforward. This structure can be applied in most types of distance-learning courses.

Table 1 indicates common pitfalls of distance learning and how the TelESOL program addressed them. It outlines a number of practical ideas and suggestions for course developers that can be employed in various combinations, depending on the learning context and needs.

TABLE 1. DISTANCE-LEARNING CHALLENGES AND HOW THEY WERE ADDRESSED IN THE TELESOL PROGRAM

Challenges	How addressed
High-tech/ low-touch trade-off	• Provide initial contact with participants at orientation or videotaped introductions for distant-learning participants. • Establish teams for submission and discussion of all work. • Assign a participant per team to the cooperative role of the encourager. • Make occasional phone calls (primarily by encourager, but as needed by instructor). • Develop team spirit, including naming teams and assigning e-mail pen names. • Send weekly chatty e-mail message from instructor to all, showcasing participants' special work/honors or current events pertaining to ESOL. • Communicate regularly with participants through individual learning logs. • Provide closure with final meeting. • Send "Keep Up the Great Work" postcards and monthly class newsletters. • Organize an optional videoconferencing session. • Offer optional seminars (or invite participants to other class sessions or events on campus) for extra credit.
Participant attrition	• Create team responsibility for completion. • Assign a participant per team to the cooperative role of encourager; give each encourager a book if his or her entire team completes on time. • Require strict deadlines.
Volume of participant electronic submissions	• Use an e-mail management program with folders for each participant. • Create a separate e-mail account for each course taught (never use personal e-mail accounts for courses). • Code all assignments and require participants to identify assignments by code in the subject area of message and as headings for the text of their message.

Continued on p. 109

TABLE 1 (*continued*). DISTANCE-LEARNING CHALLENGES AND
HOW THEY WERE ADDRESSED IN THE TELESOL PROGRAM

Challenges	How addressed
Volume of participant electronic submissions (*continued*)	• Use the vacation or autoreply function to automatically send a standard reply to all participants' messages indicating that you have received their work and will respond to it within so many days. This avoids their immediate and constant e-mailing to see if you received their work. • Ask participants to either copy and paste the text of their files into the body of the e-mail message or send attachments as rich text format (RTF) files only. • As an alternative to e-mail, use an integrated Web-based course environment and create a forum for submission of work and discussion for each course section. • Spend 30–60 minutes each day on the course, rather than letting it add up weekly.
Participant isolation and lack of interaction	• Establish teams for submission and discussion of work. • Post summaries of teams' submissions on the course Web site, which gives closure to each group's discussion and allows other groups to see what others are doing. • Include field-based assignments done locally. • Assign asynchronous group work and synchronous opportunities for extra credit (e.g., role-play chats, videoconferencing, live seminars). For role-play or problem-solving chats, make sure that each person's position is presented first on e-mail and that each person submits a summary of her or his conclusion after the chat session on e-mail. Also, be sure to assign a facilitator for each chat session. • Offer a cross-cultural key pal project with ESOL students (e.g., the project in Israel).
Confusion over course organization, procedures, deadlines, and expectations	• Provide an extensive course handbook that includes directions and samples of participant work as a model. • Provide a course packet organized in sections to correspond with the instructional cycle and explain assignments with carefully designed directions (e.g., using terms consistently). • Distribute a video guide to course packet assignments and overview of each section. • Assign previous participants to act as course veteran (procedural) mentors. This is especially helpful with initial hand-holding for new participants who are becoming accustomed to the course structure and the nature of the assignments. • Use a pyramid format, submitting team members' questions through encourager to instructor. • Distribute a master course calendar and provide a hypertext markup language (HTML) version on the course home page. Include all assignment deadlines and deadlines for cooperative role reports.

Continued on p. 110

TABLE 1 (*continued*). DISTANCE-LEARNING CHALLENGES AND
HOW THEY WERE ADDRESSED IN THE TELESOL PROGRAM

Challenges	How addressed
Confusion over course organization (continued)	• Require first assignments to be submitted 2 weeks after orientation to allow for adjustment to course and technology. • Require participants to send in questions or comments separate from assignments and to write *question* in the subject area of their message; scan daily for these messages.
Burdensome record keeping	• Code each assignment. • Require that all work be submitted according to coded format, including name at end of each message. • Assign a participant per team to the record-keeper role and create a simple form with assignment codes and spaces for participants' names. Require record keepers to submit the forms biweekly. • Use a summary table of record-keeper form information. • Collect each participant's submissions in individual mailboxes or folders in e-mail management programs.
Excessive feedback demands on instructor	• Establish teams and require team members to give feedback to each other on all written submissions. • Select specific work on which to comment/grade (i.e., portfolio components) and scan other work. Use record-keeper report codes to focus more carefully on assignments that are noted as unsatisfactory or exceptional. • Use a learning log, which enables participants to ask instructor to focus on areas of need. • Assign one participant per team to the role of summarizer, who gives instructor the big picture. • Assign one participant per team to role of record keeper, who notifies instructor if anyone submits problematic work.
Limitations of text-based content for presentation and discussion	• Provide a video with classroom footage corresponding to readings. • Develop a course Web page with team pictures, links to pertinent sites, audio clips, and video clips. • Require a substantial local field experience (e.g., case study) requirement. • Assign current teachers to serve as classroom mentors to preservice teachers, providing their classrooms for observations and offering assistance with and review of lesson plans and so forth. • Offer options for reviewing commercial videos. • Offer options for participation in traditional or videoconferencing seminars (i.e., attending specific sessions in related courses offered on campus or through videoconferencing). • Offer options for community service with local agencies. • Offer options for searching for resources and materials on the Web and adding them to the course Web site.

Continued on p. 111

TABLE 1 (*continued*). DISTANCE-LEARNING CHALLENGES AND
HOW THEY WERE ADDRESSED IN THE TelESOL PROGRAM

Challenges	How addressed
Materials and textbooks for international participants	• Bypass the university bookstore and order through Amazon.com (http://www.amazon.com) or other textbook vendors on-line; include links on course Web site. • List information on course textbook requirements on course Web site. • Put materials on electronic reserve (password protected).
Distant participant dependence on instructor as sole university contact in resolving registration and payment issues	• Put a logistics FAQ (list of frequently asked questions) on the information Web page and link each question to the appropriate division home page (and phone number) in the university or institution.
Course content/ technology updates	• Provide option for participants to search for pertinent Web sites to link to the course Web site. • Provide option for participants to write surveys of research on topics of interest to add to the course Web site. • Provide options for participants to complete and post projects (e.g., technology resource guides) on the course Web site.
Participants' technical difficulties	• Include a statement in the course syllabus indicating that participants are responsible for meeting all deadlines regardless of equipment breakdowns and provide information on the campus computer labs (where and times open) on the course Web site. • Assign participant(s) the cooperative role of technology mentor. • Arrange for e-mail or WebCT (2000) workshops if needed.

◈ CONCLUSION

As the program matures, new considerations arise. Participants are now enrolling from around the world, including Spain, the Czech Republic, Finland, Korea, and Ecuador. Because the courses were initially planned for participants in Florida, new considerations for very remote participants have arisen. Remote participants are now required to send introductory and closing videos that are shown to their team members at the orientation and final session. Having participants discuss their thoughts and experiences from such a variety of locations has enriched the courses immeasurably.

As new technologies emerge, new possibilities for their inclusion in the TelESOL courses appear. The most recent pilot is a hybrid synchronous/asynchronous course using videoconferencing and Web-based instruction. For participants who have access to a videoconferencing site, this synchronous medium for communication, demonstration, and interaction can be a powerful addition to a Web-based course. With each new technology that becomes available, the TelESOL program will be enhanced.

From two interactive e-mail courses, a seven-course distance-learning TESOL training program has evolved, and plans are under way for collaboration between two colleges to expand the program. With the investment of substantial time for planning and design, and the commitment to continuous research, reflection, improvement, and renewal, the TelESOL courses have become a viable alternative to traditional classes. Much of the credit for this success should be attributed to the participants for they have accepted the normal ambiguities of a new and evolving process and formed a supportive community of learners, with an instructor truly serving as a facilitator. The greatest lesson learned in the development of this program is to never underestimate participants' ability to construct their own meaning, to monitor their own and each other's comprehension and application of concepts and skills, and to support each other's learning.

◈ ACKNOWLEDGMENT

This project was funded by a University of South Florida Instructional Development Grant, with Joyce W. Nutta and Carine M. Feyten as principal investigators.

◈ CONTRIBUTOR

Joyce Nutta has developed and taught seven distance-learning courses and has conducted continuous research on their effectiveness. She holds a PhD in second language acquisition and instructional technology and has published and presented at national and international conferences on her approach to distance learning and the use of technology to teach ESOL and foreign languages. She coedited *Virtual Instruction: Issues and Insights From an International Perspective* (Feyten & Nutta, 1999).

CHAPTER 10

Expanding Horizons: Delivering Professional Teacher Development via Satellite Technology and E-Mail in Israel

Yael Bejarano, Esther Klein-Wohl, and Lily Vered

◈ INTRODUCTION

The choice of technology for delivery and support is an important consideration in the design of a distance-learning course. In this chapter, we describe two distance-learning, in-service EFL methodology courses for English teachers. Offered by the Open University of Israel (OU), both courses dealt with the same subject matter and were taught by the same instructors (the authors of this chapter). Nevertheless, they were delivered using different communication technologies. The first course, EFL Methodology Update for In-Service Teachers, was offered via Ofek, the OU satellite system. The second course, Methodology of Teaching English for In-Service Teachers, was offered via e-mail together with five face-to-face meetings. Given this combination of constants and variables, we thought it would be enlightening to examine the effect of the different technologies on the nature of the courses and the participants' reactions to them. In this chapter, we compare the two courses and make recommendations based on our two similar yet contrasting experiences.

Decisions about distance-learning technology should be based on parameters such as course content, participant population, accessible institutional facilities, and available staff. The decision-making process needs to take the following factors into account:

- Course content: Does the subject matter lend itself to verbal exchanges only, or does it require visual input?

- Participant population: Are the participants spread over a large geographical area? What are the participants' needs? What technology is available to them?

- Institutional facilities: What budget is available? What kinds of technology does it support?

- Staff: To what extent are staff members prepared to invest time and effort in learning and adapting to innovative ideas?

In this chapter, these and other factors are discussed in greater depth and illustrated with details from our experience.

◈ CONTEXT

EFL is a compulsory school subject in Israel. All English teachers in the school system are required to have a teaching license and expected to participate in in-service training provided by various academic institutions and accredited by Israel's Ministry of Education. Many teachers have immigrated to Israel from English-speaking countries where they worked in professions other than teaching. Others, from non-English-speaking countries, were English teachers in their native lands. Both groups are required to take specific courses to receive a permanent EFL teaching license. As a university with nationwide outreach, the OU has been actively involved for many years in providing a variety of teacher education courses.

◈ DESCRIPTION

The Ofek Satellite Course:
EFL Methodology Update for In-Service Teachers

In the spring of 1997, we planned and delivered the EFL Methodology Update satellite course, which was open to all English teachers in junior high and high schools. Seventy-eight teachers in eight centers around the country registered for the course. This 56-hour pilot course was offered via Ofek, which means *horizon* in Hebrew. A joint venture of the OU and a private company that specializes in communication engineering, Ofek is essentially an interactive educational network that broadcasts live synchronous lessons via satellite. Through the system, a lesson is transmitted by high-quality digital broadcast from a studio on the OU campus to a satellite and, from there, to any number of remote classrooms within the footprint of the satellite, which currently covers Egypt, Israel, Jordan, Lebanon, Syria, part of Turkey, and part of the Ukraine. Two-way communication turns the lesson into a live interactive session.

Audiovisual and Interactive Layers

The broadcast consists of two layers: an audiovisual layer and an interactive one. The audiovisual layer is one way (studio to centers), whereas the interactive layer is two way (studio to centers and centers to studio). The audiovisual layer enables the integration of slides, graphic material, and preselected video clips into the lesson. The instructor can take advantage of computers available in the studio for presentations, animation, ongoing displays and analysis of electronic spreadsheets, Internet surfing in real time, and other relevant computer applications. A single technician controls the entire broadcast according to a prepared script, and a professional support team prepares electronic presentations in advance.

The interactive layer enables participants, who watch lessons on a large television screen in a center near their homes, to interact with the instructor in the studio via a telephone hooked up to the satellite system. Interactions consist of voice and data communication. Open verbal exchanges are transmitted through a regular telephone headset, whereas data can be entered using the telephone keypad (e.g., for answering multiple-choice questions). These closed answers can be instantly displayed graphically on the television screens to all centers. During verbal interactions, the system identifies the participant and the conversation is heard in all centers. Any printed materials required during the lesson or as background reading are delivered to the centers before the sessions. Between sessions, participants can contact the instructors by e-mail or telephone.

Course Objectives and Syllabus

The objectives of the EFL Methodology Update satellite course were to

1. acquaint participants with current approaches in EFL teaching
2. enable participants to plan and implement instruction incorporating current approaches
3. encourage participants to reflect on the teaching/learning process in order to adapt it to their particular teaching environment

As the teaching team, we devised the syllabus, which consisted of 14 broadcasts, each 4 academic hours long, and covered the following topics, with some taking more than one session:

1. the relationship between the learner, teacher, and learning environment
2. the nature of communication and its implications for classroom practice: how these relate to oracy and literacy
3. classroom management
4. integrated group work methodology (IGM)
5. lesson and unit planning using IGM
6. technology in the EFL classroom
7. the heterogeneous class: catering to different learning styles and proficiency levels
8. the whole language approach in EFL
9. how to help nonreaders learn to read
10. the role of reflection in improving teaching
11. roundtable discussion: issues raised in the course

Teacher Training for Satellite Teaching

As none of us had previous experience with the satellite system, we received supportive training from the OU technical team. Training included observing other courses during live sessions in the studio, viewing videotaped sessions, practicing the manipulation of technology, and consulting with the graphics team. This training provided important pointers regarding the involvement of participants in discussions and group activities in the different centers, and the recommended balance between visual and oral input. The description of participant involvement was especially important as the instructor could not observe what was taking place in the centers during a lesson. The only person on hand at the centers during lessons was a technician.

Instructional Activities

Participants attended the satellite course at OU centers in or close to their hometowns. Attendance and participation in at least 80% of the sessions were required (11 of the 14 weekly sessions). Participants had to submit short, written, individual or group assignments by fax or e-mail. The final written assignment consisted of developing a teaching unit incorporating the principles covered in the course.

During the sessions, participants listened to brief lectures delivered by satellite, to which they were required to react and comment, and participated in workshops in which they interacted face to face with peers at their own center. Initially, we felt that participants' inability to observe participant interactions in other centers or to receive our feedback during these interactions because of the one-way video communication was a problem. However, as each center reported back on the interaction, it became apparent that a classroom atmosphere had been established. Quite rapidly, we began to discern the participants' personal characteristics and the group dynamics specific to each center. For example, in some centers, participants cooperated and interacted regularly, whereas in others they primarily functioned individually. As soon as both instructors and participants began to feel comfortable with the technology, we became aware of the importance of the visual media and the need to activate participants and avoid lecturing.

Early in the course it became evident that a 180-minute session with two short breaks was very demanding in terms of the participants' attention span. Therefore, we planned easier activities for the latter part of each lesson. Each session began with a short reminder of the previous one and ended with a short preview of the next session. This review/preview procedure also made the transition from one instructor to another smoother for the participants.

The E-Mail Course:
Methodology of Teaching English for In-Service Teachers

The e-mail in-service course was open to all English teachers working in Israel. Participants could enroll in the course for licensing or professional enrichment. The 60-hour pilot course was offered via e-mail together with five classroom meetings.

We planned and delivered the course in the fall of 1998. Seventeen teachers from across Israel enrolled in the course. We expected most of the participants to know how to use e-mail. Due to an administrative error, some of the participants were misinformed and registered for the course without realizing that having access to e-mail was a prerequisite. Though they were accepted, they participated using fax instead of e-mail and, as a result, missed out on the collaborative aspect of the e-mail interactions.

Course Objectives and Syllabus

The course objectives were to

1. acquaint participants with current approaches in EFL teaching

2. encourage participants to reflect on the teaching/learning process in order to adapt it to their particular teaching environment

3. relate current EFL approaches to a new centralized English curriculum in Israel

4. enable participants to plan and implement instruction coinciding with the new curriculum

We prepared the e-mail course syllabus, which was approved by the Ministry of Education and taught shortly after a new curriculum for English in Israel was published in the summer of 1998. This curriculum, which defines standards and benchmarks, spurred an interest in alternative ways to evaluate participants because it was formulated using the concepts of assessment. As a result, although the first two objectives of the e-mail course were identical to those of the Ofek course given the year before, the other two objectives related specifically to the new curriculum in terms of teaching and assessment.

The course syllabus dealt with new pedagogical issues related to language content and assessment that arose from the curriculum's publication, as well as with some of the topics covered in the Ofek course. The topics in this course included:

- the new English curriculum

- the reflective teacher

- oracy and literacy: listening, speaking, reading, and writing

- conducting a project in school

- negotiating assessment: portfolios and journals

- cooperative learning methods

- the heterogeneous class: multiple intelligences and learning styles

- extensive reading

- presentation and peer assessment

Instructional Activities

The course included the following activities:

- weekly readings collected in a printed anthology mailed to participants before the course

- an assignment to be submitted by e-mail by a prescribed day every week for each of the 10 distance-learning sessions

- five face-to-face class meetings

These face-to-face classroom meetings were intended to

- initiate participants into the e-mail procedures of the course (e.g., creating a distribution list, using the subject header to specify the nature of each communication)

- deal with administrative matters to ensure the smooth running of the course

- negotiate assessment procedures

- model and practice techniques for implementation in the classroom

Before the course began, participants received a course syllabus, an anthology, a schedule of class meetings, a description of the topics to be covered in the weekly assignments, and a guide with instructions and participant responsibilities. The course was driven by the weekly reading assignments, and the major modus operandi of the delivery system was written communication.

Participants received a list of weekly questions via e-mail. The questions were of two types: comprehension and application. For example, one of the readings assigned for Week 4 was a chapter on Writing as Process and Product in Language Learning (Cohen, 1990).

Among the comprehension questions asked were the following:

- What are the instructional purposes for writing that Cohen outlines? Which of them do you find most useful in your teaching and why?

- What example can you give to match each of the following types of writing: expository, persuasive, narrative, descriptive, and literary?

- What are the characteristic features of process writing?

Application questions for this assignment included the following:

- In what ways can cooperation between native and nonnative pupils be used to improve target language writing?

- How would you use e-mail to improve target language writing? What advantages would this have over more traditional language writing instruction?

Each participant was responsible for answering two or three of these questions by e-mail. The questions were divided among participants in such a way that more than one participant received the same set of questions. Most of the questions encouraged individual responses, although a few required collaborative efforts. Participants completed their tasks and e-mailed them to all participants and the instructor by the week's end. During the week, participants had the opportunity to interact with the instructor and fellow participants by e-mail and were encouraged to do so. The responses to all the questions, taken together, provided a bird's eye view of the content covered during that week. Within a day or two, the instructor e-mailed feedback on the assignment to the whole group. The feedback consisted of a general overview of the subject matter and personal comments to each participant. Because all participants had read all answers, the feedback was relevant to all. The instructor's comments focused on the participants' grasp and understanding of the readings as well as on the pedagogical implications that emerged from the discussions and answers. This was where the major instructional input occurred.

◈ DISTINGUISHING FEATURES

Gauging participant completion rates is one way of evaluating the value of a course. In addition, the Ofek satellite course and the e-mail course were formally evaluated by other means. Participants were asked to fill out a feedback questionnaire at the end of the course, and some were also interviewed, either by phone or in person. Participants' responses to the questionnaire, as well as their comments made in interviews, provide an enlightening window on their satisfaction with each course generally as well as the value of its particular features.

Ofek Course Completion

Of the 78 participants initially registered, 56 (72%) attended all the sessions and 38 (49%) submitted the final assignment as well as the other assignments. Of the final assignments, 12 (32%) were rated excellent to good, 20 (52%) fair, and 6 (16%) weak. As this was a pilot course, everyone who submitted the final assignment received credit for the course.

For comparison purposes, it is interesting to note that in other Ofek courses, 85% of the participants usually complete the course successfully. These courses, however, represent all other courses offered via Ofek, which are in Hebrew and, therefore, are in greater demand. They are also sometimes required by certain institutions for professional advancement. The Ofek course described here was an unrequired pilot course offered practically free (for a minimal registration fee of about $10) and given little publicity.

Ofek Course Questionnaire Findings

A standard feedback questionnaire administered in all Ofek courses was given to participants. Twenty-seven participants, almost 75% of those who completed the course, returned the feedback questionnaires. Table 1 reflects the data gathered from these questionnaires.

The salient information from these data is that 67% of respondents were very satisfied or moderately satisfied with the course. A total of 93% of the participants were very satisfied with the atmosphere in class, and 73% were very satisfied or moderately satisfied with the individual sessions. With regard to satisfaction with the individual presenters (the three instructors), opinions were evenly distributed among the three options. This may be explained because the screen personality of each instructor appealed to different participants or that the topics dealt with by each were of lesser or greater interest. It is enlightening to note that 59% of the respondents

TABLE 1. RESULTS OF THE FINAL FEEDBACK QUESTIONNAIRE FOR
THE OFEK SATELLITE COURSE (27 RESPONSES)

Question	Very	Moderately	Little/ Not at all
How satisfied were you with the course in general?	22%	45%	33%
How satisfied were you with the atmosphere in class?	93%	7%	—
How satisfied were you with the individual sessions?	50%	23%	27%
To what extent was silence maintained in class during lectures?	62%	38%	—
How satisfied were you with the individual presenters?	32%	36%	32%
How satisfied were you with the quality of the telephone/satellite connection?	67%	11%	22%
How satisfied were you with the integration of multimedia aids in broadcast?	46%	15%	39%
To what extent were you bothered by the lack of face-to-face communication with the instructor?	30%	11%	59%
To what extent do you prefer an Ofek course to a regular one?	41%	48%	11%

were not bothered by the lack of face-to-face communication and only 11% would have preferred a face-to-face course to a satellite course.

Interview Comments Regarding the Ofek Course

Participants' comments in the interviews provided additional insight on their feelings about the course. The following comments, positive and negative, give a representative sample of their views:

> During the sessions I learned a lot from the other teachers: methods, ideas, advice, solutions to problems.

> Although much of the material wasn't new to me, I enjoyed being reminded of it in an organized, attractive, and well-presented manner.

> I enjoyed the course because it provided me with new ideas and showed me that other teachers face similar problems. But I found the sessions too long and at the end could not concentrate.

> The course was interesting and good and can contribute a lot to teaching English if one decides to derive utmost benefit from it. I found it very disturbing that some of the participants kept chatting during the presentations.

> I am a very experienced teacher and learned much less than I expected. I stayed primarily for the credit. [Teachers who take in-service training courses are awarded credits that are translated into salary increases.] Perhaps if the sessions were face to face there would have been a better opportunity for feedback and mid-course improvement.

> Having several presenters enriched the course.

> Much of what was covered isn't applicable in the classroom except for the suggestions on how to use the OHP [overhead projector]. Much of what was presented via the electronic presentation would have been more useful had we received it before the lesson, enabling us to study it more in depth and save time.

E-Mail Course Questionnaire Findings

Upon completion of the e-mail course, 12 of the 14 participants (86%) filled out an anonymous feedback questionnaire developed by the evaluation team of the English Unit of the OU. The questionnaire's purpose was to evaluate the effectiveness of the course and to obtain information on course content and quality of instruction for formative evaluation purposes. The questionnaire focused on the medium, the course in general, the reading material, the weekly assignments, the classroom meetings, the course content, and general satisfaction with the course.

As shown in Table 2, participants, in general, indicated a very high degree of satisfaction with the course (4.8 on a scale of 1–5 with a standard deviation of 0.5). Responses relating to the course's impact indicated that participants gained confidence in their ability to adapt and try new ideas in the classroom and also strengthened their theoretical understanding of the field. In addition, participants felt that all the components of the course contributed positively to their learning. Responses regarding the reading materials indicated that participants were satisfied with the choice and amount of the readings and with their level of interest. In response to questions about the weekly assignments, participants felt that these assignments were

TABLE 2. RESULTS OF THE FINAL FEEDBACK QUESTIONNAIRE FOR
THE E-MAIL COURSE (12 RESPONSES)

Dimension	Mean*	Standard Deviation
Impact of the course:		
• It gave me confidence to try new things.	4.2	1.1
• It has strengthened my theoretical understanding of the field.	4.2	0.8
The reading material was relevant.	4.4	0.5
The weekly assignments helped to		
• focus my reading	4.5	1.0
• broaden my understanding of the topics	3.7	1.1
• reflect on how to apply the ideas in class	3.6	0.5
Contribution of feedback to understanding articles:		
• instructors' feedback on assignments	4.3	1.0
• peer answers to/comments on questions	3.2	1.1
Effectiveness of e-mail as a learning system	4.5	0.7
Overall satisfaction with the course	4.8	0.5

* Average score on a scale of 1–5 where 5 indicates "to a great degree" and 1 indicates "not at all."

very demanding and required intensive work. Nevertheless, the questions helped them focus their reading, broaden their understanding of the topic, and reflect on how to apply the ideas in class.

Peer Comments

One of the special features of this course was that each participant had the chance to obtain feedback from all participants and to provide feedback to others via e-mail. We anticipated that this would be a positive element; however, satisfaction with the contribution of peer input varied. In the following sample peer comment, a participant (David) responds to another participant (Shula) after she describes a writing strategy she uses in class that divides compositions into four paragraphs and clarifies for the pupil the content of each:

> Hi Shula, I read your writing strategy and I like it a lot! I want to add to it something, though: I found it very useful to let the students write a composition on something that was already talked about in class, that the vocabulary is familiar to them. A subject in which they already heard their peers express their own ideas about it.

David's comment does not really contribute to what Shula presented because it deals with a completely separate aspect of classroom writing tasks. This example may explain participants' dissatisfaction with peer comments. Perhaps in the future, instructors should advise participants about the kinds of comments that are most productive or provide appropriate models.

Face-to-Face Meetings

Responses to questionnaire items that related to the face-to-face classroom meetings indicated that the participants derived maximal benefit from the topics covered in them, especially from the last meeting at which participants presented their final projects. They all felt that the meetings were very helpful in clarifying issues as well as modeling the application of principles. An additional benefit mentioned was the opportunity to attach faces to other participants in the course and to the instructors' signatures.

Interview Comments Regarding the E-Mail Course

Further responses indicated that all the participants agreed that e-mail enabled them to cooperate and exchange ideas with other teachers and to work at their own pace. As one participant noted, "I feel reassured as a professional teacher." All of the respondents recommended taking subsequent courses via e-mail.

The overall conclusion from the participants' responses was not only that participants gained new knowledge and ideas in the content of the course, but also that the medium was ideal for distant and busy teachers because it was asynchronous and thus allowed the teachers to hand in their assignments at any hour of the day or night.

◈ PRACTICAL IDEAS

Based on information gathered formally, a review of the videotaped sessions, and impressions formed during the course, we offer the following suggestions for other distance educators. Some of these ideas apply only to satellite courses and some to e-mail courses only, but many of them apply to both.

Conduct a Needs Analysis at the Outset

For either a satellite or e-mail course, it is advisable to conduct a needs analysis before planning the syllabus. Doing this allows course planners to focus on issues that are relevant to the participating teachers.

Gain Familiarity With the Technology Before Planning the Sessions

A good understanding of a delivery system's possibilities and limitations is a distinct advantage in using it successfully. That same understanding is crucial to proper course planning.

Plan for Maximal Involvement and Variety in Activities

The more the participants are involved in the session, whether via direct communication with the instructors or through classroom interaction, the more successful the session. Therefore, in satellite courses, one should plan several group activities of relatively short duration and avoid showing a still screen (or a talking head) for more than 5 minutes. Providing a viewing guide and showing a video or a demonstration would make a good activity.

Televised Sessions Should Not Exceed 2 Hours

Being confined to a small area is extremely fatiguing for participants and instructor, and so is concentrating on even a large monitor (three, in fact, for the instructor, who must simultaneously interact with participants, monitor the electronic presentation, and work on a regular computer). Hence, sessions should not exceed 2 hours.

Avoid Lecturing for Any Length of Time

If there is an extended period of teacher lecture or explanation in a satellite broadcast, it should be accompanied by suitable visual material. Showing or doing is always preferable to lecturing.

Behave Naturally and Personably on Camera

Instructors should try to behave as naturally as possible during a satellite broadcast lesson and address participants by name. On the other hand, they should develop suitable polite techniques to handle participants who, without furthering the discussion, talk too much. The instructor, just as in a traditional classroom, is the moderator of the session and should behave accordingly.

Carefully Script Broadcast Lessons in Advance

The more detailed the script of the satellite broadcast lesson, the more relaxed and responsive the instructor will be during the actual broadcast. Although preparing a detailed script is extremely time consuming, it is well worth the investment, especially because the course can then be repeated with very little additional work.

Use Readings as You Would in Any Other Course

In either an e-mail or satellite course, the instructor should not hesitate to assign reading in preparation for a session or an assignment after a session, as long as the activity is related to it.

Roll With the Punches

No matter how good the technology and the technicians, problems do arise, and the ability to improvise when facing them is a saving grace. A sense of humor is critical here as well.

Establish Healthy Relationships With Course Technicians

Friendly and cooperative technicians are important and useful allies. Instructors should establish good relationships with them.

Offer Participants Structure as well as Freedom

To be effective, an e-mail course requires considerable structuring. Yet within the prescribed framework, participants benefit from a great degree of freedom, especially in terms of communication with instructors and peers.

Do Not Be Afraid to Be Informal

The nature of the e-mail medium allows for informality and thus creates a closer and more democratic relationship between participants and instructor.

Enjoy the Challenge

Most of all, instructors involved in any distance-learning course should enjoy the challenge of participating in something new and the opportunity to discover and learn about innovative options.

❖ CONCLUSION

Choosing the right technology for delivery and support of distance learning is important and complex. Each medium has advantages and disadvantages. Our experience was that satellite delivery is suitable for a large number of participants spread over a wide geographical area. In contrast, e-mail is suitable for groups spread over any geographical area but limited to no more than 20–25 participants per instructor. But number of participants is just one of many parameters that must be considered; another is number of communication channels. E-mail is limited because it allows verbal communication only. Demonstrations that require visual input cannot be transmitted by e-mail and, therefore, by itself, e-mail is not appropriate for all subject matters. Nevertheless, e-mail interactions have the advantage of being asynchronous; they allow for thinking and rethinking, drafting and redrafting. Also, because the workload in an e-mail course can be spread over a week or longer, it enables the instructor and the participants to work at their convenience. Additionally, the e-mail format does not require high budget, complex technology, or additional staff.

To clarify, Table 3 compares our experience with the two types of delivery systems—satellite and e-mail—according to the following parameters: the instructor, the participants, the management of the medium, and the instructional sessions themselves.

Having experienced satellite broadcast and e-mail delivery systems, we have concluded that each has its own pedagogic potential and can be fruitfully employed in distance education. Fortunately, it is not always necessary to choose one medium over the other. In fact, although we have examined them separately, we believe that they can complement each other. For example, when participants are dispersed over a large geographical area, face-to-face meetings can be conducted via satellite. Conversely, a course primarily conducted via satellite would benefit from set readings and structured assignments delivered by e-mail. Thus, a course using both media could benefit from the complementary advantages of each and be cost effective.

Although the aims of education have remained unchanged for more than 2,000 years, modern technology allows us to experiment with new ways of teaching that suit a varied participant population. We need to learn to be flexible in the use of these new methods by combining and adapting them to different teaching contexts to provide our participants with the best, most exciting, and stimulating training available today.

TABLE 3. COMPARISON OF SATELLITE AND E-MAIL MODES OF DELIVERY

	Ofek	E-mail
Role of instructor	• Precise preplanning of lesson components • Selecting a variety of visual input • Devising tasks that would generate maximal interaction • Providing feedback during sessions • Recommending readings	• Preplanning of course topics • Selecting reading texts • Devising tasks that reflect comprehension of topics and their classroom applications • Providing stimuli for on-line discussion • Devising procedures for participants' management of weekly tasks • Providing on-line feedback
Role of participants	• Attending weekly classes • Listening to presentations and reading recommended texts • Participating in workshop activities • Preparing practice assignments and sending them in	• Getting an e-mail connection and preparing a distribution list • Getting e-mail assignments and reading the assigned texts • Participating in on-line asynchronous discussions • Preparing answers and discussing them with peers • Punctually submitting the weekly assignments to the whole group • Submitting journal entries to the instructor only
Management of the medium	• Synchronous • Expensive to run; requires a studio, technical staff, and special classrooms • Approximates traditional classroom • Mostly instructor led because learner-driven learning is limited to workshop activities	• Asynchronous (except for face-to-face class meetings) • Inexpensive; does not require any equipment beyond a computer with a modem and an Internet connection • Participant studies at home • Learner-driven learning (occurs when participants read and prepare tasks) • Teacher-driven learning occurs during feedback
Instructional sessions	• Participants meet at centers, and video transmission lasts 180 minutes • Instructor provides initial input • Participants complete some workshop activities • Participants interact within and across centers • Instructor provides feedback, sums up, and leads toward next session	• Participants access Internet from home or work and class work is spread over a week • Instructor sends assignment by e-mail • Participants read texts with the assignment in mind • Participants discuss issues and problems with peers via e-mail • Participants submit answers to the whole group as well as to instructor • Instructor provides general and personal feedback

◈ CONTRIBUTORS

Yael Bejarano is head of the English Unit at the Open University of Israel (OU), where she administers language programs, is involved in teacher education, and serves as director of a reading comprehension material development program for academic purposes. Her research interests include small group teaching and interaction processes, second language testing, and EFL reading comprehension.

Esther Klein-Wohl is the coordinator of distance-learning programs at the English Unit at the OU and director of the Israel MA TESOL program at the Institute of Education, University of London. Her research interests include socio- and psycholinguistic perspectives in second language learning, teacher education and training, and distance education.

Lily Vered is the head program developer for in-service teacher education at the OU and a member of the steering committee advising Israel's Ministry of Education on the implementation of technology in EFL. She was head of the English department at the Levinsky Teachers' College and an academic consultant to Israel's educational television for a number of years.

CHAPTER 11

Teacher Education at a Distance in Canada and Thailand: How Two Cases Measure up to Quality Distance Education Indicators

Ruth Epstein

◈ INTRODUCTION

I found this program to be very comprehensive . . . If it weren't available through correspondence, I wouldn't have been able to take it.

CERTESL program participant

This is the best way for full-time teachers to learn. The content is great and it is in-service. We can learn in our free time. Sometimes I miss the interactivity of face-to-face, but the seminars helped a lot.

Thai TEFL program participant

Whether or not advanced delivery technologies are used, distance education differs from traditional education in many ways. Distance education is not simply taking a program that has been successfully delivered in a face-to-face setting and offering it at a distance. Rather, high-quality distance education requires anticipating and planning for a number of complex, interrelated factors. For learning to occur and distance education to be accepted, it must not merely claim to be, but must actually be, of high quality.

This chapter informs ESOL teacher educators who are developing distance-learning programs of an established set of indicators of quality in distance education. Examining established indicators of quality distance education (QDE) programs can inform us about the proper development of distance-delivered programs. This chapter also aims to alert program developers to the inherent components and challenges of distance education so that they can be better prepared to address these factors proactively.

Two distance-delivered teacher education programs, one in Canada and the other in Thailand, are described in this chapter and measured against a set of QDE indicators adapted from those developed at the University of Wisconsin in 1996. Examining two different ESL teacher preparation programs that employ distance education and applying the same set of QDE indicators to them illustrates how these indicators can be applied in widely varying, international contexts. These two cases also show how program planning can be systematically approached and successfully carried out using the indicators.

◈ CONTEXT

Because it differs in many ways from traditional education, distance education must be designed, described, and evaluated on its own terms, not in comparison to face-to-face instruction (Shale & Gomes, 1998). QDE indicators help stakeholders (e.g., teacher educators, participants, employers of graduates) describe the features and assess the desired program outcomes. In this way, QDE indicators are useful in comparing programs with established standards that are acceptable to the stakeholders. They are also useful in setting policies for distance education programs (Schulz Novak, 1996).

Although there are other indicators (Rowntree, 1998; Shale & Gomes, 1998), those from Wisconsin were selected because they are thorough and easily applicable to distance-learning programs. The seven Wisconsin QDE indicators (University of Wisconsin-Extension, 2000) are as follows:

1. knowing the learners
2. creating confident and committed faculty
3. designing for active and effective learning
4. supporting the needs of the learners
5. maintaining the technical infrastructure
6. sustaining administrative and organizational commitment
7. evaluating for continuous improvement

These indicators provide the context in which the main attributes of the Canada and Thai and distance education programs will be examined.

◈ DESCRIPTION

Certificate in Teaching English as a
Second Language (CERTESL) Program in Canada

The University of Saskatchewan has offered CERTESL since 1992. The program is delivered at a distance to enable teachers and potential teachers who are unable to leave their communities, work, and family responsibilities to study on campus.

The program is preservice in nature, although some participants may be teaching or otherwise employed while studying. The content is aimed primarily at preparing ESL teachers of adults but also addresses the teaching of younger learners and teaching in EFL contexts. Currently, the majority of participants are first language (L1) English speakers residing in Canada, although there are international registrants.

Registrants must have completed high school, although about half hold a baccalaureate, approximately half of which are in education. Certification is awarded upon successful completion of six courses dealing with TESL methodology, including a practicum or project (see Figure 1). Each course must be completed in one 13-week semester. The program can be completed in 1 year of full-time study, but participants

Core Courses

TESL 21:   Overview of Teaching English as a Second Language

TESL 31:   Teaching English as a Second Language: Theory and Skill Development

TESL 32:   Materials Selection and Development

TESL 33:   Applied English Grammar and Phonetics

TESL 42:   Supervised Practicum (summer on campus or distance delivered)

or

TESL 43:   Professional Project (alternative to practicum)

Electives (choose one of the following three)

TESL 34:   Teaching English as a Second Language/Teaching English as a Second Dialect for Indian and Metis Students (Metis are people of mixed French and Canadian Indian ancestry)

TESL 35:   Teaching English as a Second Language Methods

TESL 41:   Program Planning and Evaluation in Teaching English as a Second Language

Note. This slate of courses has been revised since the program evaluation.

FIGURE 1. 1995 CERTESL Courses

usually prefer part-time study for 2 to 3 years. Courses include theoretical and practical information, and this approach is also reflected in assignments.

A team consisting of a content expert, an instructional designer, an editor, and a media specialist (where necessary) develops each course. Courses are primarily print based and include a course guide, textbook(s), and an article reprints package with some audiovisual support in the form of audiotapes, videotapes, and, recently, a CD-ROM in phonology. Tutors, who hold at least a bachelor's degree in education in addition to TESL qualification and have extensive experience, are appointed to advise participants on course content and grade assignments and examinations developed by course writers. Tutors respond to participant inquiries by phone, fax, mail, or e-mail.

Currently, course registrants are mailed study packages containing the course guide, an article reprints package, and administrative documents related to assignment submission and contact with tutors. Assignments are sent to a central location where they are logged in and out and mailed back to participants after being graded. The number of assignments submitted by e-mail and fax is increasing.

Thai Teaching English as a Foreign Language (TEFL) Program

In the early 1990s, the York University English Language Institute in Toronto, Canada, collaborated with the Regional English Language Centre in Singapore to develop and implement a TEFL program in Thailand. The Canadian International Development Agency, through the Southeast Asian Ministries of Education Secretariat, funded this project. In the spring of 1994, I evaluated the pilot of this program (Epstein, 1994), which is described in this chapter.

To increase access to in-service English language teachers over a wide geographical area, the program was distance delivered. The primary delivery medium was print with some audiotape and videotape support. The program was aimed at those teaching Grades 4–12. Program objectives were "to provide participants with practical skills in TEFL combined with theoretical knowledge in the area, and to provide them with an opportunity to further develop their English language skills" (SEAMEO-Canada Programme, 1993, p. 5). Identified by the Thai Ministry of Education, participants were EFL teachers from Chiang Mai or Korat and surrounding communities and second language (L2) speakers of English, most of whom were at the advanced intermediate level of proficiency.

The content was divided into six modules dealing with classroom techniques for teaching the various language skills. The modules (classroom techniques, teaching reading, teaching oral communication, teaching listening skills, teaching writing, and teaching grammar) were further divided into units (see Figure 2). Module assignments were usually small, action research projects that learners completed in their classrooms. The program was designed to be completed in 1 academic year.

Two content experts (one from Singapore and the other from Canada), working with a Canadian instructional designer/distance education specialist, developed the courses. The print-based courses had some audiovisual support. TEFL educators at Chiang Mai and Korat teachers' colleges were hired as tutors and had advanced TEFL qualifications. Their role was to respond to content inquiries, usually by phone, and grade assignments and presentations. There were no final examinations.

The phone and mail delivery system in Thai TEFL was similar to that in CERTESL, although e-mail was not used. Participants received their course materials during a face-to-face weekend orientation seminar that included participants, tutors, course authors, and Ministry of Education officials. The orientation familiarized participants with their tutors, the design of the program, procedures for contacting their tutors, and other administrative details. The purpose of the midcourse seminar was for further sharing and clarification of course organization and content. Participants rated both seminars highly in helping them maintain motivation, meet program expectations, and improve assignments.

◈ DISTINGUISHING FEATURES

As noted previously, the curricula and purposes of the two teacher education programs were rather typical. What was noteworthy about these programs was distance delivery and how CERTESL and Thai TEFL addressed the challenges of distance education.

This section describes how various features of each program served participants according to Wisconsin's QDE indicators. However, Indicator 5, Maintain the Technical Infrastructure, is not included here because it is not very applicable; both programs were primarily print based. Print was the chosen delivery medium in both cases to ensure accessibility in remote areas, ease of revision, and cost-effectiveness. Other media were used, but only to a limited degree because of the expense of development and revision and because of intended users' limited access to technology in these contexts (Bates, 1995).

Module I: Classroom Techniques in Teaching EFL

Unit 1: Language Teaching Methodology

Unit 2: Techniques for Dealing With Large and Multilevel Classes

Unit 3: Planning

Unit 4: Testing and Evaluation

Module II: The Teaching of Reading

Unit 1: Language Teaching Methodology

Unit 2: Techniques for Dealing With Large and Multilevel Classes

Unit 3: Planning

Unit 4: Testing and Evaluation

Module III: Teaching Oral Communication

Unit 1: The Nature of Communication

Unit 2: Practical Classroom Strategies for Communication

Unit 3: Pronunciation

Module IV: Teaching Listening Skills

Unit 1: Principles of Listening

Unit 2: Listening Activities for the Classroom

Unit 3: Evaluating Listening Skills

Module V: Teaching of Writing

Unit 1: General Principles for Teaching Writing

Unit 2: Practical Techniques for Teaching Writing

Unit 3: Correcting and Grading Students' Writing

Module VI: The Teaching of Grammar

Unit 1: Grammar and Foreign Language Teaching

Unit 2: Teaching and Assessing Grammar

FIGURE 2. 1994 Thai TEFL Courses

Knowing the Learners

Learners are central in the development of any educational program. Designing for unknown learners at a distance poses particular challenges—challenges that CERTESL and Thai TEFL address in creative ways.

In CERTESL, informal and formal needs assessments (Rubrecht, 1990) provided the impetus for the program and helped identify the goals and needs of potential learners. Demographic information, including gender, age, location, and educational level, is collected each term to continually inform program developers about changes in the participant population. Participants also provide feedback in summative course evaluations and in communications with tutors. All of this feedback is relayed during biannual debriefing meetings, and feasible changes are regularly incorporated.

In Thai TEFL, the Thai Ministry of Education identified the participants' needs and demographics before program development. During the evaluation, participants agreed with the goals of increased knowledge of English and communicative language teaching. Because the Thai teacher group was relatively homogeneous in terms of their own students and previous knowledge and experience, curriculum development was more straightforward than in CERTESL. The challenge lay in writing the courses at an appropriate English language proficiency level for Thai program participants. This was accomplished by hiring developers familiar with participants' language proficiency levels and incorporating appropriate design elements.

In both program evaluations, it was difficult to obtain information for instructional design and delivery purposes on participants' learning styles and self-confidence. However, course completion rates were good, indicating fairly high levels of independence and confidence. Many rural participants in both programs said they felt isolated (discussed below). In both programs, learners complained that they were not receiving a more advanced qualification than a certificate. These are, however, administrative challenges.

Creating Confident and Committed Faculty

During the programs' development, content experts wrote the courses with the assistance of instructional designers who were also distance education experts. Programmers sought content experts who could work effectively in teams and were receptive to or knowledgeable in distance education. Orientation to distance education by instructional designers facilitated this receptivity.

In CERTESL, content experts had the right of first refusal to work as tutors of the course(s) they wrote. Course writers and tutors worked on a contract basis. Tutors received a half-day orientation to distance education at the beginning of each term, a 2-hour debriefing session at the term's end, and a tutor handbook. They were encouraged to keep in touch with course instructional designers and course administrators to suggest revisions and provide feedback. Stipends and workload expectations were based on a standard contract.

In Thai TEFL, tutors were quite separate from content experts. However, they did have the opportunity during a weekend orientation to work with the development team. Tutors received a handbook to assist them in their roles. Although the orientation to distance education and the program was intensive, tutors and administrators still expressed a need for greater depth of knowledge of distance education and distance learners. Similar feedback was not given in CERTESL. The Thai faculty also said that they needed relief from their regular workload to properly teach the program.

Designing for Active and Effective Learning

For each program, a team of language teaching experts developed a curriculum appropriate for a certificate-level program that aimed to provide a basic understanding of theory and practice, as well as opportunities for reflection. However, there were some curricular differences. CERTESL contained more theoretical content than Thai TEFL, requiring at least three times the number of study hours. Partly because of participants' English fluency, CERTESL included much more reading at a much more advanced academic level than Thai TEFL. For example, in CERTESL, an entire course of several modules was devoted to teaching approaches, whereas in Thai TEFL only one module addressed this topic. Also, Thai TEFL addressed materials selection and adaptation only briefly within modules, whereas CERTESL included an entire course of several modules on this topic. Applied grammar and phonetics constituted an entire CERTESL course but were covered in only one module of Thai TEFL. Because of the in-service nature of Thai TEFL, there were many more opportunities than in CERTESL for applying theory in the classroom. This was accomplished specifically through action-research assignments but also through participants' intrinsic motivation to try out concepts and activities in their teaching.

Reflective practice was addressed through learning activities in both programs. For example, the Thai TEFL action research projects required a section on reflection. In CERTESL, some courses required reflective journals and many assignments included a section on reflection. Telephone contact with tutors was available in both contexts and was the major vehicle for discussion. In CERTESL, case studies and interviews with ESL learners and teachers were also included. CERTESL's supervised practicum added opportunities for theory application and interaction with colleagues. In Thai TEFL, opportunities to try out EFL activities in class and share with colleagues were potentially available but not always utilized due to time constraints. A difficulty in Thai TEFL was that not all tutors had dedicated phone lines. In one case, they had to share with other colleagues in a busy staff room. Also, the remotest of learners did not have ready access to telephones. Reliable mail delivery was occasionally a problem in Thailand. However, the difficulty would have been greater at that time with a more advanced communication system (audioconference, satellite, or computer assisted). Print-based distance delivery does give rise to challenges in promoting active learning, interactivity, and application of theory, but these challenges must be weighed against the benefits of the high accessibility and low production cost of print.

Both programs used instructional designers with distance education expertise to develop courses. Such experts were well equipped to anticipate and address the challenges of distance education and print design. Isolation was a great challenge with participants in both programs. In both cases, efforts to bring learners together while studying at a distance were not successful (as previously discussed, Thai TEFL face-to-face sessions were very successful). In Thailand, communication among peers was constrained by lack of time, work and home responsibilities, program demands, cost, and distance. In Chiang Mai, this was less of a problem; learners who taught together could meet regularly.

Supporting the Needs of the Learners

Developers of both programs realized the need for learner support. Both provided academic support through contact with tutors. In Thai TEFL, tutors were located in teachers' colleges; in CERTESL, they were usually on campus.

CERTESL included the following additional supports for participants:

- administrative support through the Extension Credit Studies Office (a unit within the University of Saskatchewan's Extension Division) and a participant handbook

- academic advising through telephone or e-mail contact with the program coordinator

- audiovisual support
- off-campus library support
- study skills support through an optional distance-delivered multimedia package
- a study hints page in every course
- a document entitled "Protocol for Working With ESL and EFL Delivery Agencies"
- a booklet with community ESL contacts in Saskatchewan (not available for participants elsewhere)

Thai TEFL offered the following additional supports for participants:

- two face-to-face weekend seminars, with costs to participants covered by the program (participants rated seminars highly and suggested that they be longer)
- potential peer contact in Chiang Mai schools
- audio- and videotapes (participants wanted more of these, although some did not have playback units; production cost also was an issue)

Participants in both programs were generally pleased with the tutors' assistance. Thai TEFL participants noted that some tutors were not always available for phone calls, and some participants were reluctant to disturb busy tutors with questions. In both programs, there were some complaints about slow turnaround for assignments. In Thailand, the slow mail system was partly responsible for this. Thai TEFL learners reported home environments were not always conducive to study. Also, Thai participants had less access to library resources, although library research was not a program requirement. It was emphasized to tutors in both programs that quick turnaround times for assignments and availability by phone are crucial. However, especially in Thai TEFL, workloads and phone availability made this difficult. Poor postal service is, unfortunately, something that print-based distance education in some countries must endure.

Sustaining Administrative and Organizational Commitment

The importance of organizational and administrative commitment to distance education cannot be underestimated. Because the administration of CERTESL and Thai TEFL were quite different, each will be discussed separately below.

CERTESL

CERTESL originated in an extension unit committed to adult and continuing education that was responsible for university certificates and delivery of much of the university's distance education. The Extension Division's Centre for Second Language Instruction at the University of Saskatchewan employed ESL experts. Thus, expertise in ESL, distance education, instructional design, and technical support was readily available for program development and delivery. In addition, an effective and efficient distance education infrastructure was in place from the outset of program development. Feedback from course writers has indicated that remuneration and development time lines were somewhat insufficient. However, the contract for sessional employees has been negotiated, is standard across the institution, and, therefore, cannot be changed specifically for this program.

During CERTESL conceptualization, attempts were made to collaborate with other universities. However, because of differing mandates, the Extension Division decided to develop a certificate program on its own. CERTESL has always had the support of the university's College of Education, and Seneca College in Toronto brokers CERTESL.

The Extension Division administration has handled the marketing of CERTESL, which has expanded across Canada. Word of mouth in the TESL community has been a powerful marketing tool, in addition to brochures and conference displays.

CERTESL has been cost effective, providing a reasonable but not excessive return. Sufficient revenue is required to maintain and renew courses and meet changing needs of participants. As financial pressure on the institution increases, administrators may look to CERTESL for higher profits. However, because it is print based, CERTESL is a relatively low-cost program and has been on target in terms of university expectations.

Thai TEFL

The Thai TEFL administration knew little about the demands of distance education, but, to their credit, they employed experts, allocated resources to course development and infrastructure, and did what was possible to provide orientation to stakeholders. Still, feedback from course developers showed that the time lines were insufficient, that remuneration was barely adequate, and that the developers desired more in-depth knowledge of distance education.

As discussed previously, a Canadian educational institution, York University English Language Institute, worked closely with the Regional English Language Centre in Singapore to share expertise. Based on feedback from learners and on the fact that the program was expanded, the benefits of this collaboration far exceeded the difficulties.

Marketing of Thai TEFL was not an issue at the pilot stage. The program administration used resources wisely, given the financial and time constraints, by employing a team of very competent local and foreign experts.

Evaluating for Continuous Improvement

Both programs had the foresight to budget for evaluation and revision. In CERTESL, formative course evaluations occurred in the pilot year of course delivery. Summative course evaluations occurred at the end of each course offering. During the development phase, content experts from other educational institutions reviewed the courses. Courses are reviewed for currency on an ongoing basis and undergo major revision every 5 years.

In January 1997, a program evaluation was completed that included content evaluation as well as input by program administrators and developers, participants, and employers at ESL delivery agencies (Epstein, 1997). The results were positive. Suggested improvements usually related to expanded content (e.g., more K–12 and TEFL content), faster turnaround time on assignments, and greater administrative coordination with institutions that broker the program. CERTESL incorporated feasible suggestions and improved courses through professional editing. In addition, the course developers renewed the curriculum, and the program is currently conducting studies on participant retention, incorporation of prior learning assessment and recognition, increased classroom contact across the curriculum, and Internet interaction.

Thai TEFL had been offered only once before it was evaluated. However, course developers received tutor input at an orientation seminar before course delivery and elicited participant feedback during the midcourse seminar. Also, each course module included a feedback form, but fewer and fewer participants completed them as the program progressed. The program evaluation, completed in June 1994, consisted of a content evaluation and feedback from learners, tutors, content experts, the instructional designer, course developers, some administrative staff and participant focus groups.

Feedback on the Thai TEFL program was very positive. However, the program was challenging for participants with low English language proficiency, especially those in isolated areas. Also, workplace demands made it virtually impossible for many participants to keep up with the program. Extensions were granted to allow participants to complete their requirements. Learners in Chiang Mai had more opportunity for peer interaction and locating resources than did learners in the Korat area. By the end of the pilot program, tutors were gratified that they had participated but were glad that it was over as they had not been sufficiently relieved from regular workloads. Administrative and organizational staff personnel, however, were enthusiastic, looking forward to program revision and expansion. The course developers readily incorporated the few design and content suggestions during a revision following the evaluation. For example, with respect to content, one suggestion was to integrate grammar with other skills. With respect to design, suggestions included using more professional-looking illustrations, better quality paper, and more legible reprints.

❖ PRACTICAL IDEAS

Know the Learners

- Conduct complete needs assessments of potential learners that include all areas identified in Wisconsin's QDE indicators.
- Assume variety in learners' goals, needs, abilities, and work and home responsibilities.
- Plan for less prepared learners by incorporating flexible entry and support for study skills and language skills.

Create Confident and Committed Faculty

- Provide faculty with thorough orientation to distance education.
- Be realistic and generous in development and delivery time lines.
- Ensure that remuneration and rewards are fair.
- Allow faculty sufficient relief from other duties.
- Use a team approach to course development, involving instructional designers, editors, and technicians (as required).

- Debrief with faculty at the end of units of study and incorporate feedback.
- Provide sufficient technical support for faculty (e.g., dedicated phone lines, computers).

Design for Active and Effective Learning

- Take a collaborative approach to curriculum development.
- Take a team approach to program and course development.
- Check content and design with outside experts.
- Incorporate strategies to assist learners in developing an appropriate learning environment at home.
- Incorporate sufficient flexibility to accommodate a variety of learner goals, needs, abilities, experiences, and learning styles.
- Ensure maximum experiential and interactive opportunities within the limits of distance education and resources.
- Ensure opportunities to connect theory to practice (e.g., through observation, practica, exploration of critical incidents in real classrooms, reflective journals, portfolios).
- Ensure adequate turnaround time on assignments (i.e., learners should be able to receive feedback on one assignment before the next one is due).
- Select appropriate delivery technologies for the audience, context, and content; advanced technologies are not necessarily the most appropriate; consider accessibility, cost effectiveness, learning styles, technical support, ease of revision, and flexibility.

Support the Needs of the Learners

- Ensure administrative, academic, and personal support for distance learners.
- Ensure adequate orientation to distance education for learners.
- Ensure the commitment of tutors to learners (i.e., availability, responsiveness, thorough feedback on assignments).
- Develop a system to facilitate reliable, frequent contact between tutors and learners.
- Minimize learner isolation (e.g., through on-site workshops; pairing with peers; and advanced communications technology such as computer-mediated communication, if accessible to learners and financially feasible).
- Make library resources easily accessible through cooperating regional libraries and a library system that is willing to take mail-in, fax, or e-mail requests.
- Ensure appropriate end qualification commensurate with learner aspirations and depth of program content; be clear with learners regarding the relationship of the end qualification to the workload and depth of content.

Maintain the Technical Infrastructure

- Having selected appropriate delivery technologies, ensure technical orientation to content experts, tutors, and learners.
- Ensure that delivery technologies are well maintained, available, and tested in time for delivery.
- Ensure high-quality productions of print, videotape, audiotape, and computer applications.

Sustain Administrative and Organizational Commitment

- Orient administrative staff to distance education through meetings and a handbook.
- Appoint managers and project coordinators who are well versed in distance education.
- Consider thoroughly the advantages and limitations of collaboration with other institutions.
- Ensure through written agreements that all groups and institutions understand their roles and responsibilities in collaborative efforts; sufficient flexibility is required to address unforeseen circumstances (e.g., unforeseen resource demands, increased program demand).
- Ensure sufficient developmental resources (i.e., financial, human, time, technical) to develop a high-quality program.
- Ensure appropriate remuneration or reward for program administrators and developers.
- If applicable, incorporate marketing into the program development plan.
- Budget realistically by allocating at least as much to distance program development, delivery, evaluation, and revision as to face-to-face program development; costs will be recovered over the years of program delivery.

Evaluate for Continuous Improvement

- Budget for the inclusion of formative and summative evaluations.
- Ensure sufficient resources to allow pilot delivery of courses.
- Build formative evaluations into the pilot delivery of each course.
- Ensure program evaluations at regular intervals (e.g., about every 5 years), soliciting feedback from all stakeholders (e.g., administrative personnel, content experts, tutors, learners, ESL/EFL delivery agencies, schools).
- Ensure that feedback from all evaluations is reported and incorporated in revisions.

◈ CONCLUSION

The opportunity to take relevant training at a distance is very much appreciated. Personal accomplishment and a sense of achievement is satisfying. The program led to some wonderful teaching experiences.

CERTESL participant

Developers of distance education programs must be aware of the inherent components and challenges of distance education. Using QDE indicators such as those developed in Wisconsin helps developers anticipate those challenges that are particular to distance education so that they are better prepared to address them proactively and systematically.

Providing a high-quality learning experience for learners from different geographic regions involves familiarity with the learners, their goals and needs, and the program content. It also involves awareness of what is feasible within a given context and implementation of a design and delivery system that will be effective in the environment where the program will be delivered. This will perhaps mean thinking critically about the latest trends that favor advanced technology and using a more reasoned combination of delivery options that ensure reasonable costs to institutions and assured accessibility for learners.

◈ CONTRIBUTOR

Ruth Epstein is a faculty member at the Extension Division at the University of Saskatchewan in Canada. She is an instructional designer for distance education courses and programs and an ESL specialist. She has taught ESL/EFL and has worked in teacher education in Canada and elsewhere.

CHAPTER 12

The Pedagogy and Technology of Distance Learning for Teacher Education: The Evolution of Instructional Processes and Products

C. Ray Graham, Annela Teemant, Melanie Harris, and Ramona M. Cutri

❖ INTRODUCTION

Preparing public school teachers to meet the academic needs of language minority students is challenging in a state like Utah, which has small pockets of dense urban population and large rural areas. In such a setting, teachers and trainers look for ways of reducing the amount of travel necessary to implement in-service education programs. Our experience over the past decade with various teacher preparation programs in this setting has taught us that achieving success with distance learning is not merely a question of the delivery system—the technology—used but, most important, the pedagogy of the system.

Throughout this chapter, three aspects of our distance education program will be evident. First, our experience is marked by strong commitment to cross-disciplinary cooperation among departments at Brigham Young University (BYU). Applied linguists, teacher educators, content-area specialists, classroom teachers, and technology experts have stepped out of their zones of comfort and expertise to learn from one another and to make second language acquisition content accessible, meaningful, and practical to our in-service audience. Second, our efforts in distance learning are guided by an active university and public school partnership, which is built on shared responsibility for determining the nature of teacher preparation programs at BYU. Third, the university itself has taken a strong institutional stand by committing resources, faculty, and finances to meeting the needs of student populations served by partnership districts. These efforts at interdisciplinary and university-public school cooperation, however, have not been without their costs.

In this chapter, we describe the evolution of our distance-learning efforts for in-service teachers seeking a bilingual/ESL endorsement. Next, we describe the implementation and evolution of our use of a delivery model called *professors-plus* and detail the problems we faced and the results of program evaluations. Finally, we discuss the generations of technology and pedagogy we have considered in arriving at our current asynchronous approach to distance learning.

CONTEXT

During most of this century, the language minority population of Utah schools has been small. As late as 1985, less than 3% of the state's 400,000+ K–12 students were classified as limited English proficient (LEP) and most of those lived within the boundaries of two or three school districts (National Center for Education Statistics, 1991; Office of Bilingual Education and Minority Languages Affairs [OBEMLA], 1993). In the 6 years between 1985 and 1991, the LEP population of the state increased more than 150% (OBEMLA, 1993). By the mid-1990s, not only was almost every school district in the state affected by these demographic changes, but many schools had significant numbers of language minority students entering their programs. Teachers who had been prepared primarily to teach white, middle-class, native-English-speaking students were now being faced with students from different cultures and with varying degrees of proficiency in English.

While these demographic changes were taking place in the state, BYU was undergoing major changes in its approach to teacher education. In 1984, John Goodlad, director of the Center for Educational Renewal at the University of Washington and recognized for his research on how to tailor teacher education programs to meet the needs of local school districts and organizations, assisted BYU's College of Education and five surrounding public school districts to create what has become known as the BYU-Public School Partnership (Goodlad, 1994; Osguthorpe, Harris, Harris, & Black, 1995). In this partnership, mechanisms were set up so that district officials could have significant input into the nature of the teacher preparation programs and, at the same time, the university could strengthen the on-site practicum aspect of teacher education. As the partnership districts began to feel the pressure of the demographic changes of the 1990s, a task force was set up that included faculty members of BYU's Linguistics and Teacher Education Departments to consider ways in which the university could provide preservice and in-service education programs for teachers serving language minority youngsters.

In cooperation with the BYU-Public School Partnership program coordinator, two teacher learners from the Linguistics Department began master's theses in the fall of 1995 that examined the level of preparation of elementary and secondary school teachers in three of the partner districts (Christiansen, 1996; Guinn, 1996). These theses served as preassessments of teacher attitudes toward and preparation for teaching language minority students against which the effects of our distance-learning efforts could be evaluated.

Results of these theses showed that the majority of teachers in the three districts had had ESL students in their classes, but few (only 18% in the elementary school sample) had received any training in serving language minority students. Over-whelmingly, the teachers in both studies expressed the belief that they were not at all prepared to deal with LEP students. What is more, the most common response among secondary teachers to the question "What suggestions would you give to administrators considering additional teacher training in dealing with LEP students?" was "Students should learn English before entering [our] classes" (Christiansen, 1996, p. 90). As a matter of fact, Christiansen concludes that most secondary teachers did not want more training for dealing with language minority students at all. Rather, they preferred that the language and educational needs of these students be met through other means.

This research established a clear need for training teachers to instruct language minority students with the implication that the university should assume a major role in helping teachers receive their endorsement for working with bilingual/ESL students.

◈ DESCRIPTION

Because of the immediate need for qualified teachers in the five districts and, for that matter, across the entire state of Utah, in 1994 we began an intense effort, using existing courses and professors on overload, to create in-service classes for teachers of language minority children. The university scheduled classes for 1 or 2 evenings each week and invited schools in the partnership districts to send one or more teachers to the classes so that each school would have at least one bilingual/ESL-endorsed teacher. These courses were offered primarily during weekday evenings, and many teachers had to leave their schools after an exhausting day of work, travel for an hour or more to the site of the class, attend the class for 3 hours, and then drive another hour or more home after class. This exhausting schedule made it difficult for even the most dedicated to complete the endorsement program.

The classes were created following the newly formulated Utah State Bilingual/ESL Endorsement guidelines and consisted of six semester-length courses of 2 to 3 credit hours each and a practicum. ESL faculty in linguistics and teacher education, in cooperation with teachers who were already working with ESL students in the public schools, collaboratively designed these courses.

A Goals 2000 grant was secured to pay for most of the expenses of developing the program. Before long, we began exploring the option of offering the classes at district sites through the state's two-way audio/video communication system called *EDNET*. This distance-learning arrangement promised to allow hundreds of teachers to take ESL endorsement courses at schools near their homes, instead of having to travel to a central location.

EDNET: The First Generation of Distance Instruction

In the EDNET format, classes were taught to a studio audience near the university and transmitted to several other sites with two-way audio/video transmission facilities. Each site was equipped with a control console, two cameras, and at least two monitors. Microphones were available at each table so that participants could participate in the class discussions. A trained technician, sitting at the console, could focus the cameras on the professor, the chalkboard, a given participant in the class, or an experimental apparatus anywhere in the classroom. In addition, the technician could play a video segment on the monitors from a prepared video or show an overhead that was then transmitted to the monitors at each site.

The participants could see themselves on one of the monitors as they were presenting. On a second monitor, the technician could present visual images of participants at other sites. Therefore, any participant at any site could see, speak to, and be seen by the participants at all the other sites by having the technician switch between screens. Participation by professors and participants at the different sites was a matter of coordination among the technicians, who opened and closed screens at the appropriate moments.

Our major concern with the EDNET distance-learning format was the possibility of losing the learner community aspect of our classes in which participants shared their experiences and became resources to each other. To ensure that a sense of community would not be lost, we implemented a model in which a trained facilitator at each local site assisted the professor to conduct the instructional program. This was the "plus" part of the professors-plus model. In each session, the professor conducted brief lectures or demonstrations over the EDNET system with opportunities for responses from participants at each site. Facilitators at each site would then divide the class into small cooperative groups that would engage in hands-on learning activities related to the concepts just presented. Later, each site would report back to the professor and participants from other sites over the EDNET system. Although the inclusion of on-site facilitators increased professor preparation for sessions and required more class time for sharing between sites, the use of on-site facilitators was successful enough that we continued to work with it.

During the 2 academic years from 1994 to 1996, 50 teachers completed the entire six-course program and were recommended for state endorsement. In the 1996–1997 school year, 65 candidates completed the series of courses and received their endorsements. By the summer of 1999, the number of participants who had completed the program during the year had risen to 170. Each semester we have videotaped each class session for later examination and improvement and collected participant evaluations and suggestions.

Bilingual/ESL Endorsement Through Distance Education (BEEDE)

Those experienced in distance-learning delivery systems emphasize that one should always choose the simplest form of delivery that will accomplish the intended purpose. In spite of the successes of our EDNET approach, we have found the delivery system anything but simple. Not only does it require many hours of planning time and extensive coordination for each session, but it also requires a large amount of technological support. For example, each site has to have a technician to run the equipment that supports the professor's presentation. Schedules must be coordinated with the EDNET system months in advance and must compete for the most desirable times and days with other programs and entities wishing to use the EDNET system. Once the times are scheduled, there is little flexibility in when and where classes can be delivered. Also, times that are good for participants at one school are often not good for those at another. Furthermore, the professor and participants are always held hostage by a litany of possible technological glitches. On a given day, a particular site may be without sound or video because of some problem with equipment or the central broadcasting system.

Our experience with distance learning has taken us through various iterations of delivering instruction over the EDNET system. With each, we have made refinements in the curriculum and delivery. However, the shortcomings of on-line audio/video delivery have persuaded us to move toward a more flexible version of our professors-plus model—the BEEDE project.

BEEDE still employs a professors-plus model. The *professors* portion relies on the expertise of many nationally recognized scholars as well as experts of classroom practice. The plus portion is still a trained teacher/facilitator at each site using printed instructional guides to accompany each class. However, the *professors* part is represented by carefully crafted video segments presented by the facilitator. The video-anchored portions of each course in BEEDE are not the typical talking heads associated with some distance learning. Major course content is presented in a conversational tone through a mixture of university professors and public school experts; that is, teaching points are demonstrated or elaborated through annotation of actual classroom interaction (e.g., teacher-to-students, student-to-student) or through carefully edited interview segments with students, parents, community leaders, teachers, principals, other administrators, or experts in education and applied linguistics. In every instance when it is possible to show rather than just tell, school-based scenarios are used. Also, a narrator (a) ties together these video segments of professors and school-based scenarios, (b) introduces learning activities to be carried out off-camera with the facilitator, and (c) prompts use of the accompanying instructional guides. These study guides contain supporting information regarding the contents of the presentations, hands-on learning activities that the facilitator conducts with the groups of participants, and assignments for extending learning to real classroom practice.

In this BEEDE version of distance learning, teachers no longer need to travel to distant sites or depend on real-time technology. Instead, district facilitators who have completed our training now work within their districts to offer courses according to local district needs and demands. These facilitators, using videos with instructional guides, conduct learning activities and group discussions, collect and respond to course assignments, monitor participant performance, and communicate with professors when problems arise. With BEEDE, in-service development can take place in teachers' individual schools and at their convenience, using simple video technology the school controls. Thus, flexibility and local control are two important advantages, and more effective instruction is accomplished with less technology than through the EDNET system.

◈ DISTINGUISHING FEATURES

Delivery Features

The most critical delivery feature is the creation of learner communities through the use of the professors-plus model. The facilitator, using the instructional guides, organizes learners into cooperative learning groups that work together throughout the course. This encourages the formation of strong, supportive learning communities among teachers within the local school or district. Because these communities are school based, they continue to exist long after the formal instruction period ends. This is a critical part of the process of helping teachers to utilize the new knowledge and skills in their teaching.

Unlike independent study delivery systems in which learners sit at a computer terminal or tune in to a television station to complete course work individually, this professors-plus model considers interaction among participants essential. Participants' evaluations of the program have suggested that this cooperative approach to learning is one of its more valuable aspects.

Modeling of target teaching behaviors is another important feature of the delivery format. Not only do the instructional materials and facilitator attempt to model the teaching behaviors that they are encouraging the participants to develop, but participants are required to model these behaviors in the presentations they make to their cooperative groups. For example, when participants are given reading assignments from textbooks, one member of each cooperative group is asked to present the contents of the reading to the other members of the group using ESL strategies. That is, they are asked to summarize the chapter using graphic organizers, pictures, and hands-on learning activities that would be appropriate in content-based ESL instruction. Summaries of exemplary presentations are then frequently shared with other cooperative groups at the site.

In addition, the BEEDE model employs an active learning approach. On-site facilitators enable the monitoring of learning activities that go beyond lectures and demonstrations. The facilitator at each site can introduce a learning activity pertinent to the needs of that group, such as a science experiment that requires the active participation of the class members, and then monitor the activity and give encouragement and feedback. This provides the means for utilizing teaching strategies that once were thought to be possible only in face-to-face instruction. This active learning approach also invites learners to be "actively involved in discussing problems, seeking solutions to case studies or dilemmas, responding to simulations, participating in games, and making decisions," as suggested by Egan and Gibb (1997, p. 37).

The system's multimedia capabilities are another important feature. Professors frequently use computer graphics and videos (in the form of school-based scenarios) to enrich instruction. In contrast to the EDNET system, BEEDE's use of a video-anchored format with VHS tapes in a local VCR player avoids the technical obstacles we experienced with real-time technology. It also gives the facilitator the flexibility of stopping the video at any point and replaying it for the class. The video-anchored course content also allows materials prepared for the in-service training to be used in preservice TESOL classes. The extensive footage from classroom instruction and interviews with the various experts and professionals will be made available to university faculty for use in preservice classes through a video database.

Finally, the development of the professors-plus model is based on a strong commitment to cross-disciplinary collaboration among faculty members across university departments and with public school faculty. ESL specialists from the teacher education and linguistics departments have collaborated with content methodology specialists in the social sciences, physical sciences, mathematics, arts and humanities as well as with outstanding teachers in the elementary and secondary schools to present the most current strategies for teaching language, literacy, and academic content to language minority students. Such collaboration requires a large commitment of time and effort on the part of faculty and public school teachers.

Content Features

One distinguishing content feature is BEEDE's reliance on video-anchored course content, which means that course content is frozen. The professor does not have the opportunity to reteach or clarify last week's lesson; this is done by the facilitator. In this sense, the BEEDE version of the professors-plus model is time intensive and demands more thorough preparation—scripting, filming, editing, and piloting—before being captured on video or being available for use. Despite the technical difficulties associated with the EDNET version of professors-plus, that system allows for the dynamics of real-time teaching, albeit somewhat clumsily because of the camera and audience that can only be seen on video. In this way, BEEDE is more of a high-stakes endeavor than EDNET.

Based on evaluations from EDNET participants, we have eliminated much of the unintended redundancy that existed in the courses delivered in the earlier in-service sessions and built into the program the planned redundancy necessary for teachers to assimilate the important concepts and skills intended. In addition, we have developed extended syllabi and interactive instructional guides for the courses. The syllabus for a particular course is extended from an outline of teaching points to a script for video production. The syllabus and resulting scripts have been refined, evaluated, critiqued by external reviewers, and refined again to present a comprehensive and unified curriculum across the six courses and practicum.

A second distinguishing feature in the development of BEEDE is the effort to create an explicit and reciprocal connection between theory and practice. Whereas video segments may highlight, for example, various hypotheses about the nature of second language acquisition, school-based scenarios of classroom interaction or interview segments aim to demonstrate what those theoretical concepts look like in practice. Learning activities, such as hearing a story told in a foreign language, also reveal the connections between theory and practice.

A final feature of content in BEEDE is a commitment to reflective self-study and professional development. Course content, learning activities, and assignments push participants to engage with content and to confront conceptual change. Assignments from each course are tied to a portfolio, and participants are guided in documenting their professional development in relationship to educating language minority students.

◈ PRACTICAL IDEAS

In the process of implementing an in-service, distance-learning program, we dealt with many difficulties, some anticipated, others unforeseen, in our careful planning. These difficulties have taught us a number of valuable lessons.

Allow Time for Advance Planning and Coordination

The first lesson we learned—regardless of which delivery system we worked with—was that preparation for distance-learning teaching requires much more planning for detail than is necessary for conventional classroom teaching, perhaps as much as 10 times the planning effort. Whether the question is coordination with on-site technicians for EDNET or film production teams for BEEDE or coordination with facilitators, the sequence of instruction and learning activities must always be decided beforehand and almost minute by minute. Furthermore, there must be strict coordination between instruction and participants' instructional guides.

Deal With Delivery System Difficulties

In the EDNET version of professors-plus, the professor had to be very flexible in delivery. On occasion the system would fail, and we would lose communication with one or another site for a few minutes. On other occasions, the system for transmitting classroom videos would fail, and some other activity would have to be used in place of showing a video segment. Once we lost transmission to a site for a large segment of the evening, and the facilitator had to conduct the learning activities without the benefit of the professor's presentations on the topics. Mechanically, therefore, the distance education format placed a number of demands on the instructor and facilitators that are not characteristic of the conventional classroom setting. Our adoption of a video-anchored, professors-plus model with BEEDE has allowed us to overcome many of these technological challenges.

Learn to Teach to the Camera

Most of us who are accustomed to moving around our classrooms and creating intense interaction with learners found it rather clumsy to be tied to a microphone and to look at participants at distant sites through the video apparatus. (If the speaker does not look directly into the camera a substantial part of the time, learners at distant sites get the impression of listening in on the class rather than being a part of it.) Learning to teach to the camera was harder than most of us anticipated.

Collaborate for Course Improvement

It always takes much more time and energy to cooperate with others in the planning and delivery of content than it does to do it alone. Our project was no exception. We had our share of missed deadlines and planning problems, but we are confident that our collaborative efforts have resulted in content that is more grounded in practice— in the actual day-to-day realities of teachers' lives. The courses developed for BEEDE reflect the richness and diversity of our collaborative partners.

Consider Costs Carefully

The costs of distance-learning initiatives include not only financial commitments but also time, resources, and faculty teaching assignments. Our project is being supported by a coalition of entities, including the Goals 2000 grants through the Utah State Office of Education, the districts in the BYU-Public School Partnership, the university's Division of Continuing Education, the film studio, and our respective colleges and departments, which have allocated research assistants and reduced teaching loads.

◈ CONCLUSION

Our experience with providing distance-learning opportunities in bilingual/ESL education for in-service public school teachers has revealed the importance of pedagogy and technology. Through EDNET, the limitations of real-time technology were revealed and the promise of the professors-plus delivery format was confirmed. Our decision to move toward video-anchored technology was motivated by practical considerations and our desires to meet the growing demand for bilingual/ESL endorsements among in-service teachers.

Ongoing evaluations of our distance-learning efforts have caused us to be very optimistic about the possibilities of the professors-plus, distance-learning format. The great majority of participants during the past 2 years have noted that the program has prepared them well for the task of teaching language minority students in their classes. In their own self-evaluations, they have indicated that the program has not only helped them improve their abilities to deal with language minority students but has also helped them teach regular students in mainstream classrooms. Faculty and staff observations of participants' performance in the practicum classes have confirmed the positive effects the program has had on teaching behaviors. The most positive evaluations have come from participants' assessment of their changes in attitude toward language minority students and language minority student education. Almost universally, participants who had completed the program felt well prepared to meet the needs of language minority students in their classrooms. This is in stark contrast to the general self-evaluations of teachers in three of the partnership districts before the in-service program (Christiansen, 1996; Guinn, 1996).

Currently, the Teacher Education and Linguistics Departments are in the production phase of development for the first BEEDE course: The Foundations of Bilingual Education. It has taken us 18 months to get from teaching points to a production script. If we are indeed successful in our production of six video-anchored courses (the BEEDE program), it will be in great measure due to cross-disciplinary collaboration, university-public school partnership, and our university's commitment to teacher education and public school students.

◈ CONTRIBUTORS

C. Ray Graham is an associate professor of linguistics at BYU and has authored several articles on bilingual and ESL instruction in the public schools. He is currently the academic coordinator of BYU's English Language Center and is involved in ESL teacher education at the public school and intensive English program levels.

Annela Teemant is an assistant professor of foreign/second language education and teaches for BYU's Teacher Education and Linguistics Departments. Her teaching and research focus on ESL in K–12 public school settings and cross-disciplinary collaboration. Her main assignment is the development of the BEEDE project.

Melanie Harris is coordinator for the bilingual/ESL endorsement for the BYU-Public School Partnership. Her research interests are in school-university partnerships and professional development for ESOL instructors.

Ramona M. Cutri is an assistant professor at BYU in the Department of Teacher Education. Her teaching and research focus on multicultural and bilingual/ESL education and the moral dimensions of teaching.

CHAPTER 13

Expanding the Horizon of the TESOL Practicum via Distance Learning

Michael Janopoulos

◈ INTRODUCTION

The practicum is an integral part of most TESOL master's degree (MA) programs in North America, with almost 80% of the 208 programs surveyed in the *Directory of Professional Preparation Programs in TESOL in the United States and Canada: 1995–1997* (Garshick, 1995) reporting that some form of practice teaching is either required, recommended, or optional. The importance of the practicum in the preparation of ESOL teachers is likewise almost universally acknowledged as ". . . the major opportunity for the student teacher to acquire the practical skills and knowledge needed to function as an effective teacher" (Richards & Crookes, 1988, p. 9).

At the University of Northern Iowa (UNI), TESOL MA students are similar to those in programs described by England and Roberts (1989) and Day (1984) in terms of prior experience and perception of instructional needs. These teacher learners may be categorized into three main groups:

1. native speakers of English who either have or want to obtain overseas ESOL teaching experience

2. nonnative speakers of English who, for the most part, are experienced ESOL teachers

3. native speakers who are already practicing ESOL teachers in school districts scattered across the 99 counties that comprise the state of Iowa

Teacher learners in this third group originally began their program of study by taking TESOL courses to satisfy newly instituted state requirements for K–12 ESL certification but have now decided to pursue a TESOL MA degree.

Clearly, the inclusion of this third category of off-campus clients who work during the day poses challenges for the TESOL MA practicum in terms of content and delivery. This chapter discusses how the TESOL MA faculty at UNI has attempted to respond to these changing needs by utilizing newly emerging technological resources to provide a delivery option that offers real-time, interactive instruction in a practicum class consisting of on-campus and distance learners.

◈ CONTEXT

The Iowa Communications Network (ICN)

The ICN offers a specialized type of distance learning, one that provides for two-way, interactive, real-time instruction over a fiber optics television network. This kind of instructional medium provides educators with the "ability to establish a learning situation across wide distances . . . . With fiber optics capability, participants can interact in a two-way voice and video interactive environment. This feels just like they were sitting in the same classroom together" (Iowa Long Distance Alliance, 1995, glossary, n.p.).

According to the *Interactive Television Workshop* handbook (Iowa Long Distance Alliance, 1995), a training manual for prospective users of the ICN, as early as 1980, several Iowa universities and community colleges began to install telecommunications networks (including microwave and cable) to meet the educational needs of rural residents. It further notes that, by the fall of 1986, members of the Iowa legislature concluded that a coordinated statewide initiative was needed to most efficiently develop and deliver distance-learning technologies.

Under the terms of the so-called *Equalizing Rural Iowa* initiative of 1989, Iowa's General Assembly authorized the ICN fiber optics network project; construction began in 1991. The first two parts of the project called for installing one fiber optic *endpoint* (i.e., interactive classroom) in each of Iowa's 99 counties, additional endpoints at each of the three regents institutions (the University of Iowa, Iowa State University, and the University of Northern Iowa), one in the Capitol Complex in Des Moines, and one at the headquarters of Iowa Public Television (IPTV) for a total of 104 sites. In 1995, additional legislation was enacted to close the coverage gap, the goal being to "provide a video connection to every school district which chooses to use ICN services" (Iowa Communications Network, 2001). According to IPTV (2001), as of April 2, 2001, there were a total of 726 video classrooms operational statewide (with no indication of how many school districts are included), with the following distribution among facilities:

386 in K–12 schools	57 in National Guard facilities
100 in community colleges	39 in various state agencies
29 in regents universities	17 in various federal agencies
19 in private colleges and universities	11 in hospitals
16 in area education agency facilities	45 in public libraries

ICN Classroom Layout

The average ICN classroom is designed to accommodate one or two instructors and between 18 and 20 students in a facility that contains a standard configuration of a teacher's podium, student tables with microphones, big screen television monitors, and a fax machine. Figure 1 shows the typical layout of an ICN classroom. As can be seen in this figure, two 32-inch color television monitors flank the teacher's podium, whereas the third monitor is at the rear of the room. By looking at the two front monitors, participants at remote sites can thus follow what is happening at other sites and need only activate the nearest table microphone to join in discussion with their remote-site classmates.

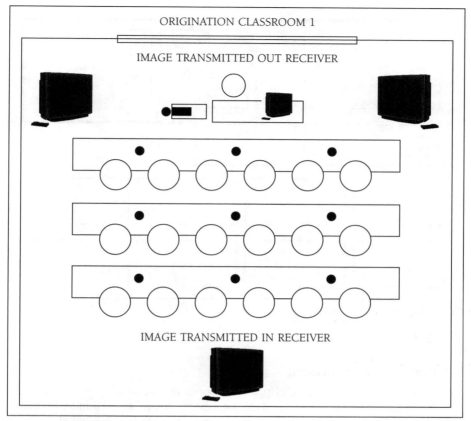

FIGURE 1. Typical Iowa Communications Network (ICN) Classroom Layout

At the origination site, the two front monitors, as well as a small monitor at the podium, show the outgoing video, which is selected by the teacher using a variety of controls on a podium-mounted computer touch screen (see Figure 2). To monitor participants' activities at remote sites, the teacher simply selects the touch pad for whatever site he or she wishes to view, and the image appears on the rear monitor. Whenever a participant at a remote site "keys" a microphone, that site is shown on the rear monitor at the origination site. In this way, the teacher always knows when someone at a remote site has a question or comment. To allow participants at all sites to view the person asking a question, the teacher simply touches the "Remote" button on the touch screen. If participants at the origination site wish to contribute, they also depress their microphone lever to speak, and the teacher touches the "Student" button so that the remote sites can "see" the speaker.

As is evident from the preceding description, the nerve center of the ICN classroom is the teacher's podium at the origination site, from which all activities are orchestrated. Teachers' podia at most sites include a VCR, a videodisk player, a satellite or cable input jack, a fax/copier machine (allowing documents to be sent directly to each of the different sites), Macintosh and IBM-compatible computers with Internet access, an audiotape player, a slide projector, and an overhead camera for display of instructional materials.

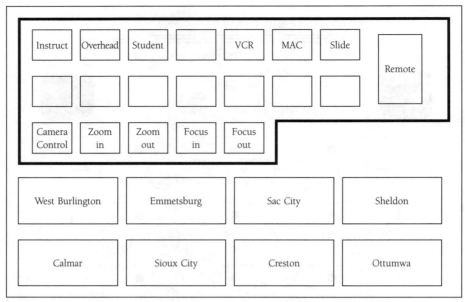

FIGURE 2. Controls on Podium-Mounted Computer Touch Screen

ICN Costs and Management

As one might imagine, the cost of such an enormous undertaking is considerable. The *Interactive Television Workshop* (ITV) handbook (Iowa Long Distance Alliance, 1995, p. 7) reports the following construction costs during the initial stage of construction:

Fiber optics cable	$960/mile
Terminal equipment	$75,000–$125,000/site
Classroom equipment	$39,000–$49,000/class

Despite the great expense involved in constructing such a comprehensive and wide-reaching fiber optics network, the actual cost to clients for using the system is extremely modest. Site rental fees for user groups (Boyd E. Sherbet, personal communication, January 29, 1999) are as follows:

Universities and community colleges	$6.30/hr
K–12 schools	$5.25/hr
Meetings scheduled by other state and federal organizations	$10.50/hr

These low costs are possible because the ICN operates like a utility, under the supervision of the Iowa Telecommunications and Technology Commission, with day-to-day operations overseen by IPTV (Iowa Long Distance Alliance, 1995).

❖ DESCRIPTION

The ICN and UNI's TESOL MA Program

Members of the TESOL MA faculty at UNI have been actively involved in using the ICN to accommodate the needs of distance learners since 1995. The ICN was originally seen as a means of reaching a wider number of clients (most of whom were teachers working to satisfy the state's ESOL certification/endorsement requirements) than could be served through the more conventional practice of teaching on-site weekend extension courses to relatively small groups of participants around the state. The use of the ICN for delivery of TESOL MA course work to participants in off-campus locations also offers several other advantages.

First, the ICN option allows for increased flexibility to off-campus participants and faculty in terms of where, when, and through which medium required courses can be offered.

Second, the ICN option enables us to greatly expand the number of courses we can offer to off-campus clients. Before the ICN, extension courses offered at one site for four weekend time blocks often failed to enroll the required minimum number of participants (usually 8–10) and so were cancelled. ICN classes, on the other hand, are far easier to subscribe the minimum number of participants (12), because those participants can be drawn from all parts of the state and attend one of several ICN remote sites on a 1-night-per-week basis. As a result, not only have we been able to extend the reach of our course offerings but, in so doing, are also able to offer more courses. Consequently, UNI's TESOL MA program has been able to offer ICN courses to off-campus clients on a regular basis (approximately one course each academic term, including summers) since late 1995.

Finally, the ICN option has allowed us to improve the quality of instruction for off-campus participants enrolled in our TESOL MA program (many of whom have been recruited from the ranks of our ESOL endorsement program) by allowing them to directly interact with their on-campus classmates. It is especially this aspect of distance learning that prompted us to offer the TESOL practicum over the ICN.

UNI's TESOL Practicum

The practicum is seen as the capstone experience in the TESOL MA course sequence at UNI. As such, it is generally delayed until the latter part of a teacher learner's program of study. The course lasts one full semester, and enrollment is generally limited to a maximum of 10 participants each term. Although a considerable amount of variety may exist with regard to specific assignments, depending on which faculty member teaches the course, the practicum traditionally requires teacher learners to participate in weekly 2-hour seminar meetings in which a variety of topics are discussed, make regular journal entries, give oral reports on assigned articles, submit a series of written reports based on observation of a range of ESOL and foreign language classrooms, and work in an ESOL classroom under the close supervision of a cooperating teacher. Duties within the ESOL class may include observation, team teaching, tutoring, the teaching of minilessons and, ultimately, a supervised teaching assignment lasting usually no more than 2 weeks or 10 instructional hours.

Until recently, the bulk of the assigned observations and the practice teaching experiences took place in UNI's on-campus Culture and Intensive English Program

(CIEP). Recently, however, our placement options have expanded to include a greater presence in the local school systems due to a dramatic influx of Bosnian refugees that began in early 1997.

Course Requirements

As is the case in our more conventional TESOL MA practica, spring 1998 practicum participants at our on-campus and remote sites were required to attend weekly 2-hour seminars. Participants at both sites were also required to complete additional assignments, including regular journal entries, written classroom observation reports, a statement of philosophy of education, oral reports on assigned readings, and practice teaching assignments. Furthermore, I formally observed everyone in both groups at least twice during the semester. The only substantive difference between the remote group and the on-campus group lay in the range of practice teaching experiences required.

For the on-campus group, practice teaching options included university-level foreign language classes (for the two participants who were assigned teaching assistantships in the Department of Modern Languages), the on-campus CIEP, and local middle schools and high schools. Participants were encouraged, though not required, to serve in two venues during the semester (e.g., 8 weeks in a local high school and 8 weeks in the CIEP) to broaden their range of teaching experience.

Because they already held full-time ESOL teaching positions, remote participants were held to slightly different standards. For example, two remote participants who were lacking in the requisite teaching experience for K–12 ESOL endorsement were obliged to observe and teach under the direct supervision of their ESOL colleagues at those levels. Thus, an elementary school teacher might also be placed in a middle school and a high school classroom as well as continuing to perform her regular teaching duties.

Another difference between on-campus and remote-site requirements is that remote participants were observed only once in person. The other observation was videotaped, with pre- and postobservation conferences being accomplished through a combination of e-mail, regular mail, telephone, and ICN communications.

Participants

Four teacher learners participated in the spring 1998 practicum from one remote site. All were teachers: two at the elementary level and one each at the middle school and high school levels. Individually, each of these teachers had at least 10 years of experience in areas other than ESOL and an average of almost 5 years of ESOL experience. All had originally started taking TESOL courses to satisfy newly implemented state ESOL endorsement requirements but were now continuing with the remaining course requirements for the TESOL MA degree.

In contrast, the on-campus contingent of teacher learners consisted of three Americans, one Japanese, one Costa Rican, and one Russian. Teaching experience for this group outside of ESOL was negligible. The group's total amount of ESOL teaching experience was 10 years, with one participant (the Costa Rican) accounting for half of that total and two participants (one American and the Russian) having absolutely no ESOL classroom teaching experience.

◈ DISTINGUISHING FEATURES

Combination of Off-Campus and On-Campus Participants

In contrast to the learning environment typically associated with Asynchronous Learning Networks (ALNs), our ICN-based TESOL MA practicum allows remote-site learners, on-campus learners, and instructors to engage in real-time audio/video interaction. Thus, what distinguishes our ICN-based practicum from the model of distance learning described by proponents of ALN learning (e.g., Sener, 1997) is that it does not concern only off-campus learners. Instead, we chose to offer a TESOL practicum over the ICN in which novice teachers-in-preparation on our campus would be brought together with experienced ESOL teachers from another part of the state to "meet" in weekly 2-hour seminar sessions. We believed that this instructional arrangement would be to the benefit of both parties.

To our surprise, the anticipated success of this combination was limited in some aspects. Despite my best efforts as the instructor, the two groups did not spontaneously interact as often or as much as I would have liked. Indeed, I was not alone in this feeling: One of my on-campus teacher learners noted on her postpracticum questionnaire that it was hard to feel like a group with the participants in the remote site.

The reasons for the existence of such a gap between the off-campus and UNI-based participants are not entirely clear, but I suspect that the gap was due as much to differences in sociolinguistic background and teaching experience as it was to mere physical distance and our on-campus participants' lack of experience in interacting with classmates at a remote site.

In other words, the very range of sociocultural background and teaching and travel experience that I was confident would be an asset may have, in some ways, become a liability. From the beginning, I sensed a certain reluctance in participants from both sites to freely engage one another in discussion regarding what I had assumed to be topics of mutual interest. Instead, my on-campus participants rarely asked for the advice of their older, more experienced classmates at the remote site on questions of lesson planning, assessment, and materials development, even though many of them were struggling to put theory into practice in what was, for some of them, their first genuine teaching experience.

Why this is so is not entirely clear to me. Perhaps my younger participants were intimidated by their older classmates' greater experience or superior teaching skills. Or perhaps it was the ICN format itself that lay at the core of the problem because a private conversation between sites is impossible unless conducted by telephone. I also could have done more to encourage and facilitate interaction between sites, instead of assuming it would occur naturally.

At least one of my on-campus participants was certainly aware of the potential benefits of sharing a course with such experienced teachers:

> I expected this course to be more class discussion in that everyone will express or share the observations made. By doing so, we can acquire more teaching tips that work well.

As for my remote-based participants, they rarely questioned their native-English-speaking or nonnative-English-speaking classmates at UNI (who as a group boasted considerable overseas teaching and learning experience and multilingual talents) regarding differences in learning styles or educational systems. As to why they were so reluctant, one participant—who coincidentally was a veteran of several INC courses—wrote: "I was hoping to share more with the other teachers informally. I think the ICN limits that kind of discussion."

Despite these areas of concern, participants from both sites reported that their expectations for the course had generally been met. Their overall opinion was that doing a practicum over the ICN had been a worthwhile experience.

Emphasis on Interaction

Another distinguishing feature of our program is that the ICN-based practicum, like ALN, seeks "to deemphasize lectures and emphasize interaction at all times" (Sener, 1997). In this way, the ICN-based practicum deviates from the synchronous learning network norm, where interaction is possible only during lectures. In the case of the ICN-based practicum, keeping the number of communicating sites to a minimum facilitates the interactions among participants. In fact, for our spring 1999 TESOL MA practicum, just two sites were on-line: the originating site (on-campus at UNI) and the one remote site. The instructor, therefore, could more easily facilitate communication between participants at both sites.

◈ PRACTICAL IDEAS

The marriage of our TESOL MA practicum to the ICN involved several innovations and taught us several lessons that can be applied to other real-time distance-learning instructional settings.

Capitalize on Participants' Diverse Backgrounds

From a technical standpoint, the ICN allowed us to bring together two geographically separated groups of clients whose diverse backgrounds and experience complemented one another. Pedagogically, this allowed for a sharing of ideas ordinarily unavailable to either group by itself.

Design Activities to Bring Participants From Different Backgrounds Together

To avoid some of the difficulties we experienced in getting participants to share their experience and expertise, instructors should design in-class activities that oblige participants at both sites to work together, especially if regular face-to-face interaction among participants is not feasible. There are certainly enough classroom-based cooperative learning techniques available to place the burden of inquiry and interaction on the participants. Perhaps pairing novices with experienced teachers from each site in lesson planning or textbook evaluation activities would help to forge closer bonds and lower affective barriers. Or perhaps having participants share videotaped segments of their teaching would open up new, productive avenues of discussion between experienced and novice teachers at the different sites.

Limit the Number of Participants and Sites to Make Activities Participant Centered

To maximize potential interaction in our ICN-based practicum, the number of participants and sites were limited. In addition, we designed seminar activities to be as participant centered as possible and to require that participants draw on each other's strengths to complete tasks. This decision was based, in large part, on previous experience with ICN classes with larger enrollments participating from as many as six different remote sites, where site-to-site participant interaction was minimal and instructional format tended toward lecture rather than discussion.

Encourage Participants to Explore and Become Familiar With Technological Resources

Use of the ICN as the medium through which these two distinct groups were combined allowed participants to become familiar with an instructional option they may have been unfamiliar with or unaware of; namely, distance learning through the ICN. To maximize potential exposure to this medium, participants were encouraged to explore and experiment with the ICN classroom's technological resources, which range from direct fax communication with the other site to the use of the overhead camera for display of graphic material.

Let Participants Conduct Class Sessions Over the Distance-Learning System

By actively participating in the conduct of the class, especially when they took control of the teacher's podium to give individual presentations, participants gained firsthand experience in how to use cutting-edge educational technology. From a pedagogical standpoint, conducting an ICN class offered valuable lessons regarding everything from planning a lesson that takes advantage of the medium (e.g., constructing visuals that conform to the shape of a television screen rather than the dimensions of a book) to learning firsthand about the importance of variety and constant attention to participant attentiveness at remote sites.

◈ CONCLUSION

The primary goal of the ICN-based TESOL MA practicum in the spring of 1998 was to meet the needs of an ever-growing number of ESOL teachers in Iowa for whom it was extremely difficult, due to distance and work schedule, to satisfy the practicum requirement in their TESOL MA program in the conventional on-campus manner. In addition, it was anticipated that by opening up the on-campus practicum to distance learners, the expected interaction between two groups of clients, one with strong experience in teaching ESOL in Iowa and the other with a much more international background but with considerably less teaching experience, would allow each group to benefit from insights offered by the other.

To the extent that these general goals were accomplished, the ICN-based practicum was a success. The program indeed allowed the group as a whole access to insights and information that it would not have otherwise possessed. In addition, participants at the remote site were afforded the opportunity to satisfy practicum course requirements—including observation assignments and practice teaching in other grade levels than the ones in which they were currently working—much more conveniently than would otherwise have been the case.

What needs to be done to improve the ICN-based practicum? First and foremost, we must improve the quality and increase the quantity of interaction between participants at the two (or three or more) sites. The reasons the two groups in this particular class did not form more of a cohesive whole are obvious: Nobody knew anybody else at the other site, and no one at the on-campus site had ever taken an ICN course of any sort before. In retrospect, I realize I should have arranged for at least one face-to-face meeting of the participants at or near the beginning of the course. In this way, participants might have formed a more personal bond, which, in turn, could have helped to establish a greater sense of community in the ICN classroom.

In closing, the key to opening the door to meaningful interaction in two-way, real-time, fiber optics-based distance learning is there. It is simply up to us to find that key. And when we do, then we will turn what was a good experience for us into something that is exceptional.

◈ CONTRIBUTOR

Michael Janopoulos is an associate professor of English/TESOL at the University of Northern Iowa. He has published on the topics of ESL composition and teacher preparation. Before his appointment at UNI, he directed an intensive English program in the United States and taught EFL in the Middle East for 8 years.

CHAPTER 14

Practicing What We Preach: Optimal Learning Conditions for Web-Based Teacher Education

Joy Egbert and Chin-chi Chao

◈ INTRODUCTION

Indiana University's (IU's) Language Education Department offers 19 Web-based courses for teacher professional development and, to some extent, beginning teacher preparation. More than 1,000 participants (mostly teachers enrolling for professional development goals) have taken these courses. The technological sophistication of the communications media used ranges from basic e-mail and class electronic discussion lists to conferencing systems, video streaming, joint work areas, and links to a host of resources. In the process of developing, offering, and refining these courses, we have learned a great deal about the strengths and limitations of on-line learning environments for teacher education.

This chapter focuses on the department's computer-assisted language learning (CALL) course on the Web and examines what this electronic venue brings to teacher education. It also reports on the challenges and difficulties instructors and course developers have faced and partially overcome in this virtual environment. In particular, we share our implementation of a model of conditions for classroom learning environments that serves as the primary course content and underlies the way in which the course is designed and taught. This implementation is important because teacher educators are often criticized for not practicing the educational methods and techniques that they ask their teacher learners to understand and demonstrate. We have tried to make this Web-based distance education course an exception, demonstrating what we think to be exemplary practice in everything we do.

◈ CONTEXT

The L530: CALL course (http://www.indiana.edu/~cell) serves as an elective in IU's Master in Language Education program, including ESL/EFL, English education, and literacy streams. The course was first offered in 1996 as an on-site course. During the following summer, we created a distance version of the same course with funding from Continuing Education at IU. Since then, IU has offered the on-site version three times and the distance version six times. Approximately 50 teacher learners have taken the course at a distance from all over the United States and some other parts of the world, whereas about 90 participants have attended the on-site version of the course.

Participants in the distance course are in-service and preservice teachers with many different educational experiences. They are from different cultures and have different teaching focus areas (e.g., EFL, ESL, bilingual education, foreign language education). During the academic year, there are more full-time graduate students in this course than practicing teachers; however, during the summer session, when the course is offered on-line only, we have not only more practicing teachers but also a greater diversity of backgrounds among participants. The demographic changes from semester to semester make it necessary to make revisions for every group. At the same time, these changes have helped us to become more sensitive to participant needs.

No matter how different the backgrounds and focus areas of our participants are, a common goal of all participants is to understand ways of incorporating computer software and applications in language curricula in an informed and educated way. According to an electronic information survey that teacher learners fill out at the beginning of the course, our teacher learners' computer skills are most often limited to word processing and e-mail. Many participants express trepidation about using computers in their classrooms and learning new computer skills, but they do see the need to become more skilled and knowledgeable in this area. The expressed fear of learning computer skills is, in fact, a challenge and also creates potentially wonderful opportunities for us to reflect on the learning process with our teacher learners. The fear, as we see it, is very much the same as that which some language learners experience when they struggle to learn a second or foreign language. Teachers often cannot relate to the fear and difficulties second language learners experience when facing a challenging learning task. There is a lot a teacher can learn about teaching just by being a learner all over again, and learning computer skills is one challenging opportunity that we can provide to the participants in this course as well as in other distance courses.

◈ DESCRIPTION

The course is intended to give participants a broad general view of CALL and the place of educational technologies in the language classroom. Course participants explore a working theory of language learning environments; use and discuss existing and potential applications of computer technology in the language classroom; and create projects to use and test knowledge gained through reading, discussion, and hands-on experience.

The course is designed for preservice and in-service teachers, technology consultants, administrators, and all others interested in CALL. Because it is an introductory workshop course at the graduate level, participants are involved in hands-on discovery and creation, in addition to perusing the literature and discussing the research. To fulfill this purpose, the class has been developed as a part seminar, part hands-on workshop. There are five important objectives in this class, which participants are expected to accomplish by the end of the course:

1. Create appropriate contexts in which language learners interact and negotiate meaning in the computer-enhanced classroom.

2. Understand how to integrate technology into the language learning environment.

3. Effectively evaluate software and technology-based projects and activities for use in their own language classrooms.

4. Develop new computer-enhanced tasks and adapt existing computer-based tasks to suit the needs of their learners.

5. Use and understand the importance of ongoing assessment in the computer-enhanced language classroom.

To reach these five objectives, the eight central modules that make up the course provide participants with a variety of information, activities, and resources. Each unit begins with a scenario of a teacher's problem related to the unit's theme. This problem is written in the first person as if the teacher were asking for course participants' advice or suggestions, as shown in the following case problem from the Interaction module:

> I can't get my students to interact in class. I give them tasks to do in groups, but often one student takes over and does the work, and the others chat or do something else off task. I would use the computer software I have that's made for groups, but I'm afraid that the same thing will happen.

Class members keep a case journal in which they analyze this case problem, propose solutions, and reflect on how they would change or adapt their solutions. To help with their reflection, the unit provides a background summary, on-line readings, and guided questions, such as the following:

Guided Questions

What is interaction? Why is interaction necessary for second language (L2) learners? What are some ways to provide students with opportunities to interact? In what ways can technology support interaction?

Background

Many researchers have noted that learning is essentially the result of interaction between learners and others (e.g., Kelman, 1990; Levin & Boruta, 1983; Vygotsky, 1978). If learning is a social process, then interaction with other people is necessary. This concept is not strange to L2 instruction, because many researchers have called to our attention the importance of meaning negotiation and interaction modification to L2 development (Long, 1985; Long & Porter, 1985; Porter, 1986; Pica, Holliday, Lewis, & Morgenthaler, 1989).

Teacher learners read material of two types. One of these is print based (e.g., journal articles). The other is on the Web (e.g., Jones, Valdez, Nowakowski, & Rasmussen, 1995). During each module, participants discuss the case problem in the electronic discussion forum and perform tasks related to the unit topic and the case. Class activity descriptions, optional assignment descriptions, related Web sites, and other resources relevant to the unit and attendant activities are included in each module, as shown in the following example from the Interaction module:

Class Activity

Evaluating a Web site is a useful activity. It makes you more discerning and critical of what you see on the Web, and it also makes you become a better designer because you are suddenly aware of what you should or should not include in your own Web site or software.

In this activity, we will be looking at a few Web sites for language learning. You can consult these pages for guidelines:

WWW CyberGuide Ratings for Web Site Design (http://www.cyberbee.com/guide2.html) (McLachlan, 1996) and the *WWW CyberGuide Ratings for Content Evaluation* (http://www.cyberbee.com/guide1.html) (McLachlan, 1997). Your main focus should be the amount and type of interaction that each page affords.

Write a brief (one paragraph) critique that deals with the strengths and the weaknesses of an appropriate Web site. Post your paragraph to the forum in the appropriate folder for this unit, and be sure to respond to other participants' critiques.

Optional Assignment

Step 1. Use a search engine to conduct a search for Web sites that deal with software evaluation. A particularly useful resource is the final project of one of our L530 class graduates: *An Educator's Resource Page to Software Review* (Reynolds, n.d.) available at http://www.hometown.aol.com/NReyno/portfoliointro.html. Another software evaluation guide (Hubbard, 1992) can be found at http://www.owlnet.rice.edu/~ling417/guide.html.

You should be able to find some professional reviews in electronic journals on the Web; you may check out several. Here is one on the Rosetta Stone: http://www-writing.berkeley.edu/chorus/call/reviews/rosetta_russian.

Step 2. Design a set of criteria and an evaluation form for selecting CALL courseware based on the condition for this unit (focus on the software's interactivity). Make your criteria clear, and make your form easy and practical to use.

Step 3. Review a courseware package of your choice using your evaluation form. Be sure to comment on how well you think the program provides for the "interaction" condition. The other conditions? If you see some problems with the courseware, how could you improve the package or its use?

Step 4. Hand in the review you did on your form.

In addition to these activities, participants e-mail individual reflections to the teacher weekly. Finally, participants complete an inquiry-based final project.

◈ DISTINGUISHING FEATURES

This course has many distinguishing features. For example, many CALL methods courses, whether on-site or distance, are arranged around different types of software and technologies, methods of language teaching, or skill areas. Instead, this course employs a model of CALL based on learning theories as its focus and as the ordering mechanism for discussion and activity. It also incorporates joint hands-on activities, such as a field trip to an electronic, Web-based virtual world (called a *MOO*, for multiuser object-oriented domain), despite the wide distribution of participants. In addition, on-site participants serve as liaisons for those who are off-site. The most important feature of the course, however, is the learning model on which it is based.

Model of Optimal Classroom Language Learning Conditions

In striving toward the goals of teaching technology skills and building knowledge about teaching, the course is based on a model of optimal classroom language learning environments into which technology skills, learning theories, and opportunities for application fit. This model consists of eight conditions that, in various strengths and configurations, create optimal classroom language learning environments for individual learners (adapted from Egbert, Chao, & Hanson-Smith, 1999; Egbert & Jessup, 1996). These conditions are

1. Interaction. Learners have opportunities to interact and negotiate meaning.

2. Audience. Learners interact in the target language with an authentic audience.

3. Authentic task. Learners are involved in authentic tasks.

4. Exposure and production. Learners are exposed to and encouraged to produce varied and creative language.

5. Help. Learners have enough time and feedback.

6. Intentional cognition. Learners are guided to attend mindfully to the learning process.

7. Atmosphere. Learners work in an atmosphere with an ideal stress/anxiety level.

8. Control. Learner autonomy is supported.

In addition to being the focus of study for the participants, this model is integrated into how the course is set up and conducted, exemplifying how these conditions look and work in classrooms.

Although each course module highlights one of the conditions, the systemic nature of the conditions in language classrooms is emphasized. The specific content and learning events of each module support the model conditions in different ways, as exemplified in Table 1.

All of these course events contribute to a supportive, participatory atmosphere that helps motivate participants to explore the potential of technology in language curricula.

Activities That Exemplify the Conditions in the Model

Instructional activities also attempt to provide good examples of the conditions. For example, to ensure that participants have enough information and feedback to complete their tasks, the instructor sends a message to the off-site participants (and their on-site liaisons, if such exist), at the beginning of each week, commenting on the previous week's discussion, listing expectations for the week, and explaining anything else that needs to be clarified. An example of a weekly message follows, in which the instructor begins with an orientation to the week's topic:

> Good morning. We are stepping into the 3rd week, and from now on we are going to zoom in and explore how each of the eight learning conditions can be supported with the computer. The first one to explore is *interaction*.

TABLE 1. COURSE EVENTS AND THE MODEL CONDITIONS THEY SUPPORT

Events	Conditions	Explanation
• Case studies	Authentic task	Focus on our participants' classrooms and engage participants in the reflective decision-making process that is required in a teacher's everyday life.
• Guided questions	Exposure and production	Provide information in a variety of media and formats for participants who want more. Help those learners who need more structure or guidance in their thinking and reading.
• Background summaries		
• Extra resources		
• Feedback from class members		
• Participant reflections		
• Example assignments		
• Class activities	Control	Allow participants to pace their own progress if they want to and provide options for learners to choose focus of interest and strategies for fulfilling the assignments.
• Optional assignments	Authentic task Control Exposure and production	Chosen by the participants; offer the option of suggesting and completing an assignment that participants feel is more relevant to their context.
• Electronic conferencing	Interaction Authentic audience Intentional cognition	Affords the opportunity to interact with a real audience of educators who want to learn from each other and ask each other's advice and comments. Promotes reflection.

Many people have difficulty imagining how interaction can possibly be promoted with computers. In fact, a colleague told me that the reason he did not want to step into CALL was that he did not believe interaction was possible. I see similar comments in some of your replies to my first question; that is, picturing computers and language learning. Yes, you are right, interaction is very important, not just for language but also for cognitive development. And yes, it is impossible if you look at computers only as a vehicle for getting software packages to work. But, if you look at it as a means for communication, a whole new picture shows up. Just think about how we interacted in the past 2 weeks in e-mail and the forum discussion! Can you see the value of promoting this kind of interaction? One concept you need to have in mind when it comes to computer-mediated communication is the difference between *synchronous* and *asynchronous* interaction. For this week, we will focus on asynchronous.

Next, the instructor describes the activities and adds information that has not been included in the module:

Hands-On Activity

The hands-on activity for this week, "Evaluating a Key Pal Project," aims to give you an opportunity to see how a key pal project is done: what preparations the teacher/students need to do and what issues/problems are involved. Just in case you do not know yet, the word *key pal* came from *pen pal*. This means students write to each other using keyboards, not pens. Details of this activity are on our Web page.

Optional Assignment

If you choose to do it, the first optional assignment is due this Friday. You need to do two assignments this semester, and I suggest that you do your assignments early in the semester. Please manage your time well because you may find yourself very busy at the end of the semester. OK. That's all for now. I will see you in the forum.

This weekly e-mail serves not only as a reminder and a motivator but also as another personal link between the instructor and course participants.

Participant-instructor interaction is common in this course, but authenticity is still an issue, especially for those participants without previous teaching experience. To help teacher learners apply their knowledge and skills, previous distance versions of this course have called on guest lecturers from various fields or integrated a series of three case studies to be addressed in teams. The current iteration attempts to develop a community of practice by tapping the knowledge and experience of in-service, computer-using language teachers to facilitate participants' problem-solving, application, and self-reflection skills.

The final project epitomizes the thinking behind this course because it incorporates all of the conditions in whatever configuration is best for the participants' contexts. The learner decides the project's content and product; the project provides feedback from experts and peers, and it results in an authentic product that teacher learners can use outside of the L530 virtual classroom. These are the instructions for the final project from the L530 Web site:

Final Project

Individuals or groups will develop a technology-enhanced solution for a problem they foresee in their specific language-teaching context. Participants will apply their knowledge and experience of optimal CALL environments and technology. There is no limit on project types, but one idea is to extend some of the class activities or assignments done during the semester.

There are three parts to this project:

1. Inquiry brainstorm

A one-page inquiry brainstorm (like the case problems we have discussed) should be handed in on the specified date, briefly explaining the following:

Who are (or might be) your users/learners? Give a short profile of each of them.

What are your goals and your learners' goals for the class?

What is a problem that you have or anticipate having in your language classroom?

What solutions are possible? Include other information that will help us to understand the problem. After reading your problem, you need to find a CALL professional who is willing to work with you during your project. You will be responsible for contacting and planning interaction with this person.

2. Technology solution

Participants will hand in their technology solution to the problem that they outlined either on disk or on the Web. Along with this, participants should include self-reflection, described below.

3. Self-reflection

In one page or less, your reflection should explain:

(a) how your project (1) solves the problem you posed and (2) meets conditions for optimal learning

(b) how/whether your own learning goals (new skills or knowledge) for the project were met (including difficulties/problems encountered and how you solved these problems)

(c) how your solution could be improved in terms of the eight conditions (if you had more time, money, or skills)

(d) how the professional you worked with helped (or did not) and what difference it made to your project

Upon receiving the inquiry brainstorm, the instructor discusses the proposal in a number of e-mail exchanges, assisting the participant in finding a feasible technology solution, helping to focus the project, and providing feedback and help. This became a labor-intensive part of the course for the instructor; therefore, in the current iteration of the course, CALL experts assume some of these responsibilities. As the project instructions indicate, participants are required to find a CALL practitioner to assist them in their project. Participants ask for help on the TESLCA-L[1] electronic discussion list or contact the author of a Web site or activity that is relevant to their project.

The final project, like all of the class activities, has been carefully designed (and redesigned) to provide learners with opportunities to experience the model's learning conditions firsthand and to facilitate the development of activities based on the model for use in participants' classrooms. In essence, we are applying the principles that our participants are learning. We have, however, encountered challenges along the way, as described in the next section.

◈ PRACTICAL IDEAS

Practical ideas to address the problems of teaching methods courses through distance education flow from our experience and the model upon which the course is built. Some of the more easily remedied problems are those with course activities, community links, technological barriers, and case studies. Those that we need more

---

[1] To subscribe to the branch list TESLCA-L, you must first be a member of the main list, TESL-L. See instructions for joining on page 66.

time and experimentation to solve are those with learning styles, practical experience, and time constraints.

Emphasize Quality Teacher Education Regardless of the Technology

We quickly realized that the geographical distribution of participants and the technology itself could not be the focus of the course; rather, the emphasis must be on offering good teacher education regardless of the context. We initially expected problems to arise from the technology itself (and there were some), but we have struggled more with important content and method issues.

Ensure That Course Activities Follow the Learning Model

The on-line readings originally used in the course, although convenient for our geographically distributed learners, did not follow the learning environment model closely enough. Currently, a text specifically developed around our model is used. In addition, to provide more continuity in the focus of the course from beginning to end, we are moving from many small class activities to the integration of one big project that combines assignments used throughout the semester.

Design Opportunities for Learners to Connect
With the Larger Class Community

Participants may feel isolated even when feedback and electronic contact are abundant because they are participating at a different time and in a different place than are members of the class community. Participants are currently required to post a photo and personal profile to the electronic conference during the first part of the class. This gives them a better idea of who their classmates are. In addition, participants complete some of the activities in groups, which helps them to make closer links to other class members by developing clear points of interaction and helping them depend on each other.

Furthermore, we found the initial links with CALL experts and other members of the CALL community tenuous and short lived. Many of the former course participants communicated only one time with an expert for their final project. Our current goal is to create even stronger links to CALL educators by incorporating guest speakers and experts throughout the course in addition to final project mentors.

Instruct Participants in the Use of the Technology

The technology sometimes gets in the way of communicating. The several different electronic conferencing systems (forums) we have used are not intuitive to participants, and there is a lot of start-up time spent that could be used for other good purposes. We developed a set of job aids that gives step-by-step instructions on how to perform the most common tasks, which has worked well for many participants. However, we need to do something more for participants who are visual learners, which may include using a more graphical set of instructions.

Provide Additional Communication Channels

Technology presents a barrier in other ways. For example, expression is limited to the written word, and reading what others have written without the benefit of pragmatic cues may cause readers to form impressions that may or may not be accurate. At this point, we send participants private e-mail messages to determine where problems may have arisen and post messages presenting important information to the electronic conference to help mediate and clarify.

Develop and Refine Case Studies Thoroughly

Participants have commented that some of the cases were ambiguous or irrelevant. We are developing and testing more authentic and detailed cases for each unit.

Guide Participants to More Independent Learning Styles

Some participants have trouble reconciling previous styles of teaching and learning with the new styles of communicating required in this course. A rethinking of how different participants can learn on-line is necessary. We need to develop ways for participants who are not used to being self-guided and self-regulated and who tend to rely on an authoritative figure for their learning to discover new ways to organize their learning. Different kinds of overviews and options may be needed for different types of participants. For example, integrating a variety of media, such as video segments and graphic tools, can provide support for participants who learn better visually and decrease the high demand for reading that is inherent in a Web-based course.

Incorporate Practical Teaching Experiences

There is no built-in mechanism for field experience for those participants not currently teaching. We cannot observe participants applying course concepts in real classrooms. One solution that we are considering is asking teacher learners to teach and videotape a lesson that has been discussed by the class and to send the videotape to the instructor for evaluation.

Reduce Demands on Instructors

It takes a considerable amount of time to develop and manage a distance course, and that burden increases exponentially with each new participant. To address this problem, we have (a) developed job aids that help to answer routine questions, (b) replaced some of the more time-intensive instructional activities with others that the participants can share, and (c) attempted to provide more opportunities for participants to support their peers. However, we are still looking for ways to maintain the quality of interaction and instruction while relieving some of the demands on the instructor.

◈ CONCLUSION

We have learned a lot through our experiences with this course, and although the fundamental structure of the eight conditions remains the same, every iteration of the course is somewhat different because of our new insights and different participant needs. We have found that the benefits of offering teacher education courses in which there is a wide variety of learners and in which communication is supported by asynchronous and synchronous technologies include the potential for

- more time for participants to reflect on their current practices and on their own learning in the course
- increased individual participation, which is more obvious when the course is offered on-line and on-site at the same time (many quiet participants choose to participate more on-line)
- more individualized feedback from the instructor and peers as opportunities for participation increase
- a wider range of opinions and views
- self-paced/self-directed learning because of more individual processing time
- resource and inquiry-based learning rather than lecture-based learning

In summary, it is just as possible to provide quality distance education as it is to provide bad instruction on-site. Because teachers often teach how they were taught, we believe it is crucial to identify the characteristics of exemplary practice and then demonstrate them in how and what we teach. Participant comments show that the participants can clearly see our conscious implementation of the learning environment conditions in this CALL methods course. We believe that, by practicing what we preach, it is more likely for them to implement the same pedagogically sound philosophy in their classrooms.

◈ CONTRIBUTORS

Joy Egbert is an assistant professor of ESL and educational technology at Washington State University, in the United States. She is interested in CALL and teaching practice.

Chin-chi Chao is a doctoral candidate at Indiana University and an instructor of the L530: CALL course. Her dissertation research investigates on-line collaboration in teacher education.

CHAPTER 15

Avoiding the Pitfalls of Test Writing in a Distance-Learning Situation: Our Experience at United Arab Emirates University

Lisa Barlow and Christine Canning-Wilson

◈ INTRODUCTION

After driving my little Honda over the last huge pink sand dunes with the sun setting behind me, I was confident. I had driven to a distance learning center on the Gulf of Oman, then to another on the opposite side of the country on the coast of the Arabian Gulf, and was now heading to the last center located deep inside the country near the Empty Quarter of Saudi Arabia. In self-satisfaction, I felt certain that this time all exams were securely locked up in the directors' offices at the nine distance learning centers. After a good 12-hour day of personally delivering the multiple versions of these final exams, I felt I had overcome the challenge of test security. It was feasible to prevent leakage. The reliability and validity had been checked beforehand. This would be a successful final exam session. But, as always, problems began to crop up the next day.

This chapter describes the challenges we faced in producing multiple versions of English language exams and administering them during a 3-week final examination period. These exams were created for learners, who were currently teachers with an associate of arts teaching certificate or learners beginning their bachelor of arts (BA) degree in education, in a distance-learning program at the United Arab Emirates (UAE) University. Our experience, which took place in the fall of 1996 and winter of 1997, illustrates not only the difficulties we encountered with test writing and test security but also how these difficulties were eventually overcome.

The first challenge we faced was how to equalize and maintain the reliability of test items and texts for up to seven versions of the exams. For reasons explained below, each distance-learning center needed to have its own individualized set of exams that, in fairness to learners, had items of equal difficulty that would produce predictable results no matter when they were administered or where the learners took the exam.

The second challenge was how to retain validity when modifying and writing up to seven multiple versions of the same exam from a limited base of course objectives. Although the course ran for a full 16-week semester, the English language curriculum did not cover a large range of objectives. This was due in part to the fact that our distance-learning arrangement did not provide modern forms of communication between learner and teacher and allowed only bimonthly lectures, thus reducing the amount of English that could be acquired at the EFL elementary level.

A big disadvantage of our distance-learning testing arrangement was that the administration did not schedule English exams on the same day for all centers. During some semesters, English exams at the same level were administered to learners over a period of 7–10 days. Thus, our third challenge was how to vary test items and text subject matter without sacrificing reliability and test security so that learners who took the exams in the first few days did not disseminate the format and possible variations of test items to learners in distant centers with later exam dates. Although the nine distance-learning centers are separated by distances ranging from 50 to several hundred miles and learners have no e-mail or Internet access available to them, they somehow manage to have or make acquaintances in each center. Thus, immediately following a testing session, learners are able to communicate freely over the telephone concerning exam format and questions. This test security challenge was probably the most difficult to overcome.

Lastly, in keeping with University General Requirements Unit (UGRU) guidelines, we needed to produce culturally sensitive, but interesting and applicable, test material for our learners. This challenge was heightened by the fact that our learners not only attended classes at centers in different parts of the country but came from different tribes.

◈ CONTEXT

The United Arab Emirates

The UAE is a country located toward the middle of the Arabian Gulf. It is bordered on the north by the Arabian Gulf, to the west by the Qatar and Saudi Arabia, to the south by Oman and Saudi Arabia, and to the east by the Gulf of Oman. The UAE government is composed of seven emirates: Abu Dhabi, Dubai, Sharja, Ajman, Umm al Qaiwain, Ras al Khaimah (RAK), and Fujaira. The federation of these seven emirates was established in 1971, with Abu Dhabi as its capital.

Since its establishment, the UAE has witnessed a remarkable and swift economic development. It has rapidly maximized the benefits obtained through its immense oil proceeds to provide for the basic requirements of society. The UAE has one of the highest per capita incomes in the world, and the main cities of Abu Dhabi and Dubai boast modern architecture and four-lane highways.

UAE University and Distance Learning

The UAE government established UAE University in 1971 as an open university where any citizen of the country could attain a degree at no monetary charge. The distance-learning program for teachers in the UAE was created in 1982 by the Faculty of Education. The purpose of the program is to upgrade elementary and secondary school teachers from their associate of arts teaching certificate to a BA in education. The teachers in this program have attended various teaching colleges throughout the UAE, and most have been teaching for 2 or more years. The exception is the learners who study at Merfa, a remote area on the road to Qatar. Merfa learners take all of their courses for a BA in education at the Merfa distance-learning center. The attainment of

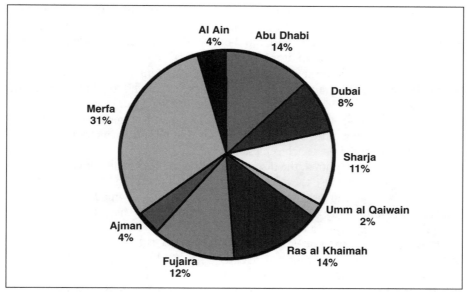

FIGURE 1. Percent of Total Learners Enrolled at Distance-Learning Centers of the United Arab Emirates University

this BA grants the teachers a substantial boost in salary and an opportunity to go into supervisory and administrative positions, and gives them prestige and confidence among their colleagues.

Nine distance-learning centers have been designated at the following sites: Abu Dhabi, Dubai, Sharja, Ajman, Fujaira, Umm al Qaiwain, RAK, Al Ain, and Merfa. Each of the distance-learning centers is run by a full-time director who handles all program administration and teaching responsibilities. Figure 1 shows the relative sizes of learner populations at each center. As can be quickly seen, the majority of learners are registered at the Merfa Center. This campus was established because busing these learners to the UAE University campus in Al Ain would be prohibitively expensive and time consuming for learners.

The learners at each of these centers receive their lectures live. That is, professors travel to each center to give their lectures on a bimonthly basis. Each center is equipped with television, video, and computer labs. However, the computers are not hooked up to the UAE University e-mail program or to the country's Internet system. One of the main reasons for this is that there are no computer support services at the centers. The center director must request a computer support staff member to come from UAE University in Al Ain whenever a problem occurs in the labs. Consequently, in these otherwise high-tech learning centers, telephone connections and university drivers (who deliver mail, books, exams, supplies, and the like to the centers) are the main modes of communication among instructors, learners, and the university.

The socioeconomic backgrounds of the learners in the distance-learning program are usually middle to upper middle class. Additionally, most of the teachers in the program are women, which means that they come from double-income homes (average marriage age in the UAE is in the range of 18–24). Because male and female learners are married with children and teaching full-time during the day, they face special challenges as far as organizing their time for study and class attendance. Although most of these women have hired help in the home and an extended family that can care for their children, it is still often impossible for them to make time for studying and attending lectures. The male distance-learning participants often have private businesses that take a lot of their postteaching hours. Fortunately, the distance-learning program does not require them to take a full load of classes each semester. It is possible for them to schedule a class with lectures only two or three times a month. Such a schedule, however, is rare, and most learners try to take a full load of three or four classes each semester.

In terms of time required, the distance-learning program is also advantageous to the learners simply because they do not have to travel to Al Ain. The establishment of the distance-learning program in the various centers has made earning a BA practical for the majority of teachers who would otherwise have to take a 2-year sabbatical from their jobs to live and study in Al Ain.

It was not until winter of 1996 that the university's UGRU began its involvement with the distance-learning program. UGRU offers freshman-level courses that all learners must complete to enter their majors. All first-year learners are required to take English, math, computer courses (taught in English), Arabic, Gulf society, and Islamic thought courses (taught in Arabic).

The university's UGRU has three levels of English, ranging from the beginning to the intermediate level. Learners are placed into the appropriate level after taking an English language proficiency exam developed exclusively for the distance-learning program. Each level focuses on reading and writing. Listening and speaking are not taught because of the limited teacher-learner contact hours and lack of need for these skills in further courses and future work. Other course objectives are to develop critical thinking skills, reading, research skills, and good study habits. It is important to note that UGRU involvement in the Merfa center means that faculty members design programs and also write and implement curriculum and tests, yet they are not included in any administrative decision making.

As noted previously, with the exception of the Merfa center, the distance-learning program serves a population of older learners who juggle work, home, and family responsibilities. Thus, the program must confront problems such as scheduling courses at times that are convenient to the learners and assigning learning tasks that cover the material yet are attainable from working learners.

Administration of Exams in Distance-Learning Settings

Although the distance-learning literature rarely addresses types and formats of testing, it does outline various methods of administering exams in distance-learning programs. For the most part, exams are given in one of the following five ways, each with its advantages and disadvantages (Daniel & Turok, 1975).

First, exams may be sent by mail to remote sites of schools that hold examinations simultaneously for distance-learning and regular learners. Staff members at the site guarantee that the examination is properly supervised and then send the papers back to the main school for grading. Results are either mailed or e-mailed to learners.

Alternatively, a written exam may be administered at the university at the end of each semester in traditional fashion. Distance-learning participants are given a date and time to come and take the exam. Their performance is then evaluated, and their grades are posted at the center. In this scenario, distance-learning participants may sit with regular university learners taking an exam for the same course taught at the university (Wedemeyer, 1977).

A third, more modern alternative for learners taking a distance-learning course by computer is to take the exam at home by e-mail. Learners usually have a time limit to complete the exam and e-mail their answers back. This type of testing usually employs an essay format in which the learner needs book and note references to complete answers (Agustsson, 1997).

Another form of computer exam can be given at the university itself. The learners are given a time period (from a day to a week) to take the exam, which is computer generated and objective in format. It consists of a large bank of items from which a subset of items is randomly selected after the learner accesses the exam. This arrangement is advantageous in terms of test security. Learners who take the exam early cannot successfully leak items to learners taking the exam later because the particular items selected by the computer at that time will, for the most part, be different (Jeppesen, 1997).

A final common way of administering exams in distance-learning programs is to give them orally. The course teacher sits at the distance-learning center and asks the learner (in person or on the phone) a number of questions. In this arrangement, the teacher can easily expand the question if the learner is weak in his or her answer. On the other hand, if the learner gives solid responses to easier questions, the teacher can quickly skip to more difficult ones.

The method we used in the UAE distance-learning program was a variation on the second approach described previously.

◈ DESCRIPTION

In our distance-learning arrangement, all of the UGRU courses were 16 hours in length. Lectures were divided into eight 2-hour seminars that were delivered by a teacher who drove to each center every other week. Although there was television, video, radio, and computer equipment at each center, it was not used for English lectures. Thus, oral teaching was limited and concentrated to a few intensive periods spread out over a 16-week semester. In between these periods, the learners studied on their own at home, with textbooks and supplementary materials provided by the university, but without the possibility of consulting teachers by e-mail, phone, or mail. Although there was a large, computer-assisted language learning program in Al Ain, these files were not downloaded onto computers in the distance-learning centers because of a lack of technical support to keep them up and running. In addition, e-mail from the Internet is not available. UAE distance-learning participants are not allowed access to the Internet due to censorship restrictions placed upon learners by the university. Thus, learners could not consult with a teacher by e-mail unless they had their own computer system at home. In most cases, communication with the teacher was restricted to the class lecture and time before and after the lecture. There were no office hours for lecturers. One full-time staff teacher kept office hours, but for only 1 day a week, and that teacher was not necessarily the one teaching the course an inquiring learner was registered in.

Learners were required to attend six of eight lectures to pass a course. All course work had to be turned in by assigned times and dates. Written assignments were turned in twice: once for teacher input and a second time by the learner with corrections and revisions completed. If one learner's homework was duplicated from another's, both were required to do the assignment again. Two quizzes are given during the third and seventh lectures. A midterm was administered after the fifth lecture (Week 10), as was a final exam upon completion of the eighth lecture (Week 16). Because all UAE University learner rules and guidelines applied to the distance-learning population also, these learners completed examinations at their distance-learning center within the same time frame specified for regular UAE University learners.

The total number of learners in the fall of 1996 was 312, spread over three levels with the majority studying at Level 3. The total population for English Level 1 (E1) was 59; English Level 2 (E2), 60; and English Level 3 (E3), 193.

The curriculum followed UGRU E1 and E2, with the exception of the listening component. E1 was aimed at false beginners and E2 to beginners. E3 departs from the UGRU curriculum in that it focuses heavily on grammar, reading, and paragraph writing skills. Each of these E3 skills is taught in a content-based unit.

◈ DISTINGUISHING FEATURES

Strong Incentives for Learners

Unlike some foreign distance-learning programs in which learners enroll out of interest and where attrition rates are high, participants in the UAE distance-learning program had strong incentives. Completion of a BA entitled the graduates not only to a substantial salary increase but also to a rise in position and status in the workplace. These incentives, along with university-imposed time restrictions for completing the degree, curbed a high dropout rate that is often lamented in other distance-learning programs (Al Rawaf, 1990; Lampikoski, 1975). They may also have exacerbated the testing challenges we faced.

Challenges in Testing

Staff administered the exams at each of the distance-learning centers during a 2-week exam period. The challenges that arose in using this approach, as well as in creating the exams, involved test reliability, validity, security, and cultural content.

Reliability Challenges

The first challenge we faced was how to equalize and maintain the reliability of test items and texts. According to Coombe and Hubley (1998), a test is considered reliable if it yields similar results when given at another date and location. In our case, this meant the test would function in the same way at each distance-learning center. Also, if a test is reliable, the score gained will approach the true score of the examinee each time it is given and in a consistent way with different examinees. For example, when Fatma in Fujaira sits down and takes the test, her score will be as true as Alia's in Abu Dhabi.

In our distance-learning assessments, one way we tried to ensure the reliability of items in the grammar sections was to write one model sentence and then vary it by one word 7–10 times, depending on the number of versions required. For example:

I _____ to the store yesterday. (go)
She _____ to the store yesterday. (go)
She _____ to the store last week. (go)

We used a more technical approach to gain an additional degree of reliability in reading texts for our exams. First, the required number of texts were written. Then, these texts were evaluated by the author, as well as the head of the course, to determine if they were truly parallel versions of each other. After this, an additional measure was employed to benchmark the level of language used in each text. They were run through one of two computer readability-level programs—Flesch Kincaid (as it appears in Microsoft Word) or Right Writer (1992). This way, whether a reading was on Mexico or Australia, learners at each center faced a text that was at the same reading level, as indicated by this additional technical measure. We realize that native-speaker readability formulas are a highly debatable measure of true readability—especially for second language learners. Nevertheless, the use of readability scales is commonplace throughout the Arabian Gulf region (Hogan, West, & Farrell, 1999).

Validity Challenges

Our second challenge was how to maintain validity when writing multiple versions of the same exam from a limited base of course objectives. By validity, we mean that the test actually measures what it is intended to measure (Brown, 1987).

When a regular 16-week university course designed for more than 140 contact hours a semester was reduced to a distance-learning course that met once every other week for a total of only 16 hours, many target and course performance objectives had to be revised or cut. Although the new course still met accreditation standards, only the bare bones of the curriculum were left. For example, only a limited number of grammar points could be taught in E2. With this minimal number of grammar objectives, our challenge as test writers was to produce items that were valid (based on course content) but not predictable. This challenge was heightened by the fact that, following UAE University policy and the norm in school systems and universities in the Arabian Gulf, the E1 and E2 distance-learning exams had to be achievement rather than general proficiency exams.

In the end, to achieve content validity, only items based on the course curriculum that was actually taught to E1 and E2 were included in the examination. In other words, no items tested general proficiency, critical thinking, or ability to expand English patterns learned previously.

Security Challenges

As Coombe and Hubley (1998) explain, security is part of reliability and validity. Further, they suggest that cultural attitudes toward collaborative test-taking are a threat to test security and thus to reliability and validity. As noted previously, distance-learning participants in the UAE have been known to contact learners at other centers immediately after taking a test and report verbatim what was on the exam. Thus, learners who have the exams on Days 6, 7, and 8 can acquire and memorize a pool of actual items before they ever take their exams.

Our third challenge, then, was how to maintain reliability while safeguarding test security so that learners who took the exams in the first few days did not effectively disseminate information about test format and items to learners in other distance-learning centers. Overcoming this challenge was not easy.

In the spring of 1996, distance-learning faculty produced 12 different exams with A and B versions for the E2 testing dates. Fortunately, E3 had fewer classes and only eight separate test dates. Yet to produce this many exams for this higher level course would have been an overwhelming task. Faculty questioned whether it was necessary to write eight exams, with A and B versions, just to ensure test security. Then we realized that we could get by with only five exams if we mixed versions when administering them. For example, if learners received exam version 3 on the first exam date, version 5 on the second date, version 4 on the third, version 2 on the fourth, and version 1 on the fifth, it would be impossible for learners taking exams on the last three dates to predict which exam they would receive. Trying to memorize and write essays for all five versions would be a monumental task for learners. Meanwhile, instead of writing so many different versions, we could spend our time creating higher quality exams.

Other test security challenges arose because UGRU faculty members have no administrative control. This means that we do not proctor our own exams—the distance-learning faculty members assigned to each center do. This arrangement led to several security problems. The biggest involved cheating due to inadequate space in the examination room (requiring learners to sit close to each other) and the small number of proctors.

Additional security problems arose, however, because of the distance-learning arrangement. For this reason, some proctors assigned to the exam did not know the learners by face. Although the UAE University provides the distance-learning participants with IDs, they are not photo IDs like the ones regular university learners receive in Al Ain. Thus, at the distance-learning center it was possible for someone to take an exam, show an ID, and still not be recognized as a nonstudent. This problem could have been reduced if the classroom teacher had been proctoring the exam.

Various cultural behaviors often lead to additional test security challenges at universities in the Arabian Gulf, and our distance-learning program was no exception. One such challenge arises when female learners take exams veiled. With her face covered with a veil, a female learner's face cannot be seen by a male proctor and she cannot be easily identified—especially by a stranger. Consequently, a registered learner can have someone else take the exam for her without anyone knowing.

To check security and reliability, the mean scores of tests given at different times were scrutinized. Comparing the results of multiple, repeated exam versions administered on different days showed that mean scores did not rise above one letter grade. Even in the E2 course, which included men and women from the same emirate (RAK) who took the exam over a 9-day period, mean scores of different administrations were virtually the same. For men, the mean score was 26.14, and for women, it was 24.19. Results from a third test (from Sharja) were scrutinized because that examination date fell equally between the two RAK testing periods for the same exam. There were no increases or differences in test scores that were significant. Therefore, we concluded that test reliability and security had been maintained.

Cultural Content Challenges

Our last challenge was how to produce culturally sensitive, yet interesting and applicable, test material for our learners. As with UGRU English texts and courses produced in-house at UAE University, our distance-learning courses avoided topics related to religion, sex, politics, and music. In addition to that, however, to be culturally sensitive, we had to be aware of additional aspects of Gulf culture. Test items and texts needed to reflect an awareness of tribal/family alliances, an intercultural hierarchy, and political and social tensions specific to the Gulf. If they did not, problems could easily result. Culturally insensitive items could produce emotional reactions in examinees that would take them off task and reduce the test's validity and reliability. Take, for example, the following sample item:

Example A. *The Shamsee tribe is larger than the Mansoori tribe.*

This sentence may seem like a simple comparative statement. However, the fact that the Al Shamsee and Al Mansoori tribes had been warring with each other for more than 100 years gives it additional meaning. Mansoori learners, who constitute the majority at the Merfa center, could easily be upset by this item.

Soccer is the number one sport in the Gulf, so the next example item might seem to be especially relevant and interesting to our learners.

Example B. *Kuwait has a stronger football team than the UAE.*

Nevertheless, this simple statement strikes a nerve with many learners. Sports competition between Gulf nations is keen, and during a past World Cup playoff, Kuwait beat UAE to go to the finals. Thus, reactions to this statement could have caused an emotional response among examinees and taken them off task.

A last example of a culturally insensitive question is one that appeared in a careers grid.

Example C. *Careers Grid: The career of a police officer does not require university education, the work is dangerous, and the salary is low.*

This item refers to the job of a police officer in rather derogatory terms. Furthermore, on the grid it was placed in the bottom position, below nurse, which is generally considered to be a much lower level career here. In the UAE, the police and military are major employers, and the job of a police officer carries high status. It requires special training and pays a higher salary than many other jobs. Thus, when the examinees saw police officer placed as the lowest profession on the grid, they could have felt that the job of their father, brother, or husband had been insulted. In a culture that considers police and military officers' work to be as reputable as a doctor's, this item could even be perceived as threatening their place in society. This discomfort could in turn cause the learners to go off task and color their attempts at producing the correct responses.

In retrospect, these culturally insensitive blunders in test writing might seem obvious. Nevertheless, when multiple test versions are required and many items must be written quickly, factors such as validity and reliability seem to require more attention, and cultural factors—especially those pertaining to learners at distant-learning centers—may be overlooked.

❖ PRACTICAL IDEAS

Creating and administering valid, reliable, secure, and culturally sensitive tests is always a difficult challenge. When these tests are given at a number of widely scattered distance-learning centers, additional challenges arise. From our experience dealing with these challenges, we can offer several suggestions to distance-learning programs concerned with testing issues. Some of these suggestions may apply only in certain cultural settings; others are more generally applicable.

Increase Test Security With Appropriate Procedures and Unified Examination Dates

Distance-learning testing should follow uniform and regulated procedures, which should be developed and standardized over time. Also, to promote test security, distance-learning programs should mandate unified examination dates whenever possible. The increased test security would lead to improved validity and practicality.

Involve Classroom Teachers in Test Administration

For cultural settings like ours, we recommend that distance-learning programs always include classroom teachers as coproctors of exams. If teachers who know learners by appearance are present, certain test security difficulties are minimized. For instance, if the examination were proctored by the regular classroom teacher and that teacher were female, she could check to see if a veiled learner was, in fact, her learner. Even if the classroom teacher were male, he might know the veiled learner by some means, such as her voice, posture, or handwriting. Without the classroom teacher present, however, the identity of the learner is simply accepted in most cases to avoid an uncomfortable cultural scene.

Consider Other Types of Assessment

Instead of traditional high-stakes testing practices, we recommend the implementation of alternative forms of testing. For example, learner assessment through written or orally presented projects would eliminate many of the problems we encountered. Another option could be the use of computer-generated examinations.

Address Testing Challenges During Program Planning

Finally, for distance-learning programs that are just starting, our most important recommendation is to understand each of the four challenges described in this chapter during the initial planning phases. Then, the potential pitfalls can be recognized, and perhaps avoided, before the first examination is given.

❖ CONCLUSION

Distance-learning challenges are not limited to the delivery of instruction. As our experiences in the UAE University distance-learning program illustrate, testing at a distance also creates some special challenges. These are not insurmountable, but distance-learning program planners will do well to keep them in mind from the earliest stages. In this way, others may be able to avoid some of the pitfalls that we have experienced.

❖ CONTRIBUTORS

Lisa Barlow is the past director of the distance-learning program for the English Unit at the United Arab Emirates (UAE) University. Additionally, she was on the testing and measurements team for the university's University General Requirements Unit (UGRU) English Unit for 3 years. She worked on the curriculum planning team for Zayed University and led the formation of the Academic English as a Foreign Language Tract at UGRU. Currently, she is a lecturer at UAE University and is working on her doctorate in education in TEFL at Exeter University.

Christine Canning-Wilson is a former lecturer and test writing specialist for the UAE University's distance-learning program. She was also on the testing and measurements team for the university's EFL Unit for 3 years. She served as a supervisor of Student Support Services and lecturer at UGRU. Presently, she is employed at Higher Colleges of Technology—Abu Dhabi CERT Campus.

References

Adult learning and literacy A.L.L. points bulletin. (1991, December). 3(6). Washington, DC: U.S. Department of Education.

Agustsson, H. (1997). The distance education program of Verkmenntaskolinn at Akureyri (VMA). *Educational Media Instruction Journal, 34*(2), 54–56.

Al Rawaf, H. S. (1990). *An open university for women in Saudi Arabia: Problems and prospects.* Doctoral dissertation, Loughborough University of Technology, Loughborough, United Kingdom.

Auerbach, E. (1992). *Making meaning, making change.* Washington, DC: Center for Applied Linguistics & Delta Systems.

Bates, A.W. (1995). *Technology, open learning, and distance education.* New York: Routledge.

Bender, W. N., McLaughlin, P. J., & Ehrhart, L. M. (1993). ADDNET network: A low-end technology success. *T.H.E. Journal, 21*(2), 96–100.

Benhalim, T., Berces, E., Dong, M., & Willoughby, D. (1993, Spring). *Information sheet.* Designed for TESOL Program Design course (FL-ED 595), California State University, Fullerton.

Bentley, L. (1993). *CSUF Extended Education distance learning orientation packet.* Unpublished materials. California State University Fullerton Extended Education.

Bowers, R. (1997, January). Using HTML for online editing. *TESOL CALL Newsletter*, p. 1.

Brooks, J. G., & Brooks, M. G. (1993). *The case for constructivist classrooms.* Alexandria, VA: Association for Supervision and Curriculum Development.

Brown, H. D. (1987). *Principles of language learning and teaching.* Upper Saddle River, NJ: Prentice Hall.

Brown, H. D. (1994). *Teaching by principles: An interactive approach to language pedagogy.* Upper Saddle River, NJ: Prentice Hall Regents.

Carroll, T. G. (2000, February). *If we didn't have the schools we have today, would we create the schools we have today?* Keynote address at the conference of the Society for Information Technology and Teacher Education, San Diego, CA.

California Teachers of English to Speakers of Other Languages (CATESOL). (1995). *CATESOL position statement on distance education for non-native learners of English.* Glendale, CA: Author.

Catterick, D. (2000). Language teaching and the online learning revolution. *SATEFL* [Scottish Association for the Teaching of English as a Foreign Language] *Newsletter, 19*(3), 6–8.

Chen, A-Y., Mashhadi, A., Ang, D., & Harkrider, N. (1999). Cultural issues in the design of technology-enhanced learning systems. *British Journal of Educational Technology, 30*(3), 217–230.

Chisman, F., Wrigley, H., & Ewen, D. (1993). *ESL and the American dream*. Washington, DC: Southport Institute for Policy Analysis.

Christiansen, D. K. (1996). *The preparedness, attitudes, and opinions of secondary school teachers concerning the education of limited English proficient students*. Unpublished master's thesis, Brigham Young University, Provo, UT.

Cohen, A. (1990). Writing as process and product in language learning. In A. Cohen, *Language learning* (pp. 103–131). Rowley, MA: Newbury House Publishers.

Collis, B. (1999). Designing for differences: Cultural issues in the design of WWW-based course-support sites. *British Journal of Educational Technology, 30*(3), 201–215.

Coombe, C., & Hubley, N. (1998, March). *Creating effective classroom tests*. Paper presented at the 32nd Annual TESOL Convention, Seattle, WA.

Cooper, L. (2000). Online courses: Tips for making them work. *T.H.E. Journal, 27*(8), 87–92.

Daniel, J. S., & Turok, B. (1975). Teaching by telephone. In E. Ljosa (Ed.), *The system of distance education* (pp. 133–140). Brighton, United Kingdom: International Council on Correspondence Education.

Davis, D. J. (1990). Text comprehension: Implications for the design of self-instructional materials. In M. G. Moore (Ed.), *Contemporary issues in American distance education* (pp. 243–259). Oxford: Pergamon.

Day, R. (1984). Career aspects of graduate training in ESL. *TESOL Quarterly, 18*, 501–514.

Dustheimer, C., & Gillett, R. (1999). The history of ELT in Korea. In G. Crocetti (Ed.), *The KOTESOL handbook: Teaching English in Korea*. Seoul, South Korea: Moonyedang Press.

Egan, M. W., & Gibb, G. S. (1997). Student-centered instruction for the design of telecourses. *New Directions for Teaching and Learning, 71*, 33–39.

Egbert, J., Chao, C., & Hanson-Smith, E. (1999). Computer assisted language learning environments: An overview. In J. Egbert & E. Hanson-Smith (Eds.), *CALL environments: Research, practice, and critical issues* (pp. 1–13). Alexandria, VA: TESOL.

Egbert, J., Chao, C., & Ngeow, K. (2000, February). Three community building strategies and their impacts in an on-line course. In D. A. Willis, J. D. Price, & J. Willis (Eds.), *Society for Information Technology and Teacher Education 11th international conference: Proceedings of SITE 2000* (pp. 216–221). Charlottesville, VA: Association for the Advancement of Computing in Education.

Egbert, J., & Jessup, L. (1996). Analytic and systemic analyses of computer-supported language learning environments. *TESL-EJ, 2*(2). Retrieved April 2, 2001, from the World Wide Web: http://www-writing.berkeley.edu/TESL-EJ/ej06/a1.html.

England, L., & Roberts, C. (1989). A survey of foreign students in MA-TESOL programs. *TESOL Newsletter, 23*(6), 5.

Epstein, R. I. (1994). *Evaluation of the RELC program of cooperation in human resource development*. Unpublished technical paper. SEAMEO Regional Language Centre & York University English Language Institute.

Epstein, R. I. (1997). *CERTESL program evaluation*. Unpublished technical paper. Extension Division, University of Saskatchewan, Saskatoon, Canada.

Feyten, C., & Nutta, J. (Eds.). (1999). *Virtual instruction: Issues and insights from an international perspective*. Denver, CO: Libraries Unlimited.

Frankel, I., & Fuchs, M. (1995). *Crossroads, Book 2*. New York: Oxford University Press.

Freire, P. (1981). *Education for critical consciousness*. New York: Continuum.

Fulford, C. P., & Zhang, S. (1993). Perceptions of interaction: The critical predictor in distance education. *The American Journal of Distance Education, 7*(3), 8–21.

Garshick, E. (Ed.). (1995). *Directory of professional preparation programs in TESOL in the United States and Canada: 1995–1997*. Washington, DC: TESOL.

Goodlad, J. I. (1994). *Educational renewal: Better teachers, better schools*. San Francisco: Jossey-Bass.

Grosse, C. U. (1999). Teaching business languages via distance learning. *Global business language*. Lafayette, IN: Purdue University.

Guinn, S. G. (1996). *Elementary teachers' perceptions of issues relating to LEP mainstreaming*. Unpublished master's thesis, Brigham Young University, Provo, UT.

Ham, V. (2000, February). *Enough of virtuality: What of virtuosity? A research agenda for the "online" delivery of teacher professional development*. Paper presented at the conference of the Society for Information Technology and Teacher Education, San Diego, CA.

Hawkes, M., & Cambre, M. (2000). The co$t factor: When is interactive distance technology justifiable? *T.H.E. Journal, 28*(1), 26–32.

Hazari, S., & Schnorr, D. (1999). Leveraging student feedback to improve teaching in Web-based courses. *T.H.E. Journal, 26*(11), 30–38.

Heinich, R., Molenda, M., Russell, J. D., & Smaldino, S. E. (1999). *Instructional media and technologies for learning* (6th ed.). Englewood Cliffs, NJ: Prentice-Hall.

Henderson, L. (1996). Instructional design of interactive multimedia: A cultural critique. *Education Technology Research and Development, 44*(4), 85–104.

Hogan, K., West, K., & Farrell, N. (1999). *An investigation into the effectiveness of the Flesch-Kincaid measure of the readability for course materials used in the English programmes at HCT*. Dubai, United Arab Emirates: Higher Colleges of Technology.

Holmes, M. (1996, September). Marking student work on the computer. *The Internet TESL Journal*. Retrieved April 2, 2001, from the World Wide Web: http://www.aitech.ac.jp/~iteslj/Articles/Holmes-ComputerMarking/index.html.

Intelecom. (Producer). (1996). *Crossroads Café* [Videotape]. Pasadena, CA: Intelecom.

Iowa Communications Network. (2001). The ICN story. Retrieved April 3, 2001, from the World Wide Web: http://www.icn.state.ia.us/about/story/history.html.

Iowa Long Distance Alliance. (1995). *Interactive television workshop* [Handbook]. Des Moines, IA: Author.

Iowa Public Television (IPTV). (2001). Video classroom data. Retrieved April 2, 2001, from the World Wide Web: http://www3.iptv.org/iowa_database/classroomStats/cfm.

Jackson, M. I'll be there. On *The best of Michael Jackson: Anthology*. Uni/Motown B000001ABC.

Jeppesen, K. (1997). Distance education in the University College Education, Iceland. *Educational Media Instruction Journal, 34*(2), 57–59.

Jolly, J., & Robinson, L. *Real-life English*. (1988). Austin, TX: Steck-Vaughn.

Jones, B. F., Valdez, G., Nowakowski, J., & Rasmussen, C. (1995). New times demand new ways of learning. In *Plugging In: Choosing and Using Educational Technology*. Naperville, IL: North Central Regional Educational Laboratory. Retrieved April 2, 2001, from the World Wide Web: http://www.ncrel.org/sdrs/edtalk/newtimes.htm.

Kagan, S. (1994). *Cooperative learning*. San Clemente, CA: Kagan Cooperative Learning.

Killion, J. (1997, April). *Establishing community in a virtual classroom*. Paper presented at the Teaching in the Community Colleges Online Conference, Honolulu, HI. Retrieved April 2, 2001, from the World Wide Web: http://leahi.kcc.hawaii.edu/org/tcc_conf97/pres/killion.html.

Kroder, S. L., Suess, J., & Sachs, D. (1998). Lessons in launching Web-based graduate courses. *T.H.E. Journal, 25*(10), 66–69.

Lampikoski, K. (1975). *Some key reasons an individual becomes interested in study by distance education*. Paper presented at the European Home Study Council Autumn Workshop, Helsinki, Finland.

Lesikar, R.V., Pettit, J. D., Jr., & Flatley, M. E. (1999). *Basic business communication* (8th ed.). Boston: Irwin/McGraw Hill.

Los Angeles Unified School District (LAUSD). (1991). *Learning English*. Los Angeles: LAUSD, Division of Adult and Occupational Education.

Los Angeles Unified School District (LAUSD). (1994). *Putting English to work*. Los Angeles: LAUSD, Division of Adult and Occupational Education.

Microsoft. (2001). Microsoft Word 2000 [Computer software]. Redmond, WA: Microsoft. (Available from http://www.microsoft.com/)

Minicz, E. (1997). *Crossroads Café partner guide*. Boston: Heinle & Heinle.

Minicz, E. (1997). *Crossroads Café teacher's resource book A*. Boston: Heinle & Heinle.

Minicz, E. (1997). *Crossroads Café teacher's resource book B*. Boston: Heinle & Heinle.

Minicz, E., Weddel, K., Powell, K., Omori, L., & Cuomo, A. (1998). *Crossroads Café assessment A*. Boston: Heinle & Heinle.

Minicz, E., Weddel, K., Powell, K., Omori, L., & Cuomo, A. (1998). *Crossroads Café assessment B*. Boston: Heinle & Heinle.

National Center for Education Statistics. (1991). *Digest of education statistics, 1990*. Washington, DC: U.S. Department of Education.

National Council of State Supervisors of Foreign Language (NCSSFL). (1990). *Position statement on distance learning in foreign Languages*. Retrieved November 16, 2000, from the World Wide Web: http://www.wnsc.org/spanish/dlsig_1990paper.htm. (A revised version of this document will be available from http://www.ncssfl.org as of January 2002)

Netscape Gold (Version 3.0) [Computer software]. (1996). Mountain View, CA: Netscape Communications Corporation. (Latest version available from http://home.netscape.com /browsers/index.html)

Newby, T. J., Stepich, D. A., Lehman, J. D., & Russell, J. D. (2000). *Instructional technology for teaching and learning: Designing instruction, integrating computers, and using media* (2nd ed.). Upper Saddle River, NJ: Prentice Hall.

Nunan, D. (1992). *Research methods in language learning*. Cambridge: Cambridge University Press.

Nutta, J., & Feyten, C. (1999). Mapping space and time: Virtual instruction as global ritual. In C. Feyten & J. Nutta (Eds.), *Virtual instruction: Issues and insights from an international perspective* (pp. 1–5). Denver: Libraries Unlimited.

Office of Bilingual Education and Minority Language Affairs (OBEMLA). (1993). *SEA Title VII data report summary*. Washington, DC: Author.

Opp-Beckman, L. (2000). *Welcome to Leslie Opp-Beckman's homepage OPPortunities in English to speakers of other languages*. Eugene, OR: University of Oregon, American English Institute. Retrieved April 2, 2001, from the World Wide Web: http://darkwing.uoregon.edu/~leslieob/index.html.

Osguthorpe, R. T., Harris, R. C., Harris, M. F., & Black, S. (Eds.). (1995). *Partnership schools: Centers for educational renewal*. San Francisco: Jossey-Bass.

Pacific Bell's BlueWeb'n update. (2000). Retrieved April 2, 2001, from the World Wide Web: http://www.kn.pacbell.com/wired/bluewebn/.

Parker, A. (1997, Autumn/Winter). A distance education how-to manual: Recommendations from the field. *Educational Technology Review, 8*, 8.

Parker, L. A., & Monson, M. K. (1980). *More than meets the eye: The research on effectiveness of broadcast radio, SCA, and teleconferencing for instruction*. Madison, WI: Instructional Communications Systems, University of Wisconsin-Extension.

Pearlman, B. (1994). Designing groupware. *ISTE (International Society for Technology in Education) Update, 6*(5), 1–2.

QuickTime [Computer software]. (n.d.). Cupertino, CA: Apple. (Most recent version available from http://www.apple.com/quicktime/products)

Ramirez, S., & Savage, K. (1999). *On common ground teacher's resource book: Distance learning edition*. Pasadena, CA: Intelecom.

Reinhardt, J., & Isbell, K. (1999, October/November). Teaching in cyberspace: Tales from the trenches. *TESOL Matters,* p. 17.

Richards, J., & Crookes, G. (1988). The practicum in TESOL. *TESOL Quarterly, 22*, 9–27.

RightWriter [computer software]. (1992). Carmel, IN: Que Software.

Rodes, P., Knapczyk, D., Chapman, C., & Chung, H. (2000). Involving teachers in Web-based professional development. *T.H.E. Journal, 27*(10), 94–102.

Rowntree, D. (1998). Assessing the quality of materials-based teaching and learning. *Open Learning, 13*(3), 12–22.

Rubrecht, P. (1990). *Accreditation of ESL teachers in Saskatchewan.* Unpublished research study for the Saskatchewan Council for Educators of Non-English Speakers.

Russell, T. (1999). *The no significant difference phenomenon.* Retrieved April 2, 2001, from the World Wide Web: http://nova.teleeducation.nb.ca/nosignificantdifference/.

Ryan, R. C. (2000). Student assessment comparison of lecture and online construction equipment and methods classes. *T.H.E. Journal, 27*(6), 78–83.

Savage, K. L., & Mooney-Gonzalez, P. (with Hoffman, E.). (1996). *Crossroads Café photo stories A.* Boston: Heinle & Heinle.

Savage, K. L., & Mooney-Gonzalez, P. (with Hoffman, E.). (1997). *Crossroads Café photo stories B.* Boston: Heinle & Heinle.

Savage, K., Mooney-Gonzalez, P., &McMullin, M. (with Weddel, K.). (1996). *Crossroads Café worktext A.* Boston: Heinle & Heinle.

Savage, K., Mooney-Gonzalez, P., & McMullin, M. (with Weddel, K.). (1997). *Crossroads Café worktext B.* Boston: Heinle & Heinle.

Schulz Novak, D. (1996). *Report summarizing the quality initiative for distance education in the Extension Division at the University of Saskatchewan.* Unpublished paper, Extension Division, University of Saskatchewan, Saskatoon, Canada.

SEAMEO-Canada Programme of Cooperation in Human Resource Development. (1993). *A distance education TEFL programme: Tutor training manual.* Singapore: SEAMEO Regional Language Centre; Toronto: York University English Language Institute.

Sener, J. (1997, March). ALN's relations: Current educational trends and concepts and their relations to ALN. Distance education/Distance learning. *ALN Magazine, 1*(1). Retrieved March 30, 2001, from the World Wide Web: http://www.aln.org/alnweb/magazine/issue1/Sener/Sener.htm.

Shale, D., & Gomes, J. (1998). Performance indicators and university distance education providers. *Journal of Distance Education, 13*(1), 1–20.

Sheridan, J., Byrne, A. C., & Quina, K. (1989). Collaborative learning: Notes from the field. *College Teaching, 37*(2), 49–53.

Smith, P. L., & Ragan, T. J. (1999). *Instructional design.* Upper Saddle River, NJ: Prentice Hall.

Soh, B., & Soon, Y. (1991). English by e-mail: Creating a global classroom via the medium of computer technology. *ELT Journal, 45*(4), 287–292.

Soliman, M., & Warschauer, M. (2000, March). *Putting the interactive in interactive videoconferencing: Tips for using videoconferencing.* Paper presented at the 34th Annual TESOL convention, Vancouver, British Columbia, Canada.

Stake, R. E. (1995). *The art of case study research.* Thousand Oaks, CA: Sage.

Sujo de Montes, L., & Gonzales, C. G. (2000, February). More than having a connection: Qualitative factors that affect learning in a Web-based university course. In D. A. Willis, J. D. Price, & J. Willis (Eds.), *Society for Information Technology and Teacher Education 11th international conference: Proceedings of SITE 2000* (pp. 177–182). Charlottesville, VA: Association for the Advancement of Computing in Education.

Thomas, K. J. (1999). Teaching via ITV: Taking instructional design to the next level. *T.H.E. Journal, 26*(9), 60–66.

University of Wisconsin-Extension. (2000). Quality distance education (QDE): Lessons learned. Retrieved March 30, 2001, from the World Wide Web: http://www.uwex.edu/disted/qde/factors.html.

U.S. Department of Education. (1991). *Teaching adults with limited English skills.* Washington, DC: U.S. Department of Education, Office of Vocational and Adult Education.

U.S. News & World Report. (1998, March 2). Best graduate schools. In *U.S. News & World Report.* Retrieved April 10, 2001, from the World Wide Web: http://www.usnews.com /usnews/issue/980302/.

Verduin, J. R., & Clark, T. A. (1991). *Distance education: The foundations of effective practice.* San Francisco: Jossey-Bass.

Wade, W. (1999). What do students know and how do we know that they know it? *T.H.E. Journal, 27*(3), 94–100.

Wagner, E. (1993). Variables affecting distance educational program success. *Educational Technology, 33*(4), 28–32.

Wallerstein, N. (1983a). *Language and culture in conflict: Problem-posing in the ESL classroom.* Reading, MA: Addison-Wesley.

Wallerstein, N. (1983b). The teaching approach of Paulo Freire. In J. Oller & P. Richard-Amato (Eds.), *Methods that work* (pp. 190–204). Rowley, MA: Newbury House.

WebCT. (2000). WebCT (Version 3.5) [Computer software]. Lynnfield, MA: Author. (Available from http://about.webct.com)

Wedemeyer, C. (1977). Independent learning. In *The international encyclopedia of higher education* (Vol. 5, pp. 2114–2132). San Francisco: Jossey-Bass.

Wild, M. (1999). Accommodating issues of culture and diversity in the application of new technologies. *British Journal of Educational Technology, 30*(3), 195–199.

Index

Page numbers followed by *n, t,* and *f* refer to notes, tables, and figures respectively.

 **A**

ABC Adult School, 30*n*
Activities
  in computer-assisted language learning,
    163–164, 165–168, 166*t*
  in EFL Methodology Update for In-Service
    Teachers, 115–116
  in Extended Education Distance Learning
    Program, 18
  in Methodology of Teaching English for
    In-Service Teachers, 117–118
  in on-line courses, 70
  in teacher education programs, 169
  in telephone courses, 57–58
  in TelESOL, 99, 107
Administration
  in City College of San Francisco program,
    31–32
  in English Business Communication for
    Executives, 44–45
  in Extended Education Distance Learning
    Program, 21, 23
  of tests, 182
Advance planning, in professors-plus
  model, 147
Advertisement
  of Certificate in Teaching English as a
    Second Language Program in
    Canada, 135
  of MiraCosta College program, 31
Agustsson, H., 177
Al Rawaf, H.S., 178

American Graduate School of International
  Management, 40
Ang, D., 2, 4
Apple, 70
Arizona, 2
Assessment. *See also* Test(s)
  alternatives to, 182
  of program success, 9
  of student progress, 9
    in Miryang National University
      program, 55–56
  by students
    of EFL Methodology Update for In-Service
      Teachers, 119–120, 119*t*
    of Methodology of Teaching English for
      In-Service Teachers, 120–122, 121*t*
Association for Educational
  Communications and Technology, 56
Asynchronous e-mail communications, 2
Asynchronous learning networks, 2
Attrition, 9–10, 27
  in South Korea programs, 54
  in TelESOL, 102, 108*t*
Audio courses. *See also* Telephone courses;
  specific courses
  community in, 78–79
  in English as an International Language,
    76, 76*f*
  face-to-face meetings in, 78
  site coordinator in, 79
  student participation in, 79
  teacher-student interaction in, 79
  technical difficulties with, 77
  visual media in, 80–81
Audiotapes, in City College of San
  Francisco program, 31
Auerbach, E., 17

B

Barlow, Lisa, 8, 9, 183
   "Avoiding the Pitfalls of Test Writing in a
      Distance-Learning Situation: Our
      Experience at United Arab Emirates
      University," 173–183
Bates, A.W., 130
BEEDE. *See* Bilingual/ESL Endorsement
   Through Distance Education
Bejarano, Yael, 2, 3, 4, 5, 6, 8, 9, 10, 126
   "Expanding Horizons: Delivering
      Professional Teacher Development
      via Satellite Technology and E-Mail
      in Israel," 113–126
Bender, W.N., 3
Benhalim, T., 14
Bentley, L., 19
Berces, E., 14
Bilingual/ESL Endorsement Through
   Distance Education (BEEDE), 144–145
   active learning in, 146
   content features of, 146–147
   multimedia capabilities of, 146
   reflective practice in, 147
Black, S., 142
BlueWeb'n Update, 67
Boruta, 163
Bowers, R., 66
Brigham Young University (BYU), teacher
   education programs of, 141–149
   Bilingual/ESL Endorsement Through
      Distance Education, 144–145
   description of, 143
   development of, 142–143
   EDNET, 143–144
   scheduling of, 143
Brigham Young University-Hawaii (BYU-
   Hawaii), English as an International
   Language at, 71–82
Brooks, J.G., 103
Brooks, M.G., 103
Brown, H.D., 18, 179
Burton, Jill, x
Byrne, A.C., 105
BYU. *See* Brigham Young University
BYU-Hawaii. *See* Brigham Young University-
   Hawaii
BYU-Public School Partnership, 142

 C

California, 3
California State University, Fullerton,
   Extended Education Distance Learning
   Program of, 13–24
California Teachers of English to Speakers
   of Other Languages, 9, 29
CALS. *See* Centre for Applied Language
   Studies
Cambre, M., 9
Canada, 3, 127–139
Canadian International Development
   Agency, 129
Canning-Wilson, Christine, 8, 9, 183
   "Avoiding the Pitfalls of Test Writing in a
      Distance-Learning Situation: Our
      Experience at United Arab Emirates
      University," 173–183
Case studies
   in teacher education programs, 170
   in TelESOL, 107
Catterick, David, 6, 7, 94
   "An Academic Writing Course in
      Cyberspace," 83–94
Center for Educational Renewal, at
   University of Washington, 142
Centre for Applied Language Studies
   (CALS), 84
CERTESL. *See* Certificate in Teaching
   English as a Second Language Program in
   Canada
Certificate in Teaching English as a Second
   Language (CERTESL) Program in Canada
   assessment of, 9
   costs of, 135
   courses of, 129*f*
   description of, 128–129
   development of, 133
   distinguishing features of, 130–136
   length of, 128–129
   marketing of, 135
   print materials in, 130
   program delivery, 133
   QDE indicators and
      creating confident and committed
         faculty, 132
      designing for active and effective
         learning, 132–133
      evaluating for continuous
         improvement, 135–136
      knowing the learners, 131–132

supporting the needs of learners,
133–134
sustaining administrative and
organizational commitment,
134–135
reflective practice in, 133
students in, 128
teams in, 129f
Chaney, 106
Chao, C., 6, 165
Chao, Chin-chi, 4, 171
"Practicing What We Preach: Optimal
Learning Conditions for Web-Based
Teacher Education," 161–171
Chapman, C., 6
Chat sessions
community and, 64
in *EnglishLive,* 63–65
error correction in, 64–65
flow of, 64
Cheating, on tests, 180
Chen, A-Y, 2, 4
Chisman, F., 25
Christiansen, D.K., 149
Chung, H., 6
City College of San Francisco, distance
learning program at, 25–38
administration of, 31–32
community and, 34
curriculum of, 26–27
delivery system, 29
description of, 28–29
design of, 29
forms developed from, 33–34, 36–38
goals of, 29
hybrid approach of, 28
implementation of, 27
instructional approach of, 27
objectives of, 28
students in, 26, 28
teacher compensation in, 32
technology used by, 31
value of program, 31–32
Clark, T.A., 1
Class size
in English Business Communication for
Executives, 49
in teacher education programs, 159
in University of Northern Iowa TESOL
MA program, 159
Classroom Connect, 67–68

Classroom layout
in Extended Education Distance Learning
Program, 15, 16t
in Iowa Communications Network, 152–
153, 153f
Classroom mentor, in TelESOL, 104
Codes, in Extended Education Distance
Learning Program, 19–20, 20
Cohen, A., 118
Collaborative learning
definition of, 105
in TelESOL, 105–106
Collier, Kory J., 3, 82
"Teaching Tomorrow's Class Today:
English by Telephone and Computer
From Hawaii to Tonga," 71–82
Collis, B., 3, 4, 8, 9
Community, 7–8. *See also* Student-teacher
interaction
in audio classes, 78–79
chat sessions and, 64
in City College of San Francisco program,
34
in computer-assisted language learning,
169
in EFL Methodology Update for In-Service
Teachers, 116
in English Business Communication for
Executives, 48–49
in MiraCosta College program, 34
in Miryang National University program,
57
in professors-plus model, 145
in teacher education programs, 157–158,
158, 169
in TelESOL, 100, 103–105, 106, 107,
108, 109t
Computer-assisted language learning
(CALL), distance learning program on,
161–171
activities in, 163–164, 165–168, 166t
final project, 167–168
hands-on, 167
optional, 167
case journals in, 163
community in, 169
context of, 161–162
description of, 162–164
distinguishing features of, 164–168
learning model of, 165, 166t
materials in, 163

CALL *(continued)*
  motivation for taking class, 162
  objectives of, 162–163
  practical applications of, 168–170
  students in, 162
  student-teacher interaction in, 167
  technology familiarity in, 169
Computers. *See also under* Technology
  technical difficulties with, 77
  testing on, 177
Constructivism
  and computer-mediated distance learning, 103
  definition of, 103
  in TelESOL, 103, 106
Contract grading, in TelESOL, 105
Coombe, C., 178, 179
Cooper, L., 8
Costs
  of Certificate in Teaching English as a Second Language Program in Canada, 135
  of Iowa Communications Network, 154
  of MiraCosta College ESL program, 30
  of professors-plus model, 148
  of telephone courses, 59
  of television courses, 14*n*
Course veteran mentor, in TelESOL, 105
Crookes, G., 151
Crossroads Café, 26–27
Cultural differences, 8, 9
  test security and, 180
Cultural sensitivity, of tests, 174, 181–182
Culture and Intensive English Program (CIEP), 155–156
Cuomo, A., 27, 31
Curriculum
  of City College of San Francisco program, 26–27
  of English as an International Language, 75
  of Extended Education Distance Learning Program, 17–18
  of MiraCosta College program, 26–27
Cutri, Ramona M., 3, 149
  "The Pedagogy and Technology of Distance Learning for Teacher Education: The Evolution of Instructional Processes and Products," 141–149

 D

Daniel, J.S., 176
Data transfer, in English as an International Language, 77
Davis, D.J., 4
Day, R., 151
Delivery systems
  in Certificate in Teaching English as a Second Language Program in Canada, 133
  in City College of San Francisco program, 29
  in English Business Communication for Executives, 48
  flexibility of, 8, 123
  in professors-plus model, 145–146
  in Teaching English as a Foreign Language Program in Thailand, 130, 133
  in TelESOL, 106, 107
Dial 101, 55
Dickey, Robert J., 3, 10, 60
  "Make It a Conference Call: An English Conversation Course by Telephone in South Korea," 51–60
Dictogloss, 58
Distance education. *See* Distance learning
Distance learners. *See* Student(s)
Distance learning
  definition of, 1
  development of, 1–2
  differences from traditional learning, 127
  in TESOL, 2
Distance teachers. *See* Teacher(s)
Distance teaching. *See* Distance learning
DLP. *See* Extended Education Distance Learning Program
Dong, M., 14
Dustheimer, C., 52
Dynamic distance learning, 102–107

 E

EAP. *See* English for academic purposes writing course
EDNET, 143–144, 146–147
EF English First, 70
EFL Methodology Update for In-Service Teachers, 113
  activities in, 115–116
  audiovisual aspects of, 114–115
  community in, 116
  completion of course, 118–119